C. T. Ulrey.

Front End Papers.

THE INTERPRETATION OF RADIUM
AND THE STRUCTURE OF
THE ATOM

THE INTERPRETATION OF RADIUM

AND THE STRUCTURE OF THE ATOM

BY

FREDERICK SODDY, M.A., F.R.S.
DR. LEE'S PROFESSOR OF INORGANIC AND PHYSICAL CHEMISTRY, UNIVERSITY OF OXFORD

WITH ILLUSTRATIONS

FOURTH EDITION
REVISED AND ENLARGED

NEW YORK
G. P. PUTNAM'S SONS
1920

First Edition - - - - - - March, 1909.

Second Edition - - - - - - November, 1909.

Third Edition - - - - - - October, 1912.

Fourth Edition - - - - - - August, 1920.

PREFACE TO THE FOURTH EDITION

In again revising this book I have conformed to the earlier plan of writing what I should have said if the lectures had been delivered in 1920 instead of 1908. The original statement has been amplified rather than modified. It has lost, long since, the appearance of challenge to existing theories which at first it may have presented.

But the subject has now grown entirely beyond the power of being fully encompassed by the original very simple and popular mode of treatment. I have thought it best, therefore, not to compress the original part unduly, as it still may serve a useful purpose to those not familiar with scientific conceptions, but to add, as a second part, a more briefly written and less elementary account of the later developments, particularly those that bear upon the problem of the constitution of the atom. It is to be hoped that even those who are not chemists or physicists, who have followed the exposition in the first part, may not be entirely unable to profit by the second part. Though, naturally, the new subject-matter, by reasons of its more general and often more speculative character—much of it still being in the making—cannot but be more difficult to understand than the original work, which dealt with distinct and easily understood steps in the progress of knowledge, made once and for all time.

FREDERICK SODDY.

The University of Oxford,
    July, 1920.

PREFACE

THE present-day interpretation of radium, that it is an element undergoing spontaneous disintegration, was put forward in a series of joint scientific communications to the *Philosophical Magazine* of 1902 and 1903 by Professor Rutherford, now of Manchester University, and myself. As its application is not confined to the physical sciences, but has a wide and general bearing on our whole outlook upon Nature, I have attempted in this book a presentation of the subject in non-technical language, so that the ideas involved, and their bearing upon current thought, may be within the reach of the lay reader. Although written in non-technical language, no effort has been spared to get to the root of the matter and to secure accuracy, so that possibly the book may prove serviceable to workers in other fields of science and investigation as well as to the general public.

The book contains the main substance of six popular experimental lectures delivered in the University of Glasgow at the beginning of the year, but being relieved from the necessity, always present in lecturing, of co-ordinating the experimental and descriptive sides, I have, while adhering to the lecture form of address, entirely rearranged and very largely rewritten the subject matter in order to secure the greatest possible degree of continuity of treatment. Certain portions of the lectures, for example those dealing with the X-rays and the spectra of elements, have been omitted, and attention thereby concentrated upon radium, the chief topic. In addition, I have briefly embodied the results of important discoveries which have appeared since the date of the lectures, particularly the experiments of Professor Rutherford and Dr. Geiger in counting the number of a-particles expelled by radium. The book also contains some account of the arrangement by means of which I have recently succeeded in detecting and measuring the quantity of the helium generated from the common radio-elements uranium and thorium.

I have borrowed freely from numerous scattered lectures and addresses bearing on the subject which I have from time to time been invited to deliver, and may mention in particular the Wilde lecture to the Manchester Literary and Philosophical Society, 1904, the Presidential and other addresses to the Röntgen Society, 1906, the opening of the discussion on the evolution of the elements in Section A of the British Association Meeting in York, 1906, and the Watt lecture to the Greenock Philosophical Society, 1908.

FREDERICK SODDY.

The University, Glasgow,
November, 1908.

CONTENTS

PART I

CHAPTER I
THE DISCOVERY OF RADIOACTIVITY

PAGE

Radioactivity, a new science—Its discovery—The four experimental effects of radioactivity—The rays of radioactive substances—The continuous emission of energy from the radio-elements - - - - - - - 1

CHAPTER II
RADIUM

Radioactivity an unalterable atomic property—The radioactivity of thorium—Pitchblende—Quantity of radium in pitchblende—The smallest quantity of radium detectable—Experiments with radium—Cost of radium—The doctrine of energy—Measurement of the energy emitted by radium—The source of cosmical energy—Radium and the " physically impossible " - - 12

CHAPTER III
THE RAYS OF RADIOACTIVE SUBSTANCES

The radiations of the radio-elements—α-, β-, and γ-rays—Test of penetrating power—Experiments with the penetrating β- and γ-rays—The feebly penetrating α-rays—Experiment with α-rays—The range of α-rays in air—The physical nature of radiation—Corpuscular radiation—The wave theory of light—α- and β- rays due to the expulsion of particles—The individual atom of matter—The spinthariscope—The decay of α-radiation—Counting the α-particles - - - - - 28

CONTENTS

CHAPTER IV
THE RAYS OF RADIOACTIVE SUBSTANCES (*continued*)

The β-rays—Deviation by a magnet—Electric charge carried by β-rays—The nature of electricity—Radiant matter or cathode-rays—The electron—Inertia or mass—Velocity of the β-rays—The radium clock—Magnetic deviation of the α-particle—Its velocity—Passage of α-particles through matter—Scattering of α-particles—Method of rendering the track of rays visible—The fates of α-particles - - - - - - 47

CHAPTER V
THE RADIUM EMANATION

The source of radioactive energy—Two alternative theories—The internal energy of matter—Radium a changing element—Disintegration in cascade—The successive outbursts of energy—The radium emanation—Experiments with the emanation—Its condensation by cold—The infinitesimal quantity of the emanation—Its radioactivity—The chemical character of the emanation—The heat evolved by the emanation—The decay of the emanation—Its reproduction by radium—Atomic disintegration—Radioactive equilibrium—Energy of radioactive change—All radioactive changes equally detectable - - 68

CHAPTER VI
HELIUM AND RADIUM

The connection of the α-particle with radioactive changes—Helium and the α-particle—The ultimate products—Discovery of helium, solar and terrestrial—Prediction of the production of helium—Production of helium from radium—Its production from uranium and thorium—Identity of the α-particle and helium—The first change of radium—Radioactive recoil - 93

CHAPTER VII
THEORY OF ATOMIC DISINTEGRATION

Questions of nomenclature—Definition of the atom—Elements and chemical compounds—The experimental facts—The nature of atomic disintegration—The chance of disintegration—

CONTENTS

The period of average life of a disintegrating atom—The unknown cause of disintegration—Determination of the period of average life—The period of average life of radium—The total energy evolved in the complete disintegration of radium — 105

CHAPTER VIII

THE ORIGIN OF RADIUM

Why has radium survived?—The reproduction of radium—The ratio between the quantities of uranium and radium in all minerals—Hydraulic analogy to radioactive change—The age of pitchblende—Uranium X—Attempts to detect a growth of radium — Existence of intermediate products — Ionium — Production of radium by uranium—The stately procession of elementary evolution - - - - - - 121

CHAPTER IX

THE SUCCESSIVE CHANGES OF RADIUM

The later changes of radium—The active deposit of radium—The radiations from the active deposit—Experiments with the active deposit—Radium A—Radium B and C—The radiation from the emanation—The later slow changes of radium—Radium D, E, and F—Polonium—The ultimate product of radium—Uranium I, and Uranium II—Uranium X_1, and Uranium X_2 (Brevium)—Radium C and Radium C_2 - - 136

CHAPTER X

RADIOACTIVITY AND THE NATURE OF MATTER

Ratio of quantities of polonium and radium in minerals—Table of the ratio of the quantities of all the products of uranium—Impossibility of concentrating many of the products of disintegration—Increase of activity of radium with time—The rarity of elements—The currency metals—The nature of atoms—The velocity of α-particles—Stability and survival of elements—Connection between range of α-rays and period—Pleochroic halos—Uranium and thorium halos - - - 152

CHAPTER XI

RADIOACTIVITY AND THE EVOLUTION OF THE WORLD

The potentialities of matter—Why radium is unique—The total energy evolved by uranium—The importance of transmutation—Primitive man and fire—Source of cosmical energy—Radium in the earth's crust—Various possible fates of the earth—The most probable view—Radioactivity and mythology—The new prospect - - - - - - - 168

PART II

CHAPTER XII

THE THORIUM AND ACTINIUM DISINTEGRATION SERIES

The thorium disintegration series—Mesothorium and radiothorium—Radioactivity of thorium—Mesothorium—The thorium emanation—Radiothorium—Experiments with the thorium emanation—Thorium A—The actinium disintegration series—The origin of actinium—Multiple atomic disintegration—Branch series of thorium and radium—The actinium branch series—The actinium emanation—Actinium A—Eka-tantalum or proto-actinium—Uranium Y—Table of complete disintegration series—The unsolved riddle of matter - - 186

CHAPTER XIII

THE ULTIMATE STRUCTURE OF MATTER

A flood of knowledge—The nature of mass—Sir J. J. Thomson's model atom—The periodic law—Electrolytic dissociation—The outermost region of the atom - - - - 209

CHAPTER XIV

THE NUCLEAR ATOM

The innermost region of the atom—An artificial transmutation—Atoms compared and contrasted with solar systems - 220

CONTENTS

CHAPTER XV
ISOTOPES

Elements which are chemically identical—The periodic law and radioactive changes—The atomic number—Isotopic elements—The problem of the ancient alchemist - - - - 227

CHAPTER XVI
THE X-RAYS AND CONCLUDING EVIDENCE

The X-ray spectra of the elements—The γ-rays—The intermediate region of atomic structure—The homogeneous characteristic X-rays of Barkla—The atomic mass or weight—The element lead—The separation of isotopes—Neon and Metaneon—The general prevalence of isotopism—The problem of transmutation—Conclusion - - - - - - 234

INDEX - - - - - - - - 253

LIST OF ILLUSTRATIONS

FIG.   PAGE
1. Becquerel's uranium radiograph of an aluminium medallion ⎫
2. Welsbach mantle, taken by the rays from the thorium contained in it ⎬ *To face* 7
3. Photograph and radiograph of a piece of pitchblende (Sir William Crookes) - - - " 15
4. Photograph of silk tassel electrified by friction ⎫
5. The same discharged by the rays of radium ⎬ " 18
6. Radium writing on a photographic plate ⎫
7. Box of compasses taken by γ-rays of radium ⎬ " 31
8. Diagram of coated flask and radium-covered dish for showing α-rays - - - - - 35
9. Photograph of the same apparatus - - *To face* 35
10. Diagram of Spinthariscope of Sir William Crookes - - - - - - 43
11. Photograph of the Spinthariscope - - *To face* 35
12. Photograph of the electro-magnet for deviating the β-rays - - - - - " 47
13. Diagram of magnetic deviation of β-rays - - - 49
14. Diagram of Crookes' tube to show magnetic deviation of cathode-rays - - - - - 54
15. Diagram of Strutt's radium clock - - - 59
16. Photograph of radium clock - - *To face* 47
17. Tracks of α-particles photographed by C. T. R. Wilson - - - - ⎫
18. Track of a single α- and of a single β-particle ⎬ " 65
19. Tracks of two α-particles—one straight, one twice deflected - - - - ⎭
20. Photograph of tube containing willemite ⎫
21. Photograph of the same tube by its own light when containing radium emanation - ⎬ " 78
22. Diagram of apparatus for showing the condensation of the radium emanation - - - - 81
23. Diagram of the first disintegration of radium - - 94

xv

LIST OF ILLUSTRATIONS

FIG.   PAGE

24. Photograph of the spectrum-tube in which the production of helium from radium emanation was observed — *To face* 99
25. Photograph by Dr. Giesel of the spectrum of helium produced from radium
26. Photograph of apparatus for detecting and measuring helium produced from uranium and thorium — „ 100
27. Diagram showing the first change of radium — 103
28. Diagram for the first disintegration of uranium — 129
29. Diagram of the uranium-radium disintegration series (initial changes) — 133
30. Diagram of the first four disintegrations of radium — 139
31. Diagram of apparatus for obtaining the active deposit of radium — 141
32. Photograph of the same apparatus — *To face* 141
33. Diagram of the later disintegrations of radium — 146
34. Diagram of the complete uranium disintegration series — 150
35. Microphotograph of uranium and thorium pleochroic halos (Joly) — *To face* 166
36. Enlarged photograph of uranium halo showing ring due to Radium A
37. Diagram of the complete thorium disintegration series — 190
38. Diagram of the complete actinium disintegration series — 199
39. The branching of the thorium series — 201
40. The branching of the radium series — 202
41. Initial part of uranium series showing branch actinium series — 206
42. Table showing complete disintegration series — 207
43. The periodic table of the elements — 214
44. Chart showing α- and β-change and periodic law generalisation — 230

THE INTERPRETATION OF RADIUM AND THE STRUCTURE OF THE ATOM

PART I

CHAPTER I

THE DISCOVERY OF RADIOACTIVITY

Radioactivity, a New Science.

ONE of the main duties of science is the correlation of phenomena, apparently disconnected and even contradictory. For example, chemistry teaches us to regard under one aspect, as various types of combustion or oxidation, the burning of a candle, the rusting of metals, the physiological process of respiration, and the explosion of gunpowder. In each process there is the one common fact that oxygen enters into new chemical combinations. Similarly to the physicist, the fall of the traditional apple of Newton, the revolution of the earth and planets round the sun, the apparitions of comets, and the ebb and flow of the tides are all phases of the universal law of gravitation. A race ignorant of the nature of combustion or of the law of gravitation, and ignorant of the need of such generalisations, could not be considered to have advanced far along the paths of scientific discovery. The phenomena with which I am concerned in these lectures belong to the newly-born science of radioactivity and to the spontaneous disintegration of elements which the study of radioactivity has revealed to us. It is a natural inquiry to ask—To what most nearly are these new phenomena correlated? Is it possible to give, by the help of an analogy to familiar phenomena, any correct idea of the nature of this new phenomenon " Radioactivity " ? The answer may surprise those who hold to the adage that there is nothing new under the sun. Frankly, it is not possible, because in these latest developments science has broken fundamentally new ground, and has delved one distinct step further down into the foundations of knowledge.

During the century which has just closed there occurred, it is true, at an ever-increasing rate, a ceaseless extension of our knowledge of the nature of matter upon which physical science is largely based. Yet this advance was for the most part an expansion rather than a deepening. It was concerned with what may be termed atomic and molecular architecture, the external qualities of atoms and the construction and study of complexes built of atoms—that is to say, molecules. As buildings are built of bricks, so compounds can nowadays be built up out of atoms. The atoms are to the chemist and physicist what bricks are to the architect—the units supplied ready-made to a certain limited number of standard specifications and dimensions capable of an endless variety of combinations and arrangements, each with its own peculiarities and external relationships.

The century which has just begun has seen the first definite and considerable step taken into the ultimate nature of these units of matter or atoms, which is in one sense not merely an extension of existing knowledge or principles, but a radically new departure. Radioactivity is a new primary science owing allegiance neither to physics nor chemistry, as these sciences were understood before its advent, because it is concerned with a knowledge of the elementary atoms themselves of a character so fundamental and intimate that the old laws of physics and chemistry, concerned almost wholly with external relationships, do not suffice. This first step has indeed emphasised how superficial our knowledge of matter has really been. If one were to demonstrate to an architect that the bricks he habitually and properly employs in his constructions were under other circumstances capable of entirely different uses—let us say, for illustration, that they could with effect be employed as an explosive incomparably more powerful in its activities than dynamite— the surprise of the architect would be no greater than the surprise of the chemist at the new and undreamt of possibilities of matter demonstrated by the mere existence of such an element as radium.

In this first lecture our attention will be mainly directed to the one outstanding feature in connection with radium, and the property of radioactivity which it exhibits to an extraordinary degree, in which the whole range of its remarkable features are epitomised. The radioactive substances evolve a perennial supply of energy from year to year without stimulus and without exhaustion. It would be idle to deny with regard to this that physical science was taken completely by surprise. Had any one twenty-five years ago ventured to predict radium he would have been told simply that such a thing was not only wildly improbable, but actually opposed to all the established principles of the science of matter and energy. So drastic an innovation was, it is true, unanticipated. Radium, however, is an undisputed fact to-day, and there is no question which would have triumphed in the conflict, had its existence conflicted with the established principles of science. Natural conservatism and dislike of innovation appear in the ranks of science more strongly than most people are aware. Indeed, science is no exception. There was, however, never the slightest ground for assuming that because the new facts were startling and unexpected they must necessarily conflict with older knowledge. That would be to pay science a poor compliment. Some of the new facts we shall discuss in the lectures appeared at first, and may even yet appear to you, almost incredible, but that is only on account of the entire newness of the whole region to which they belong. Into this region the older chemistry and physics have, as we have seen, never before penetrated. It is not until we begin to apply to the new facts the established principles of science, which have served so well of old, that their full significance gradually becomes evident. Keep in mind that our knowledge of Nature is always of necessity partial, and is bounded in all directions by certain inevitable but too often forgotten limitations connected, for example, with the briefness of human life and the physical impossibility of pursuing investigations except under conditions where the life of the investigator can be maintained. The laws and principles of physical science, old and new, are alike subject to these perpetual limitations, and are necessarily only true within these limits. From this point of view there is nothing in the many surprising properties of radium which conflicts with a single established principle of older science. Physics and chemistry remain almost unchanged where they were, and radioactivity, so far as it is concerned with the correctness of their principles, has, as a matter of fact, given to the old laws and theories a fuller and truer significance than they had before. The extension of the old theories which has been rendered necessary has not been revolutionary in any destructive sense. It is wonderful how accommodating a true theory is to new truth, apparently of a diametrically opposite character, and this not in any sense of mere ingenuity of explanation, but in a manner that arrests the investigator, and is his sign that he is on safe ground. It may seem a paradox, but from the first the best proof of the newer views, to my mind, was in the completeness with which the strange, newly-won knowledge of radioactivity harmonised with the old views of the chemist about atoms and elements. On the other hand this gratifying harmony, where conflict might have been expected, is not a surrender. On every hand new vistas of thought are opening out. We see the simple and direct answer to many problems before deemed insoluble. We recognise now causes at work where before we only saw effects, many of them so familiar and ingrained in our consciousness that the necessity for a cause had been almost overlooked, or, if felt at all, met perfunctorily and wholly inadequately by existing knowledge. Highly technical and complicated as many of the researches on radioactivity are, the main conclusions of the science are as simple and certain as they are fundamental, and of general interest. It is the duty of every educated man to make himself aware of the chief bearings of these conclusions, for they touch human life strangely at many points, and are destined in the future to influence profoundly the course of philosophic thought. In a few years the elementary principles of radioactivity will be taught in all schools as belonging to the very beginnings of physical science. To-day, while all is strange and new and the very name of the science even unfamiliar, it may appear a far cry to attempt to foretell the effects these discoveries, concerned primarily with the ultimate nature of matter, are destined to exert on our conceptions of the ultimate destiny of man. But already the most direct connection is apparent. Indeed, this aspect of the advance is perhaps the most revolutionary. We shall be able to see more clearly at the end how this has come about. At present it is sufficient to indicate that radioactivity has introduced a new conception into the fundamental problems of existence. By its conclusion that there is imprisoned in ordinary common matter vast stores of energy, which ignorance alone at the present time prevents us from using for the purposes of life, radioactivity has raised an issue which it is safe to say will mark an epoch in the progress of thought. With all our mastery over the powers of Nature we have adhered to the view that the struggle for existence is a permanent and necessary condition of life. To-day it appears as though it may well be but a passing phase, to be altogether abolished in the future as it has to some extent been mitigated in the past by the unceasing, and as it now appears, unlimited ascent of man to knowledge, and through knowledge to physical power and dominion over Nature.

The Discovery of Radioactivity.

The first discovery of the property we now call radioactivity was made in the year 1896 by M. Henri Becquerel in Paris, and, like many other great discoveries, the actual experiment itself owed something to luck or chance or accident. Looking backward, however, it appears rather that only the particular day or month of the discovery was a matter of chance. The time was just ripe for the event, and it is certain that its coming could not long have been delayed. Some slight historical sketch of the conditions preceding and immediately following the discovery is necessary before considering wherein lies its great significance. The memorable discovery of the X-rays by Professor Röntgen, in 1895, which is known to all, familiarised scientific workers with a type of radiation able to traverse objects opaque to light. The X-rays are themselves invisible to the unaided eye, but are able to affect the photographic plate. This led to experiments being made in order to see if similar types of rays were not produced in other ways. As you all know, certain substances exposed to sunlight shine afterwards in the dark, and this property, which finds an application in the manufacture of luminous paint, is known as phosphorescence or fluorescence. Is phosphorescent light entirely stopped by opaque objects? Or does it in part consist of invisible penetrating rays like the X-rays? M. Becquerel wrapped a photographic plate in black paper and placed on it a

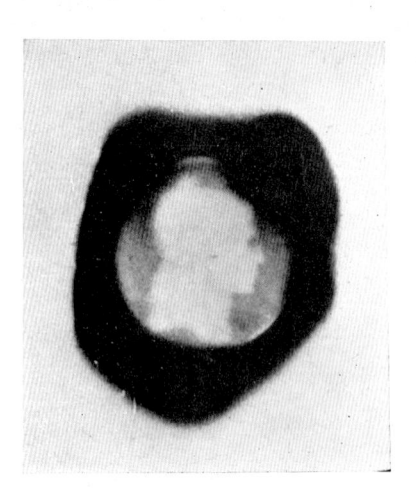

FIG. 1.—BECQUEREL'S URANIUM PICTURE.

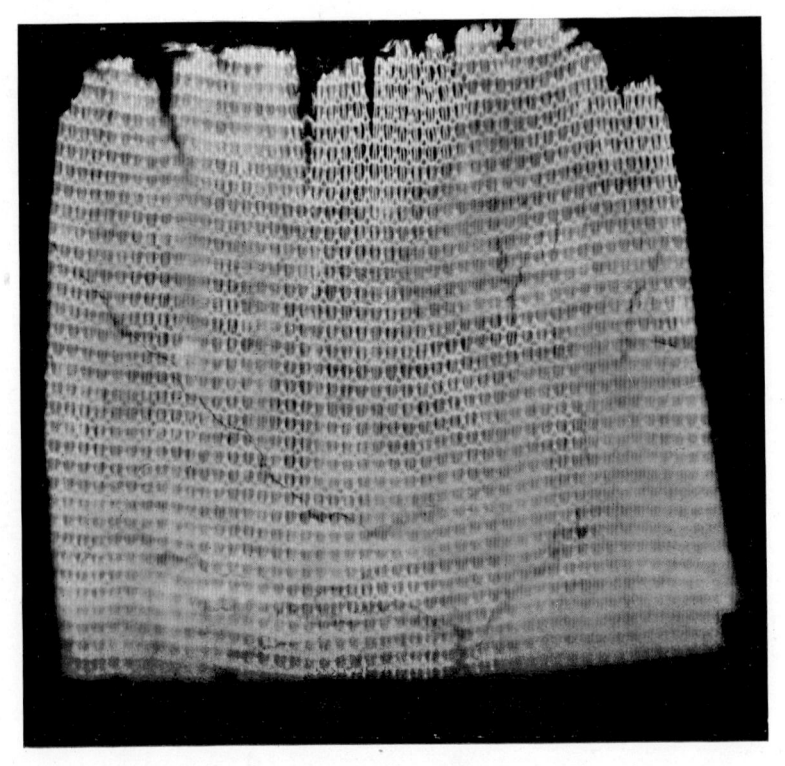

FIG. 2.—WELSBACH MANTLE IMPRINTED BY ITS OWN RAYS.

To face p. 7

phosphorescent substance which was then exposed to sunlight. By great good fortune M. Becquerel chose as the particular phosphorescent body a preparation of *uranium*, and found as the result of the experiment that the photographic plate beneath the preparation was darkened. The preparation had given out rays which, unlike sunlight, were capable of penetrating the black paper. It was soon found that these rays, like the X-rays, even penetrated thin plates of metal, for when such a thin plate was interposed between the preparation and the film darkening still occurred. But one day, the sun being obscured, the plate and the phosphorescent uranium preparation upon it were set aside in a dark drawer for some weeks, and M. Becquerel, wishing to see if any darkening had occurred without the sunlight, developed the plate as it was. It was found that darkening had gone on just as much in the darkness as in the light. Further experiments soon established that neither sunlight nor phosphorescence had anything to do with the experiment. The action is an entirely new inherent property of the element *uranium*. No other phosphorescent body would have darkened the plate even in the sunlight, while all preparations containing uranium do so, whether they are phosphorescent or not, in total darkness as well as in the light. Fig. 1 shows one of the photographs by uranium rays obtained by M. Becquerel. Between the patch of the uranium preparation and the plate was placed an aluminium medallion, stamped with a head of a figure in relief, which partially shielded the plate beneath from the rays. The impression under the thinner portions of the medallion is darker than under the thicker portions, thus causing the head of the figure to be clearly apparent in the photograph.

The Four Experimental Effects of Radioactivity.

Although the radioactive process is itself without analogy in science, the main effects which it produces can almost all be more or less nearly imitated, and were all more or less perfectly studied prior to its discovery. The main effects of radioactivity with which we are most concerned are four. Firstly then, radioactive substances affect a photographic plate in the same manner as light and many other agencies. Secondly, they excite phosphorescence or fluorescence in certain substances when brought in their neighbourhood. Thirdly, radioactive bodies cause the air and other gases to lose the insulating power they normally possess and to become partial conductors of electricity. In consequence, any electrified object has its electricity rapidly discharged in the neighbourhood of a radioactive substance. The passage of the rays through the gas shatters the electrically neutral gas molecules into oppositely charged particles or, as it is termed, ionises the gas. But the same effect is produced by X-rays, by incandescent bodies, and even by a lighted match. The instrument employed to detect this effect is the gold-leaf electroscope, the first and simplest electrical instrument to be invented, and for this purpose capable of so great refinement that it affords the most delicate and sensitive test it is possible to employ in the detection of radioactivity. Lastly, radioactive bodies generate heat, as does coal or any other substance burning. The photographic action and the discharge of electricity from insulated charged bodies are clearly shown by radioactive substances even in the form in which they occur in Nature, as all unsuspected they have been handled and examined by men for centuries. Hence you will understand how it is that the discovery of radioactivity could not under any circumstances have been indefinitely delayed. But only the more powerfully radioactive substances, like radium, give appreciable phosphorescence or heat effects. In the naturally occurring radioactive substances these effects are far too small to be readily detectable.

The Rays of Radioactive Substances.

Exact physical experiments have demonstrated that all these effects of radioactivity owe their origin to the fact that the radioactive substances emit "rays." These rays are invisible to the unaided eye it is true. In this they resemble Röntgen's X-rays. There are three different types of rays given out by the radioactive substances, which are known respectively as the α-, β-, and γ-rays. Each will require detailed future consideration. But they all bear less resemblance to light than to the recently discovered types of rays, of which the X-rays of Röntgen are typical, produced when an electric current is forced by powerful appliances to traverse a nearly vacuous space, a path which it much prefers not to take if it can avoid it.

The first effects of most new things are old. Motorcars and railways do the old work of horses. In commercial life a really new effect is generally valueless until it has ceased to be new, as many inventors know to their cost. In scientific discovery a new effect does not usually proclaim itself from the housetops. It often needs new instruments and the way must first be paved for its discovery, while old effects are generally recognised first. It is natural that the first effects of radioactivity to be discovered should be those more or less familiar. But for the development to perfection of that marvellous thing, the photographic plate, radioactivity would not have been discovered in the way it was, and we should still be without one of the readiest methods of detecting it. But for the work on the conduction of electricity through gases immediately following the discovery of the X-rays, the only other method of detecting radioactivity in the natural state would be unknown, and therefore also in all probability radioactivity itself. On the other hand, if radioactive substances exhibit any entirely new *kind* of properties— and it is quite possible that they do—it is very likely that their very novelty would delay their discovery.

The Continuous Emission of Energy.

Why then, you may ask, if all of the effects of radioactivity are shown in other ways do I insist that radioactivity is a phenomenon unparalleled in science? The distinctive feature of radioactivity is not, however, so much in the rays the radioactive substances emit, though we shall find upon a closer examination that these are distinctive and most remarkable. The main interest of the new property consists in the spontaneous and continuous emission of *energy* of which the rays are but one manifestation. Heat and light may be obtained in numerous ways, but it is a new thing to find it being given out by a substance, as it is by radium, year in, year out, without apparent intermission or diminution, and without the substance being in any apparent way consumed or altered. This was the arresting fact. The radioactive substances apparently were performing the scientifically impossible feat of evolving a store of energy presumably out of nothing. So long as radioactivity was known only on the scale and in the degree exhibited by uranium, it was perhaps possible to explain away this aspect of the question because of the minuteness of the amount of energy involved and the difficulty of proving that it was not in some way derived from the surroundings. But the work of M. and Mme. Curie, by their discovery of radium, made the world familiar with an element over a million times as radioactive as uranium. In this case the energy evolved is great enough to produce effects which are obvious to all and which cannot be explained away. In a strictly scientific sense there is no difference of principle between the radioactivity of radium and that of uranium. The difference is one of degree only, but it is so great that radium, though, as we shall come to see, not so wonderful in reality as uranium, rapidly acquired a monopoly of public interest and attention.

CHAPTER II
RADIUM

Radioactivity, an Unalterable Atomic Property.

It is worth while to stop to consider the starting-point of Mme. Curie's discovery. Chemistry analyses all known substances into their component constituents or elements, all of which are fundamentally different, the one from the other, and inconvertible the one into the other. Uranium is such an element, gold, silver, lead, and many of the common metals are others, but uranium is distinguished by having relatively the heaviest of all known atoms. The atom is the minimum unit quantity of an element. The relative atomic weight of an element is one of its most important characteristics, and as a first approximation the atom of hydrogen is chosen as the standard and is assigned unit value. For exact work it is more convenient to choose oxygen as the standard, with the value 16. On this basis the atomic weight of hydrogen becomes 1·008, and that of uranium 238·18.

Now radioactivity is an intrinsic property of the element uranium, and therefore of the atom of uranium. This Mme. Curie first recognised, and it formed the starting-point of her work. In the case of uranium, the element itself and all its various compounds are radioactive, and the radioactivity of each compound is conditioned simply by the relative amount of uranium it contains. It does not matter where the uranium comes from—it is always to the same degree radioactive. Non-radioactive uranium is unknown. Not only so, but it is absolutely impossible really to affect the radioactivity of uranium or any other of the radioactive elements in the slightest degree. In this the process is utterly unlike any other process previously known in Nature. Radioactivity is part and parcel of the very nature of the element which possesses the property, and therefore of the atom or unit quantity of the element. The attempts that have been made artificially to alter or to stop the radioactivity of an element have met with signal failure. This is still an impossible feat —a thing modern science cannot do—and yet, as we shall come to see quite clearly in the sequel, a thing which science must do if mankind is to realise to the full the destiny these discoveries have for the first time unveiled. There is another still impossible feat, to the accomplishment of which all the appliances of modern science have been directed in vain, as well as all the utmost power of man from the earliest time. It is transmutation, or the conversion of one element into another.

Radioactivity is the one process going on in matter we cannot influence or stop, while transmutation is the one process in matter we have so far signally failed to effect. The juxtaposition of radioactivity and transmutation is not a fanciful one, because it will appear, as we proceed, that the two processes are most intimately connected.

The Radioactivity of Thorium.

Radioactivity being a property of the element uranium, it was natural to ask whether uranium alone of all the eighty elements known possessed it. This was the starting-point of Mme. Curie's illustrious researches in the subject. She found only one other element among those known which possessed the property—the element thorium, which, at one time rare and little known, has come into industrial prominence of recent years in the manufacture of the Welsbach incandescent gas mantle,[1] of which it forms the main constituent. To the electrical or ionisation test—the power of discharging a gold-leaf electroscope—thorium preparations are of about the same degree of radioactivity as uranium; but to the photographic plate thorium is far less active than uranium, owing to the fact that the type of rays which affect the photographic plate most strongly are not those with most effect on the electroscope. The radioactivity of thorium is a fact which can be beautifully demonstrated by any one acquainted with the process of photography. An incandescent mantle, after burning off the fibre, is cut open and pressed as flat as possible on a card. A photographic plate, which has first been wrapped in a light-tight envelope, is laid upon the flat mantle, and the whole is left undisturbed for a fortnight or longer. On developing the plate it will be found that an image of the mantle has been formed on the plate in the dark by the rays from the thorium contained in the mantle. Any one can do this simple experiment for himself.

Fig. 2 (facing p. 7) shows the result I obtained with a very thin piece of aluminium foil between the film and the mantle. The foil, while quite opaque, allows the α- as well as the β-rays to go through. Paper would stop the α-rays entirely.

The radioactivity of thorium, though producing the same general effects as that of uranium, differs from it entirely in detail. Indeed, by a few simple tests on the radioactivity, any one of the radioactive elements can be recognised and distinguished far more quickly and certainly than by any of the other chemical or spectroscopic tests, even when present in very minute quantities. In the historical development of the views now held in radioactivity thorium played a leading part. But, as it is quite foreign to my intention to give anything approaching a detailed systematic account of the subject, and as radium lends

[1] The cause of the action of the gas-mantle in generating light is quite unconnected with the property of radioactivity.

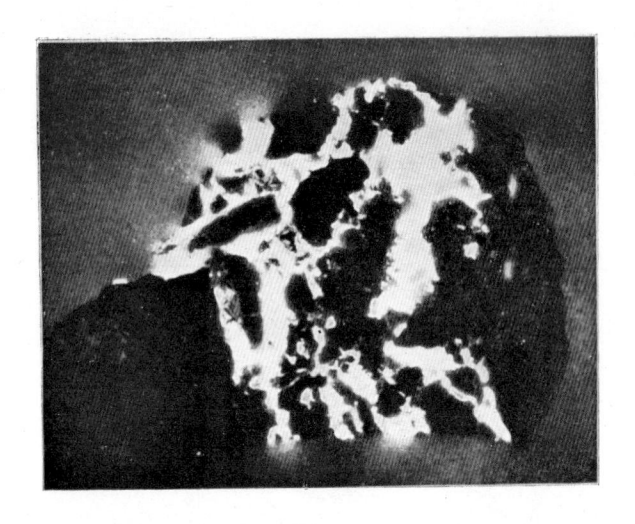

FIG. 3.—SIR WILLIAM CROOKES' PICTURES OF PITCHBLENDE.

The lower figure is a daylight photograph.
The upper was imprinted in the dark by the rays from the substance.

To face p. 15

itself more readily to experimental demonstrations, I shall confine myself at first to the properties of the latter substance.

PITCHBLENDE.

Although uranium and thorium were the only two known elements possessing radioactivity, Mme. Curie found that the natural minerals containing uranium are more radioactive than can be accounted for by the uranium present. Certain minerals, called pitchblende, particularly the variety from the celebrated Joachimsthal mine in Austria, contain often more than 50 per cent. of uranium in the form of uranium oxide. The radioactivity of pitchblende to the photographic plate is beautifully shown by two photographs of Sir W. Crookes (Fig. 3). The lower figure shows the polished face of a piece of pitchblende photographed in the ordinary way by daylight. The upper figure was taken by placing the polished face of the mineral on a photographic film wrapped in light-tight paper. The lighter portions of the figure indicate where the plate has been acted on by the rays from the radioactive matter in the pitchblende. Some pitchblendes are from three to four times as radioactive as pure uranium oxide. This could only be the case, Mme. Curie correctly argued, if there existed in the minerals one or more unknown elements more powerfully radioactive than uranium. By the ordinary process of chemical analysis it is easy to separate out the various constituent elements in pitchblende. There are a great number of elements in pitchblende, though most of them are present in very small amount. A fact that will be found significant later is that lead is *always* present in important quantity. Mme. Curie found that of the elements so separated two in particular, the bismuth and the barium, were strongly radioactive. Now ordinary bismuth and barium are not at all radioactive, and the radioactivity of these elements, when separated from pitchblende, is really due to the presence of two new elements in minute amount mixed with them. The one associated with bismuth was discovered first by Mme. Curie and named *Polonium*, after her native country. Its consideration is more profitably delayed till later. The other, which was discovered very soon afterwards, is associated with the barium, and is *Radium*.

Quantity of Radium in Pitchblende.

The exact quantity of radium in pitchblende and other uranium minerals is a fact of considerable importance. There is one part of the element radium for every three million two hundred thousand parts of the element uranium in pitchblende. The pitchblende may be of any degree of richness, from only a few per cent. to over 50 per cent. of uranium. But of even the richest pitchblendes between 100 and 200 tons would be needed to produce an ounce of pure radium. The compound usually sold, hydrated radium bromide, the formula of which is written $RaBr_2 \cdot 2H_2O$, contains, if pure, 54·33 per cent. of radium. But what it lacks in quantity radium makes up for in quality—that is to say, in radioactivity. It is like the myriad of roses we are told go to make a single drop of the real attar, which is almost priceless. The radium that is extracted is a million times more radioactive than the mineral, and several million times more than pure uranium itself. Conversely, just as you can buy quite a large bottle of rose-water for a small sum, so quantity is not the only consideration to be taken into account in the buying of radium preparations. A very small quantity of radium is sufficient to confer on a large quantity of an inactive salt many of its own peculiar properties. Particularly is this the case with the property of glowing visibly in the dark. Weak radium preparations, which contain usually barium, shine by themselves in the dark more strongly even than the pure radium salts, owing to a phosphorescent action of the barium salts, although they may hardly contain enough radium to affect an X-ray screen through a piece of metal. If you mix a very minute quantity of radium with a quantity of a very highly phosphorescent body, like sulphide of zinc,[1] it will shine in the dark so brilliantly that an inexperienced person might well be deceived into believing that it must contain a large quantity of radium. So great has become the need that radium preparations should be of definitely ascertainable quality that in 1910 an International Radium Standards Committee was formed, with the result that there is now preserved in Paris an International Radium Standard prepared by Mme. Curie, and consisting of a tube containing twenty-two milligrams of the most carefully purified radium chloride. By comparison with this standard secondary standards have been prepared and supplied to the official testing institutions of the various countries, and now there is as much definiteness about the milligram of radium as there is about a pound of tea.

The Smallest Quantity of Radium Detectable.

It is an interesting digression to consider here the smallest absolute quantity of radium which can be detected and identified with certainty in the laboratory. One fifty-millionth of a milligram, or one three-thousand-millionth of a grain of radium is quite easy to recognise, whilst with special care one-tenth of this amount could probably be detected. This is far less than could be detected in the case of any non-radioactive element by any method known, not excluding even the spectroscope. If the half of a grain of pure radium bromide, which is in this room to-night, were divided equally among every human being at present alive in the world, and one such portion were returned to us, it would prove sufficient for detection and identification by means of a gold-leaf electroscope with the greatest ease. With half a grain of a pure radium compound the main effects of radioactivity, which in the case of uranium or thorium would either be too feeble to show or would require the

[1] This mixture now finds extended application in " Radium Watches " and the like, for painting the dial figures and tips of the hands.

use of inconveniently delicate instruments, can be shown in a striking and convincing manner to you all in the simplest possible way.

Experiments with Radium.

Of the small amount of radium bromide, which by a labour of love certain chemists have succeeded in extracting from pitchblende, I am fortunate to possess about a grain, or sixty-five milligrams. Half of this quantity, which I shall use for most of my lecture experiments, is contained in a small ebonite capsule. The other half is dissolved in water and not brought into this lecture-room, but kept in the laboratory half a mile away. With the room dark the radium in the capsule is hardly visible to you, because the rays do not of themselves affect the unaided eye, but if I bring some crystals of the fluorescent substance, barium platinocyanide, near to it, you will see that the crystals shine out at once with a beautiful green light. An ordinary X-rays fluorescent screen, which is simply a piece of card painted over with the same fluorescent substance in the form of powder, is very convenient for these experiments. When thin pieces of metal foil are placed between the radium and the crystals you see their brightness is only slightly reduced, while several shillings can be interposed one above the other without altogether stopping the rays from the radium. Those in the front will see the crystals still shining faintly, although the rays from the radium have first to traverse more than half an inch of solid silver before reaching the crystals. The electrical effect of radioactivity can be shown in a very rough and simple way with this, comparatively speaking, large quantity of radium. A silk tassel is stroked with a rubber tobacco-pouch and so electrified. All the threads then repel one another and stand out as you see (Fig. 4). The moment the radium is brought near the threads collapse at once (Fig. 5). Lastly, the photographic action of the rays is seen in the photograph (Fig. 6, facing p. 31)

FIG. 4.—SILK TASSEL ELECTRIFIED.

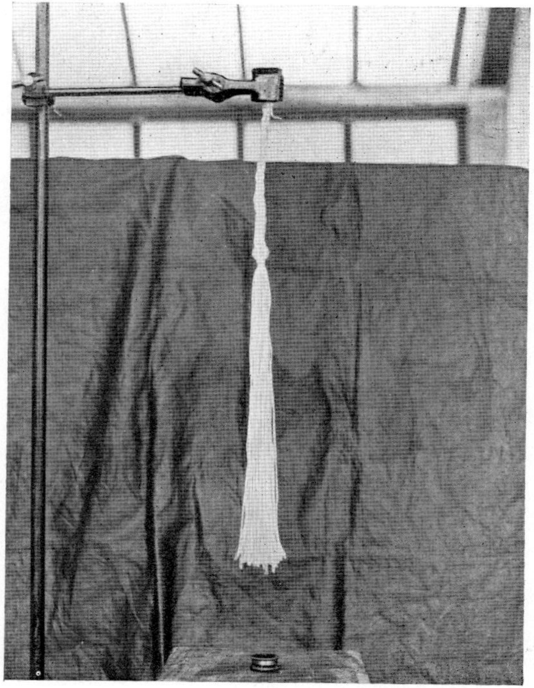

FIG. 5.—SILK TASSEL DISCHARGED BY THE RAYS FROM RADIUM.

which was obtained by slowly writing, with a small tube containing a small fraction of a grain of radium bromide as if it were a pencil, over a photographic plate wrapped in black paper, and then developing the plate without exposure to light.

By the aid of delicate thermometers it could also be shown that this small quantity of radium is always a few degrees hotter than the surrounding air.

Cost of Radium.

The one fact about radium, which every one is aware of, is its tremendous cost. When you consider that even of the best ore several hundredweights must be worked up to obtain the small quantity here exhibited, you can understand that the price is necessarily very high. The price rose rapidly from about 8s. the milligram for radium bromide in 1903 to about £15 the milligram in 1912, and even at the latter price very inferior preparations have found a ready sale. During the war, in which radium found several applications for illuminating rifle sights, compass cards and the like, over £20 a milligram was paid, and it is likely to remain at this high level. We shall see, as we proceed, that from its very nature any strongly radioactive body like radium must always be excessively rare. Indeed, in the degree of radioactivity we have a scientific standard of rarity, and therefore of " value." There are unfortunately some fields of scientific investigation, of which radioactivity is one, which cannot be thoroughly explored without continuous and considerable expenditure. The old boast of science, that some of her grandest discoveries were made with very simple apparatus, largely built up of wire and sealing-wax, costing little or nothing, does not apply to any of the discoveries with which we are now concerned. The investigations of Mme. Curie naturally have cost many thousands of pounds, provided in part by the Austrian Government and the Rothschilds. This radium we are using to-night we owe to the work of a German chemist, Dr. Giesel, who undertook its extraction on a large scale in the early days when the raw material was to be obtained in the market, and who very unselfishly distributed much of the radium he prepared among workers in all parts of the world.

The chief source of radium at the present time (1920) is American carnotite, which contains 2 per cent. of uranium in the form of a uranium potassium vanadate, mixed with sandstone. Its use in medicine and, later, in war has produced results as startling in the field of common sense as in that of physical science. "A great industry has sprung up." The creator of the wealth, the scientific investigator who discovered the material and the methods of winning it, and made a free gift of all his hard-won knowledge to the community, is now unable to afford to buy radioactive materials, even in the modest quantities he needs for scientific investigation.

The Doctrine of Energy.

To-night it is not my intention to take you through the various phases of the new properties of radium. We have to face squarely the great general question which its simple existence has demanded of physical science. Last century will remain for ever memorable on account of the development and establishment of the great doctrine of energy. Those were splendid days for physical science in Scotland, for that doctrine, which lies at the root of all modern industry and enterprise, took its rise largely in Scotland, and was developed by Tait, of Edinburgh, and Lord Kelvin, of Glasgow.

For a full account of these stirring developments you should read Tait's *Recent Advances in Physical Science*, which, in spite of the fact that it is now over forty years old, still continues fresh and inspiring. The first law, that of the conservation of energy, states that energy is a real entity, and has a real existence no less than matter, and no more than matter can energy be created or destroyed, although the forms it may assume are legion. The second law, that of the availability of energy, is sufficiently accurately stated for present purposes by saying that the same energy is available for useful work but once. To obtain useful work from any source of stored-up or potential energy, it is necessary to transform it into new forms which are kinetic, and by which something is made to move. As motion is invariably attended by friction or similar processes, ultimately the energy passes into heat. It is said to be degraded into low-grade or waste energy, for although all forms of energy tend, after assuming the kinetic form, to turn into heat, the transformation of the waste heat so produced back into useful forms cannot be practically effected. The conversion is not altogether impossible, but requires for its accomplishment the degradation of more fresh energy than is gained, and so is practically out of the question.

The practical aspect of the question may be summed up by saying that if you want useful energy you must pay for it like any other commodity, and the value of the energy, though not the energy itself, is destroyed by use. The up-to-date street car driven by the electric motor, which has displaced the old horse-tram, although it has not the same obvious incentive to locomotion as its predecessor, nevertheless does not go by itself. It requires energy or power, which is bought and sold and has a value as strictly as the oats and hay which energised the now emancipated horse. The driving power of the machinery of the modern world is often mysterious, but the laws of energy state that nothing goes by itself, and our experience, in spite of all the perpetual motion machines which inventors have claimed to have constructed, bore this doctrine out, until we came face to face with radium. Nothing goes by itself in Nature, except apparently radium and the radioactive substances. That is why, in radioactivity, science has broken fundamentally new ground.

I cannot too plainly insist that available energy,

though immaterial and intangible, has a definite and real physical existence. Were it not so, coal would not be the very expensive commodity it unfortunately is rapidly becoming. No one burns coal for the sake of polluting the atmosphere, but simply and solely because it gives out during combustion a certain amount of energy as light or heat. Last century civilisation may be said to have attained its majority and to have entered upon the control of an inheritance of energy stored up by the sun in fuel during the long ages of the past, and now it is dissipating that inheritance as quickly as it can. With the light-heartedness and irresponsibility of youth, it is taking no thought of the future, but confidently assumes that the supply of natural energy, upon which at every turn it is now entirely dependent, will continue indefinitely. Well ! if it does not do so, new stores of energy cannot be created to order, and there will be an end to the age of energy in which we are living, and to civilisation as we have come to understand it.

Measurement of the Energy emitted by Radium.

Energy is susceptible of exact measurement and, though it exists in many varieties, all forms of energy can be most readily and completely converted into heat and measured as such. The energy given out by radium, although it is in nature new, is no exception to this rule. Practically the whole of the energy is transformed into heat when the radium is kept in a leaden vessel, so that the rays are absorbed in the surrounding metal. The actual amount of heat given out, for instance, by this small quantity on the table is, of course, very small, but, in comparison with the quantity of substance producing it, it is very great indeed. Exact experiments have proved that 1 gram (=15·4 grains) of radium gives out 133 calories per hour.[1] The amount of heat evolved by

---

[1] The caloric is the quantity of heat required to raise 1 gram of water 1° Centigrade. Spelt with a capital C, the Caloric is 1,000 calories

any quantity of radium in three-quarters of an hour is as much as is required to raise a quantity of water equal in weight to the radium from the freezing-point to the boiling-point. Radium bromide, if it is dry, consists roughly of three-fifths by weight of the element radium and two-fifths of the element bromine. Half a grain of radium bromide thus evolves two and a half calories every hour. This specimen of half a grain of radium bromide has been in my possession for sixteen years, and the outpouring of energy has been going on ceaselessly day and night at a steady rate. A simple calculation shows that in this time about 350,000 calories have been evolved. To obtain an idea of what this means consider the amount of energy given out in the burning of coal. A weight of coal equal to the weight of this radium bromide would give out during complete combustion only about 250 calories, so that this radium has evolved in sixteen years 1,400 times the energy obtainable from the same weight of coal. I have chosen coal for the comparison because the combustion of carbon furnishes the modern world with its main supply of energy. During the last sixteen years this radium has given fourteen hundred times as much energy as could be obtained from an equal weight of any other kind of substance in any way known. Coal is no longer coal when it is burnt and consumed. Gunpowder and dynamite, once they have exploded and evolved their stored-up energy, disappear as such, and there remain incombustible and non-explosive solids and gases, out of which no more energy can be drawn. But this radium is as active as ever. So far, careful measurements have failed to detect the least diminution in the radio-activity of radium with time. Rather it increases steadily, rapidly in the first month and slowly for the first few years after preparation, for certain profound reasons we shall have to go into subsequently. These show also that after some thousands of years the evolution of energy must cease. But the calculated diminution is only some four per cent. per century.

The Source of Cosmical Energy.

In the face of a new fact of this character it is obvious that this doctrine of energy, which we thought so well founded, requires further consideration. Based as it has always been on the results of our experience and the practical impossibility of achieving perpetual motion of any kind, it is confronted with a natural example, going on apparently for an unlimited space of time under our very eyes, which not only does not come to a stop, but which cannot be stopped by any means whatever. Now, although the doctrine of energy accords well enough with our terrestrial experiences, the student of the physical sciences has only to turn his thoughts from the laboratory to the heavens to see there, in the larger laboratory of Nature, an example of practical perpetual motion on the grandest and most majestic scale. What, for example, is the source of the apparently inexhaustible supply of energy from the sun, upon the receipt of a minute and insignificant fraction of which life on this planet absolutely depends for its continued existence from year to year? This is a question which has been frequently asked and only imperfectly answered by physical science. It has been the custom vaguely to connect the apparently endless and inexhaustible outpourings of energy going on everywhere in the universe with its vast scale and dimensions. In the background there has always been the tacit assumption that the supply of fresh energy is only apparently inexhaustible, and that in some remote future a time will at length arrive when the supplies of fresh energy are exhausted and all things will come to a stop and remain at rest for ever. We have applied the teachings of the laboratory, our knowledge of the laws of energy and its conservation, and the impossibility of perpetual motion, without modification to the cosmos, only making allowance for its enormous scale.

Astronomers, in consequence of the new discoveries,

are no longer compelled to regard cosmical evolution as proceeding on these old conventional lines. It is not so certain as it was that it is only a question of time before the sun and planets cool down to a dead uniform temperature. In former days this point of view was the only possible one. A hot body radiating heat and light into space, even when all possible sources of energy, such as the accretion of meteorites, shrinkage, etc., have been allowed for, must ultimately radiate away its energy. The same is still true but with a difference. Thus Professor Tait, in his *Recent Advances in Physical Science* (1876), says (p. 169): "If we were to trace the state of affairs back, instead of to ten millions, to a hundred millions of years, we should find that (if the earth then existed at all) if that collocation of matter which we call the earth was then actually formed, and if the physical laws which at present hold have been in operation during that hundred million years, then the surface of the earth would undoubtedly have been liquid and at a high white heat, so that it would have been utterly incompatible with the existence of life of any kind such as we can conceive from what we are acquainted with. Thus we can say at once to geologists, that granting this premiss—that physical laws have remained as they now are, and that we know of all the physical laws which have been operating during that time—we cannot give more scope for their speculations than about ten or (say at most) fifteen millions of years.

"But I dare say many of you are acquainted with the speculations of Lyell and others, especially of Darwin, who tell us that even for a comparatively brief portion of recent geological history three hundred millions of years will not suffice.

"We say, so much the worse for geology as at present understood by its chief authorities, for, as you will presently see, physical considerations from various independent points of view render it utterly impossible that more than ten or fifteen millions of years can be granted."

Again (p. 154): "Take (in mass equal to the sun's

mass) the most energetic chemicals known to us, and in proper proportion for giving the greatest amount of heat by actual chemical combination, and, so far as we yet know their properties, we cannot see the means of supplying the sun's present waste for even 5,000 years. . . . This question is totally unanswerable, unless there be chemical agencies at work in the sun of a far more powerful order than anything that we meet with on the earth's surface."

Radium and the "Physically Impossible."

I do not quote these utterances with any wish to revive the old controversy between geologists and physicists, long since tacitly abandoned by both sides mutually as barren and unprofitable, but because of their present extraordinary aptness. To-day, science has come to know, by means of radioactivity, of agencies at work on the earth's surface of a far more powerful order than anything that was known in the time of Professor Tait. The discovery of radioactivity and the revelation it has given of unsuspected stores of energy in Nature available for cosmical purposes, of necessity put the whole question of the evolution, the past history and the future destiny of the universe in a new light. This is one of the conclusions of clearly general interest which follow from the recent discoveries.

There is nothing of the vast scale and dimensions of the universe about this tiny scrap of radium. Yet it is giving out energy at a rate, relative to its mass, which no sun or star is doing. Suppose, for example, our sun, instead of being composed of the materials it is, which we know by the spectroscope are practically the same as those of the earth, were made of pure radium. Provided only that every part of its mass gave out energy at the rate this radium on the table is doing, there would then be no difficulty in accounting for its outpourings of energy. Rather, the light and heat that would be given out from such a sun would be of the order of a million times greater than they actually are. On another count also one's thoughts almost unconsciously revert from radium to the transcendental phenomena of the larger universe, for in no other phenomena are we so reduced to the position of onlookers, powerless alike to influence or control. All the powerful resources of the modern laboratory—extremes of heat and cold, and of pressure, violent chemical reagents, the action of powerful explosives and the most intense electrical agencies—do not affect the radioactivity of radium or the rate at which it works in the slightest degree. It draws its supplies of energy from an hitherto unknown source and obeys as yet undiscovered laws. There is something sublime about its aloofness from and its indifference to its external environment. It seems to claim lineage with the worlds beyond us, fed with the same inexhaustible fires, urged by the same uncontrollable mechanism which keeps the great suns alight in the heavens over endless periods of time. This tiny speck of matter we can hold in our hands exhibits in perfect miniature many ancient mysteries, forgotten almost in their familiarity, or mistakenly and too easily dismissed as belonging and appropriate to the infinitely great dimensions of the universe. The " physical impossibility " of one era becomes the commonplace of the next, and in the controversy between the geologists and the physicists we have a good illustration that no theory can claim a universal application. It is of necessity partial, and bounded on all sides by the unknown and unexplored. It is rarely proved false, so surely and truly are the foundations of modern science laid, but it is liable at any moment to be restricted in its application to the particular cases for which it was formulated and found not to apply in new spheres at the time of its inception unsuspected. As we shall see, the law of the conservation of energy is not necessarily controverted by any of the new facts with reference to radium, but prior to these discoveries our knowledge of the available sources of energy in Nature has been partial and superficial to a degree.

CHAPTER III
RAYS OF RADIOACTIVE SUBSTANCES

THE RADIATIONS OF THE RADIO-ELEMENTS.

IN the previous lectures we have considered the bare fact that radium and the radioactive substances are continually evolving from themselves a perennial supply of energy, and the fundamentally new ground which this discovery opens up in physical science. To-night our inquiries will be directed to one special portion of the subject, namely, the nature of the rays emitted by the radioactive elements, by means of which, or rather of the effects of which, the property was first discovered. These rays themselves, apart from their effects, we have hitherto scarcely considered, but they play an essential part in the theoretical scheme by which the activity of the radio-elements is now interpreted.

The tracing back of the main effects of radioactivity, photographic, fluorescent, electrical, and thermal, to definite *radiations* emitted by the radio-elements came very early in the subject, but it must not be forgotten that such tracing back is of the essence of the discovery. Too frequently it is wrongly assumed without such evidence that any substance capable of simulating one or other of the various effects of radioactivity is therefore a radioactive substance. Naturally, the exact study of the new radiations has been mainly the work of physicists. They have succeeded, not only in clearly analysing into distinct classes the complex radiations involved and distinguishing the part played by each alone, but also they have advanced very far towards a solution of the real nature of each class of radiation emitted. Much of this latter work, however, is based upon reasoning of too specialised and intricate character for general presentation, and as these lectures are intended primarily for the general public, and not for trained physicists, I propose concentrating attention for the most part on the conclusions which are universally accepted and of the greatest general interest. Although the reasoning is difficult, the chief conclusions are very simple and easily followed, and they fit in with the general scheme of the cause and nature of radioactivity in a way which makes the whole subject clearer and more easily visualised.

α-, β- AND γ-RAYS.

The first analysis of the complex radiations emitted by each of the radio-elements—uranium, thorium, and radium—was done by Sir Ernest Rutherford, and much of the work we are considering is his, and has called forth in their highest degree his well-known experimental genius and energy. He classed the rays into three main types, the α-, β- and γ-, distinguished from one another by enormous differences in their power of penetrating matter. I may say at once that the α-rays of radium, for instance, are readily distinguishable in penetrating power from the α-rays of uranium, and the latter again from those of thorium. Moreover, the α-rays of radium are themselves complex and consist of no less than four separate types readily distinguished. The same is true of the β- and γ-rays of radium, which are themselves complex and recognisably different from the β- and γ-rays of uranium or thorium. But the differences between the α-rays as a class, for example, are small and unimportant relatively compared to the enormous difference between any α-ray and any β-ray or γ-ray. The most penetrating α-ray known is not much more than twice as penetrating as the least penetrating known, whereas the β-rays as a class may be considered to be approximately a hundred times more penetrating than the α-, and the γ-rays a hundred times more penetrating than the β. Again, the kind of matter penetrated, although it has a certain influence which may be different for different types of rays, is only of secondary importance. For these rays, like the new X-rays, and unlike light, are absorbed by matter roughly in proportion to its density, and quite independently of its optical qualities of transparency and opacity. The first result of these researches was to bring into prominence the α-class of rays, which at first sight are of apparently little importance, and to diminish relatively the importance of the β-class of rays which had been operative in the photographic effects hitherto mainly studied. For the α-rays are completely absorbed by very thin screens—even by a sheet of thin paper, or by three inches of ordinary gaseous air,—and they produce but little action on the photographic plate in comparison with the β-rays, which are able to pass through a visiting card or piece of tinfoil with ease. To the electrical test—the discharge, for example, of an electrified silk tassel or electroscope—the α-rays are immensely more effective than the β- and γ-rays together, and from this fact Rutherford concluded, and the conclusion has been wholly borne out by subsequent developments, that the energy possessed by these feebly penetrating, and not at first sight very striking, α-rays is always immensely greater than that of the other two types taken together. In fact, the β- and γ-rays at most possess but a few per cent. of the total energy of radiation, and therefore are in this fundamental respect relatively of less consequence than the previously neglected α-class. Although less suited to lecture experiments than the other more penetrating types, the α-class have proved far the most instructive and important in the theory of radioactive change.

FIG. 6.—WRITTEN BY RADIUM IN THE DARK.
(From a Radiograph by R. Hill Crombie, Esq., *Journal of the Röntgen Society*, Dec., 1906.)

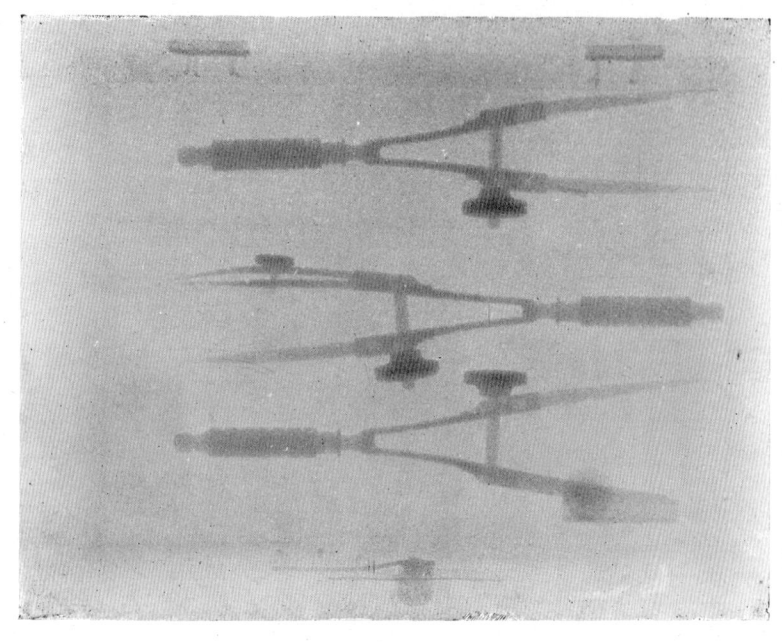

FIG. 7.—CLOSED BOX OF COMPASSES TAKEN WITH THE γ-RAYS OF RADIUM.

Experiments with the Penetrating β- and γ-Rays.

The small capsule in which my radium is contained is closed by a thin sheet of mica, which effectively stops all the α-rays, so that in working with the capsule only the β- and γ-rays are operative. The platinocyanide salts fluoresce most brilliantly under the β-rays. On interposing successive thicknesses of thin copper or aluminium foil the fluorescence is weakened, very rapidly at first, but a point is soon reached when the feeble fluorescence remaining is not much further weakened by additional thicknesses of foil. This is because the β-rays have all been absorbed, and there remain only the relatively feeble but extraordinarily penetrating γ-rays. These γ rays are always very feeble, and comparatively unimportant, but their chief interest lies in the fact that they are by far the most penetrating type of radiation at present known. If the capsule is completely closed in a box of steel, half an inch thick, and a platinocyanide crystal laid on the top, those in front can readily see that the crystal still fluoresces, and stops the moment it is taken away from the radium. Through a pile of twelve shillings, or pennies, the effect can still be observed, while by means of a sensitive gold-leaf electroscope it has been shown that a minute proportion of the rays can penetrate a foot thickness of solid lead.

The rays from radium are not well adapted for the taking of radiographs of the kind produced by X-rays. The β-rays are hardly sufficiently penetrating for this purpose, so that the flesh as well as the bones of the hand, for example, casts a heavy shadow. The γ-rays, on the other hand, are far too penetrating, and the bones hardly cast a shadow at all. (The picture (Fig. 7), however, is a good example of a radium radiograph taken by the γ-rays of radium. A small box of compasses with the lid shut was placed on a table. Over it, film down, was placed an X-ray plate wrapped in a light-tight envelope.

On the floor beneath, at a distance of twenty-five inches from the plate, was placed one-tenth of a grain of pure radium bromide sealed up in a tiny glass tube. The radium was placed between the poles of an electromagnet, as recommended by Mme. Curie, to deflect away the β-rays which tend to blur the distinctness of the picture. In this way the γ-rays of radium were alone used. The exposure was five days. It will be seen that the shadow cast by the wooden box is scarcely noticeable, while even the metal compasses and fastenings of the box by no means entirely stop the rays. The metal parts appear in the negative only slightly darker than the unprotected portions of the plate. The negative was reduced and intensified before reproduction.

At first the γ-rays appeared to be a secondary radiation produced by and accompanying the β-rays, much as X-rays are produced by and accompany cathode-rays. The β- and γ-rays seemed always to go together, any variation of the β-rays being accompanied by a similar variation of the γ-rays. This is now known, however, not to be invariably the case, and the opinion is gaining ground that the β- and γ-rays are not necessarily connected. The question of the real nature of the γ-rays was the last to be solved, and as the rays are not of primary importance at the present stage we may, with these experiments and remarks, defer the subject and pass on to the more detailed consideration of the two more important types of rays.

The Feebly Penetrating α-Rays.

Before proceeding to show experiments with the α-rays it is necessary to touch on certain considerations which come into play on account of their very great absorption in passing through matter. In the first place, radioactivity is a mass or volume phenomenon. That is to say, every part, not the surface only but the inner portions also, of a radium salt, for example, is giving

THE FEEBLY PENETRATING RAYS

out α-, β- and γ-rays. All these rays are absorbed by the substance itself very considerably, for the salts of radium are dense or heavy. But this absorption naturally does not affect the more penetrating rays nearly so much as the feebly penetrating α-rays. That part of the latter, generated inside the salt, does not escape at all. Only a very thin surface film contributes to the α-radiation. The consequence is that whereas, with the small quantities of radium that we have to work with, the strength of the penetrating rays is more or less proportional to the quantity of radium employed, with the α rays this is no longer the case. The weight of the substance is less important than the amount of surface exposed. A very small quantity, say a milligram, of radium bromide, spread out as a thin film on a large plate, will give out immensely more α-rays than the same quantity in the form of a small crystal. In order to free the β- and γ-rays from the α-rays, or the γ-rays from the β-rays, it suffices to interpose screens of successively increasing thickness until the more easily stopped type is completely absorbed. But it is not possible so easily to eliminate by physical methods the β- and γ-rays from the α-rays in order to leave the latter by themselves. For practical purposes, however, this result can be achieved very simply. If we take a very minute quantity of radium salt spread over a very large area, the β- and γ-rays from so small a quantity will be so feeble as to be practically negligible, whereas the α-rays under these circumstances will reach their greatest intensity. For practical purposes a thin film of pure radium salt can be used to give α-rays by themselves, essentially free from β- and γ-rays.

EXPERIMENTS WITH α-RAYS.

Such a thin film I have prepared for these experiments. On this shallow platinum dish, about a square inch in area, I have evaporated down a solution containing about a milligram of pure radium bromide, and the dish, with its precious film open to the air, is carefully preserved when not in use in a special tube containing a desiccating agent to keep it dry, so that without undue risk of loss I can work with a bare film of radium salt and show you the α-rays. Over the bare film I bring the electrified silk tassel. It collapses instantly, in fact, much faster than it does when brought over the whole thirty milligrams of radium bromide contained in the mica-covered capsule. The α-rays from one milligram of radium produce more electrical effect than the β- and γ-rays from thirty milligrams. Now I cover the bare film of radium with a single sheet of thin writing-paper, which stops the α-rays completely, the β- and γ-rays scarcely at all. You observe the tassel remains now charged as if the radium were absent. The β- and γ-rays from so small a quantity hardly appreciably discharge it.

But if I displace the paper ever so slightly and expose a tiny part of the bare surface, the tassel instantly collapses. From these experiments, and the fact that it was the fashion at the time to cover radioactive substances when experimenting with them, you will have no difficulty in understanding how it was that these feebly penetrating but intensely powerful α-rays remained at first neglected and almost unknown.

The Range of α-Rays in Air.

I now have to show you a very striking experiment indeed, suggested by some profound investigations of Professor Bragg in Adelaide, on the α-rays, to which we shall again have occasion to refer. So readily are these α-rays stopped that a few inches of air suffice entirely to absorb them. But the α-rays show this remarkable peculiarity not exhibited by any other type known. Each individual α-ray of any one homogeneous type travels exactly the same distance in an absorbing medium, and is stopped sharply and completely when a certain thickness of matter has been penetrated. The

Fig. 9.—Apparatus to show Absorption of α-Rays by Air.

Fig. 11.—The Spinthariscope of Sir William Crookes.

To face p. 35

consequence is that if we work with a homogeneous beam of α-rays, just without the distance of complete absorption, there is absolutely no effect, while just within there is a very large effect. I have said that the α-rays derived from radium are complex, consisting of four different types, each with a definite " range," as it is termed, or distance, it will travel in any given absorbing medium. For the purposes of this experiment, however, it is necessary to consider only the most

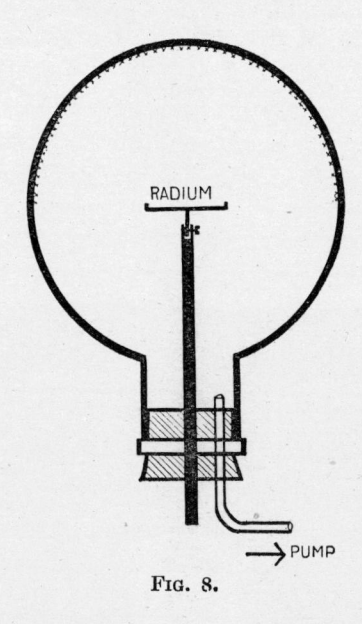

FIG. 8.

penetrating type, which Bragg found could travel in air at atmospheric pressure and ordinary temperature, 71 millimetres (or just under three inches) and no more. Now this flask (Figs. 8 and 9) is a little more than six inches in diameter, and it has been coated on the upper hemisphere of the inside surface with a phosphorescent film of zinc sulphide. For these α-rays the usual phosphorescers (*e.g.*, the platinocyanides, willemite, etc.), employed for the β- and γ-rays, are far less sensitive than crystallised zinc sulphide, or, as it is called, Sidot's hexagonal blende. The coated flask is arranged so that I can plunge my platinum dish with its bare radium film upward inside the flask and hold it centrally by a cork. In the dark, the flask being full of air, you observe hardly any glow. The three inches of air surrounding the radium film on all sides suffices completely to stop all the α-rays, and the β- and γ-rays, from so small a quantity of radium, produce only a negligible effect on the zinc sulphide. But I have connected the flask to an air-pump and can pump out the air. At the very first stroke of the pump the whole globe flashes into luminescence, and as I continue pumping the glow gets stronger and fairly illuminates the immediate neighbourhood with its soft white light. I now readmit the air, and the glow disappears as suddenly as it came. So that you see, with somewhat carefully designed arrangements, and keeping in mind the peculiar properties of these α-rays which physicists have exactly worked out, it is possible even from a minute amount of pure radium bromide to obtain quite a fair amount of light, whereas the same quantity of radium less cunningly disposed would give very little effect. Radium compounds are usually preserved in sealed tubes so as to prevent them absorbing moisture from the atmosphere. Under these circumstances the effects produced by these α-rays are not observed.

The Physical Nature of Radiation.

Problems connected with the real physical nature of radiation are, it is well recognised, among the most fundamental in physics, and they involve more deeply perhaps than any others the great underlying metaphysical relationships between the external world of physical fact and the subjective mental processes by which we attempt to visualise these facts and obtain some sort of a reasonable explanation of them. Take, for example, the great problem that is always before us of the real nature of light. Is there anything more difficult of mental comprehension ? The difficulties are not minimised but rather increased by the very definite view we take to-day of energy as a separate entity having a real physical existence.

Contemplate for a moment, if you can, the origin of the energy which impels every moving thing in earth or sea or sky. With the exception of a very small and practically negligible movement contributed by the tides and by volcanic agencies, and, it must not be forgotten, by the radioactive substances themselves, all things which move do so directly or indirectly by virtue of the energy reaching this earth *as radiations* in the form of the sun's light and heat. Great masses move hither and thither here because of happenings at some time past, remote or recent, 90 millions of miles away in the sun. Inevitably, when we begin to contemplate radiation phenomena, we are driven to inquire into *the medium* filling the outer void of space by virtue of which this immaterial, but vital entity—*energy*—reaches us from far distant worlds. It is true we call it *ether*, and try to give to it all sorts of material, or pseudo-material, characteristics. Lord Kelvin seems to have spent a large part of his leisure time trying as it were to dematerialise matter into ether, that is, trying by all sorts of mechanically ingenious arrangements and analogy from material models—the only possible models our minds can yet grasp—to obtain a possible construction which would simulate the elusive but all pervading ether. Others, on the well-known principle that topsy-turvydom, if only consistent and all-embracing enough, results finally in a system no less logical and rational than the original one, have given to the ether inconceivably great density, and to the atoms of matter the character of holes or voids in it. The necessity for the existence of a universal all-pervading medium, or ether, capable of transmitting energy, no one in these days of wireless telegraphy would deny, but on the question of its real nature opinion is as divided as it well could be.

The tendency, however, in modern physics to-day is rather to derive and explain material phenomena from the properties of the ether than to attempt to construct an ether on a material or pseudo-material model. As yet, however, we know little about the properties of the ether itself. One definite thing we do know, for certain, and have known for a very long time, namely the velocity at which influences are transmitted across the ether. It is 185,000 miles a second, the speed of light. So far as we yet know, all influences that are transmitted by the ether travel at this one definite velocity. Not only light, but also the electro-magnetic radiations employed in wireless telegraphy, the magnetic storms, as they are termed, which reach us from the sun, and also, we believe, the X-rays, travel through the ether at this one definite speed.

Corpuscular Radiation.

The great mind of Newton two centuries ago appreciated to the full the fundamental difficulty in the explanation of radiation, and proposed the only way of escape from the more modern doctrine of an ether which, so far as I know, has ever been put forward.

Light, on the Newtonian hypothesis, consisted in the emission from the glowing body of excessively minute material particles or corpuscles travelling with immense velocity. This corpuscular theory, so far as light is concerned, failed when subjected to a closer examination, and gave way to the present undulatory theory that light consists in a transverse vibration of the ether, the existence of which, it was beginning to be recognised, was as great a necessity for the transmission of gravitational, magnetic, and other forms of energy which reach us from outer space as it was for the transmission of radiation itself. Though proved wrong so far as light is concerned, this idea of corpuscular radiation, strangely enough, will rank as one of the most suggestive flashes of Newton's genius, for it, in fact, anticipated by two

CORPUSCULAR AND WAVE-RADIATION 39

centuries the march of experimental discovery. To-day, thanks to radioactivity, science has been enriched by the discovery of α-, β-, and γ-rays, and two, at least, out of these types, the α- and the β-rays, are not, like light, vibrations of the ether, but consist of the emission of excessively minute material particles (atoms and corpuscles) travelling with immense velocity. This is one of two chief main lines of evidence that radioactivity is an accompanying manifestation of " atomic disintegration."

Into this aspect of the matter, however, I do not propose entering to-night. Its consideration is more conveniently deferred. It is sufficient to say that the α- and β-rays, or, as I shall henceforth also refer to them, α- and β-particles, comprise the lighter fragments, as it were, of the disintegrating atoms of the radioactive substance. In ordinary circumstances radium appears to be expelling both α- and β-particles together, but this as we shall come to see is due to the fact that several successive disintegrations are occurring, and the effect is a composite one. The nature of these rays is so utterly different from that of light that it is worth while to stop and examine the difference a little more closely.

THE WAVE THEORY OF LIGHT.

The wave theory of light has often been illustrated by what happens when a stone is dropped into a pool. Ripples extend outwards in concentric circles from the disturbance. The water, as the ripple reaches it, first rises above, then immediately afterwards falls below the normal level. The disturbance is propagated *transversely*, that is, outwards horizontally by a vertical, or up and down wave-movement of the water. The surface discloses the nature of the disturbance, but the same type of disturbance is taking place below the surface, and each circular ripple is in reality the section of a hemispherical shell. It is not possible to get an ether surface like a water surface, since the ether is all-pervading. Light travels out from an incandescent point in all directions in spherical ripples, in which a to-and-fro motion of some kind is going on in the ether, transverse to the direction of propagation of the light. Contrast with this what is believed to be the nature of the α- and β-rays given out from a radioactive substance. The rays are given out uniformly in all directions, not as a succession of spherical waves, but as the random flight of immense swarms of tiny projectiles ejected from the radioactive substance. For shortness I shall call this the "discrete theory," as contrasted with the wave theory, because the radiation is considered to be due to the flight, radially outward from the substances like the spokes of a wheel, of swarms of free-flying, independent discrete particles. You could hardly imagine two more different phenomena, and yet that it is not easy to distinguish between their effects is shown by the fact that for a long time a controversy raged between the two views regarding the nature of light itself.

α- AND β-RAYS DUE TO THE EXPULSION OF PARTICLES.

I must anticipate a little here for the sake of clearness. It is now an old story that in the tiniest grain of matter there is a mentally inconceivable myriad of separate atoms. In this tiny quantity of radium bromide, weighing half a grain, we know with fair certainty there are fifty million billion (5×10^{19}) separate atoms of radium, assuming that the compound is pure. It has been proved that, roughly, one two-thousandth of these disintegrate yearly. There are about 32,000,000 seconds in a year, so that in every *second* of time rather less than one thousand million of these radium atoms disintegrate, giving some small multiple of this number of α- and β-particles. So mighty a host projected outwards in all directions at random, as you may suppose, fill the surrounding space with their trajectories to all intents and purposes as completely as if they advanced as one continuous spherical wave-front. In other words, if only the number of projected particles is sufficiently great a discrete radiation will be, in many of its general effects and laws of propagation, not different from a wave-radiation. It is true that such a radiation will show neither regular reflection, refraction, nor polarisation in the manner that light does, and the absence of these phenomena for the α- and β-rays is part of the evidence in favour of their discrete nature. If, however, we continuously reduce the number of particles ejected, in other words, if we continuously diminish the quantity of radium employed, there should come a point when the discrete radiation should no longer simulate the wave-type. It should, as it were, break up and show discontinuity, much as some of those faint continuous light-patches in the heavens, known as the planetary nebulæ, when investigated by more and more powerful telescopes, begin to break up and show discontinuity, and finally are resolved into an innumerable host of separate twinkling stars. Is it possible so to resolve a swarm of α-rays?

The Individual Atom of Matter.

The older physicists who first deduced by accurate computation the weight and measure of the single individual atom and evaluated the number of billions contained in the smallest portion of matter perceptible to the senses, had they been soberly asked whether it would be possible ever to observe a single atom of matter, would have scouted the bare possibility. A single atom of matter! A single atom of matter! I recall this one exclamation, repeated over and over again with varying intonation by a distinguished foreign visitor, whose years had been spent at the microscope on the borderland between the perceptible and the imperceptible worlds, when the question we are now considering was under discussion at a British Association meeting.

Let us, however, now make a few calculations to see whether there is any hope whatever of being able to detect the effect of, say, a single α-particle expelled from radium, in the same sense as it has been found possible in astronomy to detect the individual stars which go to make up a planetary nebula.

In an earlier lecture (p. 17) I alluded to the smallest quantity of radium that could be detected by the aid of the gold-leaf electroscope, that is, therefore, by means of the α-rays emitted. It was one three-thousand-millionth of a grain. Half a grain, as we have seen, gives out a few thousand million α-particles every second. So that the smallest quantity of radium detectable by the ordinary electroscope must be giving out only a few individual α-particles per second. From a very early stage it appeared not inconceivable to Rutherford that a discontinuity in the emission of a-rays might actually be detected by using a very minute quantity of radium.

The Spinthariscope.

The problem was actually solved, almost unawares, by Sir William Crookes, by means of an instrument he devised and called the Spinthariscope. The instrument is the only genuine instrument worked by radium that it is at present possible to buy at the optician's in the ordinary way, and it can be bought—radium and all—for a few shillings. The reason for this apparent paradox is to be found in the fact that it is in the essence of the result to be attained to reduce the amount of radium to the smallest possible quantity, and this unusual condition allows of a practically unlimited number of spinthariscopes to be made out of an almost invisible quantity of radium bromide. The amount of radium in each instrument is absolutely unweighable and invisible. A needle, A, is made to touch a tiny phial which once contained radium, and is then mounted (Figs. 10, and 11 facing p. 35) centrally in a little brass tube, the size of a small reel of cotton, at the bottom of which is a phosphorescent screen, B, coated with zinc sulphide. At the other end of the tube is a lens, C, for magnifying the screen and, by means of a little screw, D, outside, the needle point may be moved nearer to or away from the screen. If now in a dark room the screen is observed through the lens, it will be seen to be luminous, and this luminosity can be concentrated or spread out by screwing the needle point nearer to or farther from the screen. After the eye has become used to the darkness it will be seen that the luminosity is not just a quiet

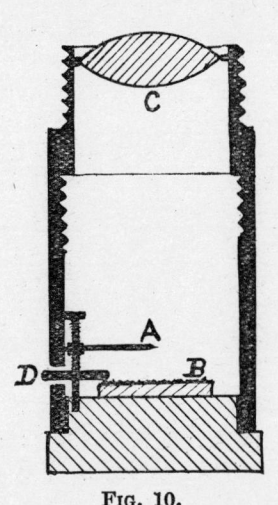

FIG. 10.

continuous glow. The light, like that of the planetary nebulæ, has been resolved and shows discontinuity. It resembles most nearly a shower of shooting stars. Bright momentary flashes of light or scintillations, too numerous at any instant to count, are appearing and disappearing in the field of vision. These flashes are caused by the α-particles of radium. This minute insignificant trace of radium is positively belching forth α-particles. It seems incredible that the incessant bombardment of the screen can be caused by such an infinitesimal amount of radium. Yet so it is, and in a month's time, if the instrument is re-examined, it will be found that the scintillations are as numerous and as brilliant as formerly. After a time, perhaps a year, the phosphorescent screen *itself* will be worn out by the incessant bombardment, will become insensitive and need renewal. But replace it by a new one and the radium will be found to be as energetic as ever. The owner of the instrument will pass away, his heirs and successors, and even his race will probably have been forgotten before the radium shows any appreciable sign of exhaustion.

The actual α-particle itself must, of course, be extremely small. How else could a mere speck of radium send out such an incessant and numerous swarm? As we have still to prove, the α-particle is an atom of helium, the second lightest atom of matter known. A grain of radium bromide expels every second about ten thousand million α-particles, and if we contemplate this mighty swarm expelled once every second of time throughout many centuries we may begin to have some idea of how many atoms there must be in a single grain of matter, and how small must be the single atom. The philosophers of only a generation ago would have ridiculed the hope that we should ever be able to look through a magnifying-glass to see the effect of a single atom of matter, yet each of the scintillations of the spinthariscope is nothing else.

Decay of α-Radiation.

The spinthariscope was the original, but to-day it is only one of many lines of evidence which have established the discrete character of the α-radiation and the nature of the α-particle. We know of many radioactive substances—polonium is one—emitting α-radiations, which gradually and completely lose their radioactivity with the lapse of time. Anticipating, we may say that the disintegration of polonium proceeds so rapidly that it is complete in the course of a few years. Were the process at all similar, for example, to the case

COUNTING α-PARTICLES

of a hot body cooling, one would expect a gradual alteration in the character of the radiation with the diminution of its intensity with lapse of time; whereas the character of the radiation is exactly the same at the end, when it has nearly all decayed, as it is at the beginning. This is explained simply on the view that the number of α-particles expelled grows less as the activity decays. The individual α-particles have the same velocity and other characteristics, whether expelled at the end or at the beginning of the process. Professor Bragg's discovery that each α-particle has a definite " range," characteristic of it, is quite inexplicable on a wave theory. The range of the α-particles emitted by polonium, for example, is thirty-eight millimetres of air, and though in the course of a few years the α-radiation of polonium decays always completely, the range of the α-particle expelled at the end is exactly the same as at the beginning.

COUNTING THE α-PARTICLES.

In this connection, finally, I may mention some really wonderful work recently done by Professor Rutherford and his co-worker Dr. Geiger, in which they have actually succeeded in counting directly the number of α-particles expelled from a given quantity of radium every second. As you may know, if two points are connected to an electrical machine, or other method of generating an electric force or tension, a spark will pass between them under suitable circumstances. Now suppose the distance apart of the two points is just so great that no spark will pass with the particular electrical tension applied, and that some radium is then brought near to the points. Then a spark will pass. The rays from radium by making the air a conductor of electricity facilitate the passage of the spark, so that under their influence the discharge will leap across a greater distance than it otherwise would. Substitute for the crude method of detecting the discharge by means of a spark a highly refined electrical instrument, known as the electrometer, in which, as in the galvanometer, a spot of light is reflected from a mirror attached to a needle, which can be arranged to move when a discharge passes across the gap, and you have the essential principle of Rutherford's arrangement. Such an arrangement can be made so excessively sensitive that the passage of a *single* α-particle from radium through what corresponded to the "spark gap" of the first arrangement described, is sufficient to cause the spot of light from the needle of the electrometer to move with a sudden jerk. The experiment consists, then, in counting the number of these sudden jerks of the electrometer needle in a given time, when a known quantity of radium is placed at a known distance. The radium has to be placed many yards away from the apparatus, and the α-rays are fired along a long exhausted tube with a small window at the end to admit the passage of a very minute definite proportion of the total number of α-particles, which proportion can be calculated. In the actual experiments the distance of the radium and the size of the window through which the α-particles passed were such that, roughly, only one out of every 100 million α-particles expelled found their way into the apparatus. The total number of α-particles actually expelled per second by a grain of radium in its normal condition was found to be about ten thousand million. Per milligram of radium the exact number per second is 136 million. These results were also checked by counting the number of scintillations per second in a special form of spinthariscope. There have always been scientific men who have regarded the atom and the atomic theory with suspicion, and have never tired of insisting upon its "hypothetical" character. It may therefore be rightly regarded as one of the greatest triumphs of science that an observer can now actually sit down in front of a vessel and with the aid of a watch count the number of atoms entering it every minute from a quantity of radium outside.

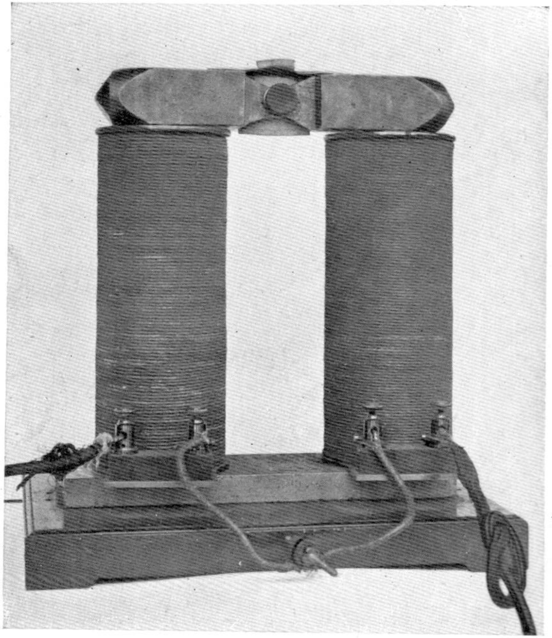

Fig. 12.—Electro-magnet.

The capsule of radium is fixed on the near side of the pole-pieces so that the rays pass between the poles to the screen on the far side.

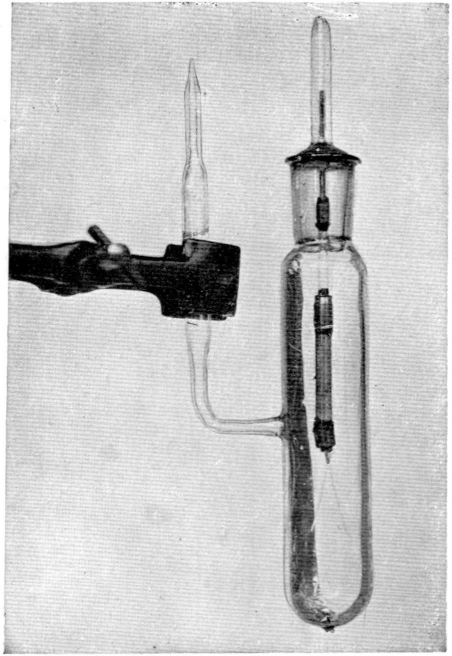

Fig. 16.—Professor Strutt's "Radium Clock."

To face p. 47

CHAPTER IV

RAYS OF RADIOACTIVE SUBSTANCES—*Continued.*

THE β-RAYS.

IN addition to their varying power of penetrating matter, there is another test which has proved of great service in analysing the three types of rays from radioactive bodies and in determining the real nature of each. The trajectories of some of the rays are powerfully influenced by a magnet, others are slightly, and others not at all affected. Thus the β-rays of all radioactive substances if caused to traverse the space between the poles of a magnet are very strongly deflected, and if the magnet is a powerful one may be completely coiled up into closed circles or spirals.

Faraday imagined that between the N-pole and S-pole of a magnet there existed actual *lines of magnetic force*. In the electro-magnet on the table (Fig. 12), which is formed so that the N- and S-poles are bent round so as to face one another, the lines of force between the opposite faces of the two pole-pieces are straight lines following the shortest distance between them. It is convenient to imagine with Faraday the actual existence of such lines of force. An electro-magnet is simply an arrangement in which a bar of soft iron can be magnetised at will by passing an electric current through a coil of wire wound round it. Soft iron of good quality, unlike steel, retains no appreciable permanent magnetism. It is very easily magnetised by an electric current, and its magnetism continues just so long as the current, and ceases practically completely when the current is switched off.

DEVIATION OF β-RAYS BY A MAGNET.

Now suppose a beam of β-rays of radium to be fired through the space between the pole-pieces at right angles to the lines of magnetic force. The path of the rays is bent. The rays tend to coil round the magnetic lines of force in circles. Suppose we look along the lines of force stretching from the N-pole to the S-pole, that is to say, suppose the eye to be placed at the centre of the N-pole and to be looking towards the centre of the S-pole. Then the β-rays will be coiled round into circles in a direction of rotation opposite to that of the hands of a clock, that is, as we say, counter clock-wise. If we look from the S-pole to the N-pole the direction of rotation is clock-wise. Now if the radium is placed behind the poles of the electro-magnet, and a screen of platinocyanide of barium is placed in front, and the distance between them is so adjusted to the strength of the magnet that when the latter is excited by an electric current the β-rays from the radium are coiled up into circles of lesser diameter than the distance between the radium and the screen, none of the β-rays will now reach the screen. This will be seen from Fig. 13. In this figure the eye is supposed to be at the centre of the S-pole of the magnet, looking towards the face of the N-pole. The rays from the radium passing up between the N-pole and the eye, in the top diagram, reach the screen. In the lower diagram the magnet is in action, and the rays are coiled clock-wise into circles, none reaching the screen.

The radium is contained in its mica-covered capsule so that only the β- and γ-rays are dealt with, the α-rays being suppressed. In the darkness you see the phosphorescent screen brilliantly luminous so long as the magnet is not excited. I switch on the current and the light of the screen at once goes out almost completely. The faint luminosity left behind is due to the γ-rays, which are not deviated at all, so far as we know, even by the strongest magnetic forces. If I interpose a penny in

MAGNETIC DEVIATION OF β-RAYS

front of the radium so that the γ-rays have now to traverse it before reaching the screen the faint luminosity is hardly diminished. Now I switch off the exciting current and the magnet almost instantly loses its magnetism, the β-rays spring back out of their circular into straight trajectories, strike the screen and cause it

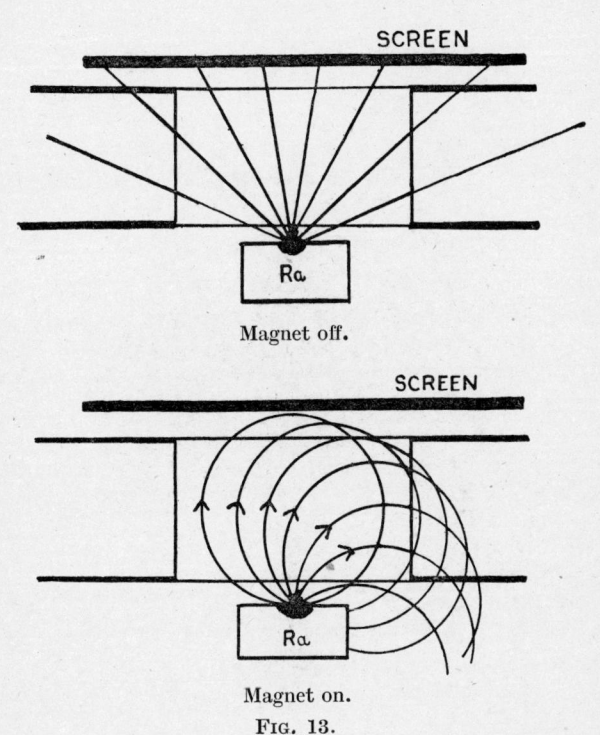

Magnet off.

Magnet on.
FIG. 13.

again to flash out into brilliance. Now the introduction of a penny causes the luminosity practically to disappear, all but for the faint glow due to the γ-rays.

ELECTRIC CHARGE CARRIED BY β-RAYS.

To a trained physicist the interest of this behaviour is due to the fact that it is exactly what would happen to a current of electricity if it were made to flow between the poles of a strong electro-magnet. If we employed a piece of ordinary wire to carry the current, the wire would tend to coil up into a circle exactly like the β-ray, and there would be a battle between the natural stiffness of the wire and the deviating magnetic force, and it would depend on their relative strengths which prevailed. With care, however, it is possible to use a fluid wire, which has no stiffness. If a strong current is passed through a thin aluminium wire it, of course, gets hot and finally melts, but retains its original form without breaking, hanging by virtue of its weight as a beautiful loop of glowing molten aluminium. Such a loop provides an extremely sensitive means of investigating the laws of action of magnets on currents, and you can see how violently and powerfully it is deviated if it is hung between the poles of the electro-magnet and the magnet then excited. The β-rays, as they traverse their course, behave exactly like a current of electricity. If they consisted of extremely rapidly moving particles—*charged with electricity*—we know that such a stream would behave to a magnet exactly like a current flowing in a flexible conductor.

The Nature of Electricity.

Now we do know the direction in which the β-rays are moving, namely *from* the radium, but we do not know, or at least did not till recently know, the direction in which the electricity is moving in an electric current. However, by long usage we speak in a purely conventional way of the + and − ends of a wire in which a current is flowing. We do not yet know for certain whether there are two kinds of electricity, a positive kind and a negative kind, but the probability is that there is only one kind, the negative kind, and that the effects of the opposite kind are due to a relative electrical scarcity or vacuum. It is much the same with heat and cold, except that we know the real thing is heat, and cold is the absence of it. A trained physicist

POSITIVE AND NEGATIVE ELECTRICITY   51

will speak of so much heat, or so little heat, or of one body having so much less heat than another, but he will not speak of so much cold, or one body having more cold than another, although often such a method of expression would be convenient and would lead to no error. In this sense we may speak both of positive and negative electricity without error. A current of electricity flowing along a wire from the positive to the negative we may look upon as due to the transport of *positive* electricity in the direction from + to −, *or* as the transport of *negative* electricity from − to +. The two ideas are equivalent and, in fact, identical for the present purposes. On the view that there is only one kind—the negative kind—of electricity, a positively charged body or atom is merely a body or atom with less negative electricity than is normally present in an " uncharged " or electrically neutral body.

In the β-rays we have a movement of charged particles *from* the radium, and we have to find out whether the particles are positively or negatively charged, using the terms positive and negative in their conventional electrical significance. If the rays were deviated in the same sense as a current flowing from + to − in the same direction as the rays, obviously we should conclude the β-rays were + ly charged. As a matter of fact we find the opposite is the case. When the β-rays are deviated clock-wise by the magnet a current of the kind described would be deviated counter clock-wise. To simulate the deviation of the β-rays the electric current must be a negative current, that is to say, must be either negative electricity flowing in the direction of the rays, or positive electricity flowing in the opposite direction. As there is no reason to doubt that the β-rays do come *from* the radium, the electric charge they carry must be negative.

Modern views are definite on the point that *if* there is only one electricity, that one is the kind which by convention has, unfortunately, been styled negative. The negative is the real electricity. The positive may, like cold, be the mere deficit of the real kind, or it may have a separate existence, the mirror image as it were of the other kind. I personally have always preferred the view that negative electricity is "electrical heat" and positive electricity "electrical cold," but a real answer to this question would no doubt prove itself to be a very fundamental step, and would require much further consideration.

The behaviour of the β-rays in a magnetic field associates them at once with some previously known radiations from the electrical discharge tubes exhausted to an extremely high degree of vacuum which are known generically as Crookes' tubes, from their first systematic investigator. Into this field of work I have no intention of entering in detail, for it is the one aspect of this subject which has received the most adequate treatment in the accounts of radioactivity written for the benefit of the public. A brief resumé only must suffice.

Radiant Matter or Cathode-Rays.

The β-rays are very similar in nature to the "Radiant Matter" (also called "cathode-rays" or "cathode-streams") of Sir William Crookes, obtained when an electric discharge or current is passed through a vessel exhausted to a very high degree of vacuum. The requisite degree of vacuum can be obtained with a little trouble by the aid of a mercury pump, based on the same principle as Torricelli's celebrated experiment with the barometer. But far quicker and more efficient methods have lately come into use. One such consists in absorbing the last traces of gas in the pores of the charcoal of cocoa-nuts cooled to the temperature of liquid air, according to the discovery of Sir James Dewar. Another method consists in absorbing the last traces of gas with the vapour of metallic calcium heated to a very high temperature in a special vacuum furnace. The discharge from the cathode, or negative pole, in a high vacuum then consists of radiant streams of particles travelling in straight lines and producing vivid green phosphorescence where they strike the glass walls of the vessel. Any obstacle placed in their path casts a sharp shadow, the glass beyond not fluorescing where protected from the bombardment by the obstacle. These particles also carry charges of negative electricity, and have great energy, heating to whiteness a piece of platinum interposed in their path, and causing the most intense fluorescence of willemite in the same way as the radium rays. Like the β-rays they are deviated by a magnet, and in the same sense, only very much more easily. Here is a form (Fig. 14) of Crookes' tube, designed to show the cathode-rays and their deviation by the action of a magnet. The electrodes consist of plates of metal, which are attached to the terminals of an induction coil, or an electrical machine or other sufficiently powerful source of electric tension. One electrode A is connected to the positive pole, and the other electrode B to the negative pole of the coil, and we have to concentrate our attention on the negative electrode, this being what is also called the "cathode." The tube has been exhausted by a pump until there is only about one ten-thousandth of the air left, and was then sealed up. Under such conditions the glass of the tube shines with a brilliant fluorescence when a discharge is forced through it. This fluorescence has been traced to "rays" inside the vessel, proceeding from the cathode at right angles to its surface and travelling in straight lines through the tube. Wherever they strike the glass they cause it to glow, just as the radium rays do.

In front of the cathode is a piece of mica with a slit cut in it, which stops all the rays except a narrow pencil passing through the slit. Along the length of the tube is fixed a fluorescent screen in the form of a plate painted with powdered willemite, and as the narrow pencil of rays impinge on this plate they trace out their path as a bright line of green fluorescence. Now if one pole of a magnet is brought behind the tube the rays are bent sharply to the left or right, depending on whether the

Without magnet.

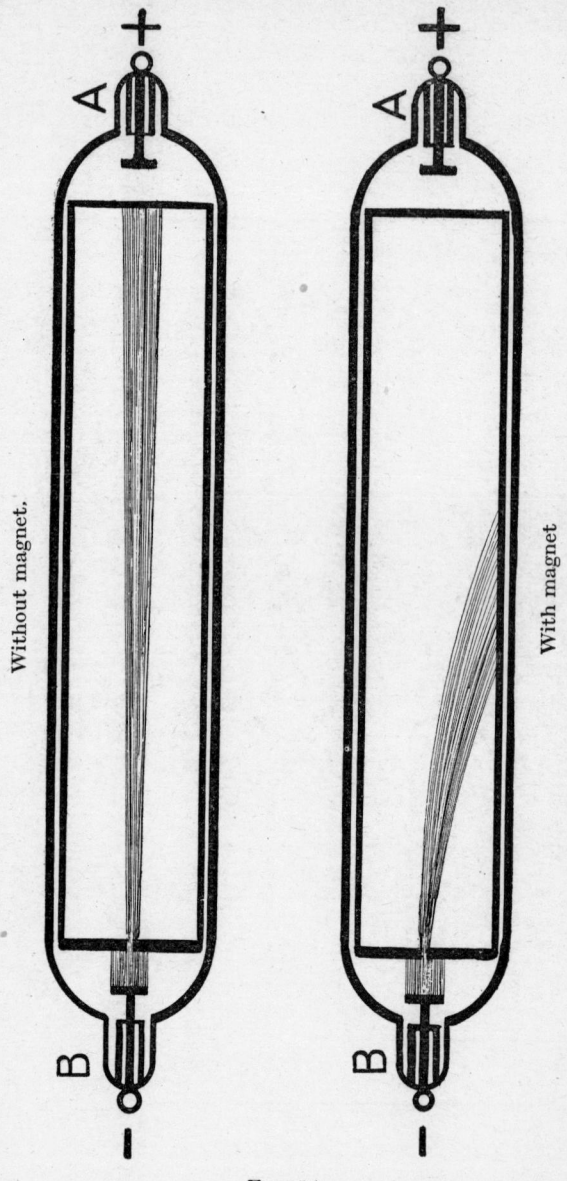

With magnet

Fig. 14.

THE ELECTRON

N- or the S-pole of the magnet is presented to the tube. The direction of the deviation is the same as with the β-rays, and before even the β-rays had been discovered the cathode rays of the Crookes' tube had been definitely shown to consist of minute particles charged with negative electricity flying off from the cathode with immense velocity.

The Electron.

What are these particles? Crookes thought they were matter in a new or fourth state. To-day we know they are "electrons." The electron is a new and somewhat startling conception to minds trained on the older lines, although traces of it date back from the discoveries of Faraday of the laws of electrolysis. We owe largely to the well-known investigations of Sir Joseph Thomson, and his school at the Cavendish Laboratory, Cambridge, the recognition of the electron as an atom of electricity, divorced from matter. The cathode-rays consist of these separate individual and isolated electrons, repelled out of the metal of the negative pole under the action of powerful electric stress, and, in the absence of gas, gathering terrific speed in their passage through the exhausted tube. Whatever the manner in which these electrons are produced, under whatever circumstances they result, they are always identical in their main characteristics. Their charge is always the same, and also their "mass," although their velocity may and does vary according to the conditions within very wide limits. They and their motion are responsible for the most varied and apparently unconnected phenomena in Nature, and in the empire of matter they seem often to occupy a rôle in comparison with the more massive material atoms analogous to the part played by the planets in relation to the central sun of a solar system. The mass of the electron is only one two-thousandth part of that of the hydrogen atom, the smallest particle previously known.

The methods employed depend upon tracing the

paths of the cathode-rays when they were subjected simultaneously to electric and to magnetic fields. Both fields deflect the cathode-particle but in different ways, and from the results the charge, mass, and velocity of the particle were separately found.

Inertia or Mass.

In some ways we know far more about the electron than about the atom of matter. The electron cannot move without disturbing the medium which occupies all space continuously, and which we, not yet knowing too much about its real nature, call the ether. It is the motion and change of motion of the electron which give us light, the X-rays, and the long ether waves used in wireless telegraphy. It is the reaction of the ether on the moving electron which gives it its "mass." Now this "mass" of the electron, applied as the term was to the atom of pure electricity entirely unassociated with matter, needed very careful and clear thinking, or it would appear utterly contradictory to the older conceptions of matter. The term *mass*, used in this sense, has nothing to do with the effect of gravity or weight, as it is still absolutely unknown whether electrons obey the law of gravitation.

In this region of new ideas we are now entering, more difficulty, perhaps, is to be anticipated in the meaning attached to the terms employed than in the actual ideas themselves. Mass is often equivalent to "weight," but here it is not so. The mass of, meaning the quantity of, matter, is a fundamental idea, while weight is a derived idea due to the earth's attraction. A given quantity of matter throughout the universe has an unchanging mass. Its weight, of course, depends upon the proximity and mass of the world attracting it. What then is the measure of mass as distinct from weight ? Weight is, as a matter of fact, invariably used on the earth to measure mass because it is so convenient. Yet if we can imagine ourselves isolated in space at a great distance from all worlds

INERTIA

with a given quantity of matter it is desired to know the the mass of, we should still have no difficulty in distinguishing the greater mass, say of a sphere of lead, from the lesser mass of a similar-sized sphere of wood. We should know the difference by the difference of *inertia*. If we struck each a similar blow the wood sphere would start to move many times as fast as the lead sphere. Neither would have appreciable weight under these circumstances, but their relative inertia would still be in proportion to their masses. A collision between two " weightless " railway trains meeting in mid-space would work just as much havoc to the trains as it would if it occurred at the same speed upon the earth. Hence when a physicist speaks of the " mass " of a β-ray particle, or of a cathode-ray particle, no considerations of weight are in his mind.

Sir J. J. Thomson, first with these cathode-rays, afterwards with the β-rays, showed how it was possible, by measuring the extent to which they were deviated by magnetic and by electric forces, to determine the velocity, the charge, and the mass of the particles which constitute them.

The application of these methods resulted in the proof that the charge and the mass of the β-particle were identical with that of the cathode-ray particle of vacuum tubes, but the velocity of the β-particle was far higher than that of the fastest known cathode-ray. Thus the β-particle ejected from the radium atom was already known. It is true it is ejected more violently by radium than in any previously known case, but in its essential characteristics, its charge, or the quantity of electricity it carries, and its mass—it is the *same* particle as Sir William Crookes dealt with in his vacuum tubes thirty years ago. He christened them in a prophetic moment with the name of " Radiant Matter," and was, like many another prophet, ridiculed for his pains.

Velocity of the β-Rays.

The cathode-ray particle, and also the β-ray particle, were found to carry the *same* amount of electricity as the charged hydrogen atom. Hence, whatever else the β-particle of radium is, it is certainly an atom of negative electricity. With regard to the velocity, just as the mass of these particles is smaller than any known material particle, their velocity is appropriately almost inconceivably greater than that of any previously known material particle. It approaches that of light itself, which has a velocity of 185,000 miles per second. The average velocity of the cathode-ray particle of the vacuum tube is from 5,000 to 10,000 miles per second; while that of the fastest of the β-particles of radium is so nearly that of light as to be indistinguishable from it. Most of the β-rays, however, travel with a velocity from 40 to 80 per cent. of that of light.

This is one of the most general, as it is one of the most remarkable, features about radium. The effects produced by its rays, even the rays themselves in some part, are not entirely new. They can be simulated to some extent by artificial means. In passing from the effects produced artificially to those produced by radium spontaneously, we are aware of great resemblances, and at the same time of great differences. By the use of exceedingly powerful electrical appliances, and the expenditure of a considerable amount of energy, we can simulate to some extent the β-rays of radium, but no instrument maker at the present time can provide you with the means of impressing upon the artificially generated cathode-ray electron of the Crookes' tube more than a small fraction of the velocity with which the β-ray electron is being spontaneously expelled from radium. It is the same in other matters. The utmost we are able to effect by the most powerful forces at our disposal falls far short of what is being done spontaneously by a mere speck of matter undergoing atomic disintegration.

THE RADIUM CLOCK.

Before leaving the subject of β-rays, I have to show you an interesting instrument devised by Professor Strutt,[1] and popularly called the radium clock (Fig. 15). It is the nearest approach to perpetual motion that has yet been devised, and it consists of a gold-leaf electroscope, worked by the negative electricity carried away from the radium by means of the β-rays. A few milligrams of a salt of radium are contained in a thin-walled closed glass tube, A, through which the β-rays can easily penetrate, and this tube is supported from an insulating rod of quartz, B, within a highly exhausted glass vessel. The tube in turn carries at its lower end two gold leaves, C, after the manner of an electroscope. The β-rays shot out from the radium carry away negative electricity, and therefore the radium itself left behind becomes positively charged. The gradual accumulation of this charge causes the gold leaves attached to the tube to diverge little by little, until they touch the sides of the vessel and are discharged, when the cycle of operations recommences. The instrument on the table (Fig. 16, facing p. 47) was constructed many years ago, and has been functioning about once every three minutes ever since. There is no reason why it should not do so for at least a thousand years more, though at a slowly decreasing rate. Though not a true perpetual motion machine, it is one so far as only our lives are concerned.

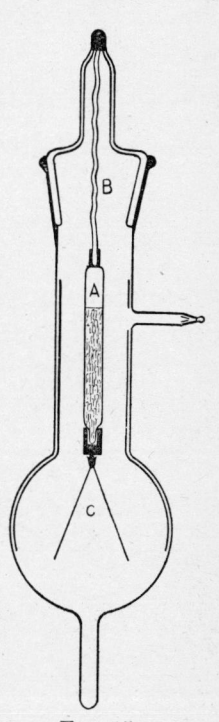

FIG. 15.

[1] Now Lord Rayleigh.

MAGNETIC DEVIATION OF α-PARTICLES.

The methods we have been considering which led to the elucidation of the real nature of the β-rays—the determination of the nature of the expelled particle, its mass, charge, and velocity—have been applied successfully also to the elucidation of the real nature of the α-rays, though here the task was very much more difficult experimentally. Rutherford, to whom we owe our knowledge of this subject, worked for a long time before he could detect any influence produced by the most powerful magnets on the course of the α-rays, so slight and insignificant it is compared with the effect on the β-rays. Finally, he proved that the α-rays were deflected both by electric and by magnetic forces, but to an extent of the order of one-thousandth part of the effect that the β-rays suffer under similar circumstances. The deviation of the α-rays, moreover, is in the opposite direction to that of the β-rays. Where the β-rays are coiled clock-wise, for example, the α-rays would tend to turn counter clock-wise. By these, and numerous other experiments, it has been shown that the α-rays consist of positively charged particles. The α-particle is, however, not, like the β-particle, only a disembodied electrical charge. It is a charged material *atom*. At first it was thought to be twice as heavy as the hydrogen atom, on the assumption that it was charged with a single " atom " of positive electricity. Now, however, it has been proved to carry two charges of positive electricity, and to be an atom four times as heavy as hydrogen. This is in accord with the whole of the rest of the evidence of radioactive changes still to be considered, which points unmistakably, though indirectly, to the conclusion that the α-particle is an atom of the element helium. The atomic weight of helium is four, or, in other words, the helium atom is four times as massive as the hydrogen atom, which is always taken as unity. In our most recent view, to be later considered, the α-particle is the nucleus of a helium atom that has lost the two electrons that accompany it as satellites in the normal " uncharged " atom.

Velocity of the α-Particle.

Waiving the case of the β-rays which, as we have seen, are electrical rather than material in nature, the α-rays of the radioactive substances furnish without doubt one of the most wonderful phenomena at present known. If radium did nothing else but send out these α-particles, that alone would of itself constitute a new epoch in our knowledge of nature. Take their velocity, for instance, which, though lower on the average than that of the β-rays, reaches in some cases the very handsome value of over 12,000 miles per second. This is hundreds of times faster than the next fastest known material thing moving in earth or air or space. The swiftest flight known previously is that of some of the shooting stars, which attain sometimes to a speed of from twenty to forty miles a second, and from the attack of which we are largely protected by the fact that their velocity is so great that they are quickly dissipated into vapour by the simple resistance of the air. While such a meteor was traversing the distance to the moon an α-particle would, given an unimpeded path, reach the sun.

Such a velocity multiplied by itself, or squared, gives us a measure of the *energy* possessed by the α-particles. If their velocity is, say, half a thousand times faster than any previously known, the kinetic energy they possess is, mass for mass, a quarter of a million times greater than any we have ever had to do with before. In this fact lies the key to many of the surprising revelations of radium. When we speak of being able to detect the effect of a single α-particle, and therefore of a single atom of matter, we mean the detection of its energy, which is a quarter of a million times as great as that of any other kind of atom known to us. Similarly, when we speak of being able to detect in a few seconds by radioactive methods the course of a change which would have to proceed continuously for geological epochs before it produced an effect detectable by the most sensitive chemical test, it is because, firstly, we detect the energy evolved by the change, not the change itself; and, secondly, because the energy is at once so relatively enormous and at the same time so much more easily detected compared with any other kind of energy outburst previously known to us.

Passage of α-Particles through Matter.

Matter moving with the speed of 10,000 miles a second is so novel and strange to us at present that it is doubtful whether our ordinary conceptions afford much guide or analogy. The muzzle-velocity of a cannon-ball, for instance, is a small fraction of one mile per second. Now we have seen that the α-particle of radium is capable of traversing very thin aluminium leaves and also several inches of gaseous air. It is extremely interesting to inquire what happens during the collision of an α-particle with a molecule of gas or metal. Some at least of these collisions must be full and direct, not simple grazing or glancing coincidence; and it seems at first sight difficult to believe that an α-particle striking a gas-molecule full and fair should not be stopped, however fast it is moving. Nevertheless, it is not so. Upon this matter the researches of Bragg and his colleagues have thrown a flood of light. His conclusions are as remarkable as they are definite. "Each α-particle pursues a rectilinear course, no matter what it encounters; it passes through all the atoms it meets, whether they form part of a solid or a gas (or, in all probability, of a liquid), suffering no deflection on account of any encounter until, at any rate, very near the end of its course. . . . A thin metal plate may be placed in the way of the stream, and so rob every particle of some of its energy, but not a single one is brought to rest by collision with the atoms of the metal, and the number of particles in the stream remains unchanged." Surely this vivid picture of the flight of a swarm of α-particles raises anew the old metaphysical conundrum of the schoolmen, whether two portions of matter could occupy the same space at the same time. For the only possible meaning of Professor Bragg's conclusion is that the α-particle must go *clean through* the atoms of matter it penetrates as though they were not there, and therefore at the instant of collision the two atoms do occupy the same space at the same time. This power of the interpenetration of masses is one of the peculiar properties of matter moving at these, what may be termed ultra-material, velocities. We know for certain it is not a normal property of matter. The only apparent consequence of the passage of the α-particle through the atoms it encounters is that it ionises them, that is, they become charged, some with + and some with − electricity, after the collision. It is probable that the α-particle possesses its charge when it is expelled from the atom. But whereas in the case of the β-particle the charge of electricity *is* the particle, in the case of the α-particle the charge would almost certainly result as a consequence of the velocity with which the particle is moving, even if it were uncharged initially. At least it is certain that no atom moving at 10,000 miles a second would continue uncharged. The very first collision with an atom of matter would " knock out an electron or two," that is to say, charge the moving particle positively.

Scattering of α-Particles.

Since the above quotation was written by Professor Bragg it has been proved that some of the α-particles do suffer a deflection or scattering in their passage through matter. For the vast majority of the α-particles this deflection is exceedingly slight, but for a very small proportion of the whole the deflection may be so great as practically to turn the α-particle back the way it came. This is extremely interesting. The α-particles alone have access to the real interior of the atom of matter, and a close study of this phenomenon has resulted in information being obtained as to what the atoms of matter consist of. Hitherto science has been completely confined to the external characteristics of atoms, but the α-particles, after their passage through these atoms, will afford some clue, which will be later considered, as to the nature of the unknown territory which they have traversed.

The quotation from Professor Bragg (p. 63) pursued the question of what happens to the α-particle on collision only as far as the initial stages. Each atom of matter penetrated robs the α-particle of some of its energy, and its velocity is therefore diminished as it pursues its path. But the more slowly it moves the more energy is withdrawn from it in passing through any given obstacle. In addition, the slower it moves the more easily is it deviated from its course, or scattered. In consequence, the speed is more and more quickly reduced as the end of its path is approached, and the α-particle thus passes out of the range of detection somewhat suddenly.

A Method of rendering the Tracks of α-Rays Visible.

By an ingenious arrangement, C. T. R. Wilson has succeeded recently in making the paths of many of the new radiations in air, or other gas, visible to the eye, and in actually photographing them. These rays ionise the gas, and leave in their tracks columns of ions, which are molecules of the gas carrying an electric charge, and which, although really moving about like all gaseous molecules at great speed, are, by comparison with the much swifter rays producing them, almost at rest. Now these ions, the negative variety more easily than the positive ions, afford nuclei for the condensation of moisture from a supersaturated atmosphere. Dust plays the same part, but all dust can readily be removed. When moist air in a closed space is suddenly expanded

Fig. 17.

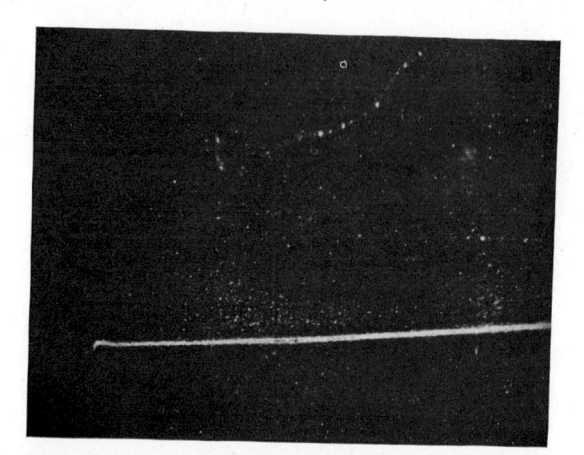

Fig. 18.

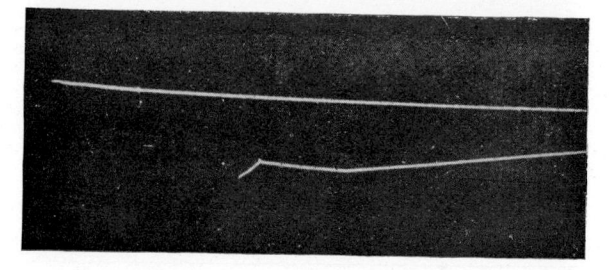

Fig. 19.
Cloud-Tracks of α-Rays of Radium.

TRACKS OF α-PARTICLES

the air is cooled and the moisture condenses as mist or rain on the dust particles and carries them down, so freeing the air from such impurities. If the pure air is now suddenly expanded within certain well-defined limits, in the absence of ions or dust, no condensation is produced. But if the air is traversed by any of the new ionising radiations, the tracks of the rays, when the ionisation chamber is suitably illuminated, appear momentarily as long spider-threads of mist whenever the air is suddenly expanded and chilled. If a flash of light is arranged to take place just after the expansion, the threads may be photographed. In Fig. 17 is shown the α-rays proceeding from the needle point of a spinthariscope (p. 43), and in Fig. 18, in the lower part of the picture, an enlargement of the end of the track of a single α-particle.

The tracks left by the α-particles are almost all perfectly straight, but a very few show abrupt large deflections, and sometimes actually the direction of travel is nearly reversed. The β-rays, on the other hand, give very zigzag tracks. These rays are known to be scattered and turned very readily by their encounter with the molecules of matter, and owing to the ionisation they produce being less intense than in the case of the α-rays, their tracks are much fainter. In the upper part of Fig. 18 is seen the end of the track of a β-particle, just before it stops and ceases to ionise. At first when the β-particle is travelling at high velocity its track, which in air may be several metres long, is very much straighter, and it may travel for several centimetres without sensible deflection. The photograph has caught the end of the track when its energy is feeblest and its liability to be deviated greatest. In Fig. 19 are shown the photographs of two α-ray tracks, one the normal practical straight path, and the other showing two abrupt changes of direction in its length. To quote C. T. R. Wilson's own words: " The α-particle has thousands of encounters with atoms of the gases of the air in each millimetre of its course by which ionisation is brought about, as we know from measurements made by the electrical method, and in accordance with this the cloud particles (which are simply ions magnified by condensation of water) are so closely packed that they are not separately visible in the photograph. It is remarkable that only two encounters out of the many thousands occurring in the course of its flight should succeed in deviating the particle visibly from its course and that in these cases the deviations should be quite large." We shall have occasion to refer to this again as these phenomena have thrown much light on the internal structure of atoms. The experiments have also thrown light on the nature of the γ-rays, and have made it appear probable that these rays do not ionise the gas directly, but first cause the molecules struck to emit a kind of cathode- or β-radiation, and it is these secondary radiations which produce the ionisation.

The Fate of the α-Particle.

Fluorescent, photographical, and electrical actions all cease simultaneously. It is estimated that at the moment the α-particle ceases to be detectable it is still moving with the velocity of several thousand miles a second. For all that is known the particle may then suffer a sudden stop, or it may continue its course without ionising the atoms it encounters.

For us who are concerned, for the most part with the broad limitations of our past and present knowledge, the most interesting feature of this phenomenon is that it indicates quite definitely that an α-particle expelled with an initial velocity below several thousand miles a second could not by any of the present known methods be detected. Any of the apparently stable and non-radioactive elements might be disintegrating and expelling α-particles, but if these did not attain this limiting speed we should have no evidence of the fact. It is really by a somewhat slender margin of velocity

THE VASTNESS OF THE UNKNOWN

that the α-particles have come within our knowledge at all. The light we have gained has but served to intensify the darkness by which we are surrounded on all sides. Processes similar to and but little less energetic than those which produce radioactivity, may be going on suspected everywhere around us, without producing any yet detectable effects. Radioactivity is to be regarded rather as a benevolent hint given to us by Nature into secrets we might never have guessed, rather than as the necessary and invariable concomitant of the processes of atomic disintegration.

CHAPTER V

THE RADIUM EMANATION

THE SOURCE OF RADIOACTIVE ENERGY.

IF we are to continue to regard energy in the modern way as something having a definite existence, we have to answer the question, " From where does the energy of radium come ?" That it comes from nowhere, or that it is being newly created out of nothing by radium, is a view it is not possible to entertain for a moment without destroying the basis upon which nineteenth-century physical science has largely been reared. "How has it got the energy in it to do it ?" is the first question that naturally arises in the mind with regard to radium, but obviously we should first ask, " Has it the energy in it ?"

TWO ALTERNATIVE THEORIES.

If the doctrine of energy is true, there are fortunately only two possible alternatives to be considered. Either the energy must be derived from within the radium, which we shall call the first, and as we think the true, alternative, or it must be supplied from outside the radium, and this we shall call the second alternative. This simple narrowing down of all the possible issues to two alternatives may appear to you somewhat trite, but in reality it carries with it far more than appears on the surface. In the first place, being an intrinsic property of the element, radioactivity is therefore a property of the atom, and if we take the first alternative and say the energy comes from within, it means from within the atom. and therefore that there must exist an enormous and not previously suspected store of energy in matter, or at least in radioactive matter, in some way inside its atoms or smallest integral parts.

On the second alternative, which has often been advanced, radium acts merely as a transforming mechanism. There are electrical transformers dotted all over this city, receiving the economically transmitted but dangerous high-tension currents from the central power station and delivering the comparatively safe low-tension currents to your houses, which are wasteful to transmit for long distances. Are the atoms of radium acting as the transformers of a mysterious and hitherto unknown source of external energy, first receiving it and then delivering it up again in a form which can be recognised? It may be said at once that so vague a view, postulating the existence of illimitable and mysterious supplies of energy from without, cannot be directly disproved. At first it seemed to provide a way of escape from some of the more unpalatable logical consequences of the first alternative and was eagerly adopted. In reality, instead of a way of escape, it proves to be a veritable will-o'-the-wisp, luring on its followers beyond the limits of credulity into a quagmire of unsubstantial hypotheses, so bottomless and unreal that even the facts of radium are a wholly inadequate justification, and, even so, incapable of throwing any light on the facts when these are more nearly examined. Nevertheless, we must pursue both alternatives impartially, if only to leave no doubt that both have only to be fairly considered for one to be dismissed.

On the second alternative the radium owes its activity to a supply of energy from outside. One has only to isolate the transformers which light this city from all connection with the outside central station to plunge the city in darkness. But we have seen that to quench radioactivity or to modify it in any way is one of the things science cannot do. Experiment has proved that even in the natural state in the mine, hundreds of feet deep down in the earth, pitchblende exhibits its normal radioactivity. So that if it derives its energy from without, this must be of a kind entirely different from any at present known, for it must be capable of traversing without loss hundreds of feet of solid rock. This is as far as we need pursue the second alternative for the moment. Provided we can call into existence a new kind of radiant energy unlimited in amount, permeating all space and unimpeded by passage through matter of any thickness, we may, but only so far as we have yet gone, seek a bare explanation of the energy of radium on the second alternative. Such a view would accord at first sight with the continuous and permanent activity of radium for an indefinite time, and there would be no reason why radioactivity, however intense and powerful, should decay or diminish with the lapse of time.

But if the first alternative is true, and the energy comes from within, large as the store of energy in the atom must be to explain radioactivity, it cannot be infinite, and therefore it is to be expected that the activity will slowly decay with the lapse of time. If two radioactive bodies, one much more powerfully radioactive than the other, are compared together, it is to be expected on this view that the activity of the more powerful body will decay faster than that of the other. But for both a time will come, as soon as the internal stores of energy are exhausted, when the radioactivity will come to an end.

By far the most important consequence of the first alternative, however, has still to be considered. Radium, if we call by that name the substance containing the unevolved store of energy, can no longer be radium when the energy is lost. Coal is not coal after it is burnt. When energy is obtained from matter the matter changes, and before it can be regained in its former state the energy evolved must be put back. In no case is it possible for matter to part with its store of energy and remain the same, for otherwise you will readily see a perpetual motion machine would be easy enough to

INTERNAL ATOMIC ENERGY

construct. Indeed, most of those attempted involved this impossible assumption.

But we have seen that if the energy is stored up in the radium it must be within the atom, and, therefore, if radium changes, it must be a change of the atom and of the element itself. This change of an element would be transmutation, which is a more fundamental and deep-seated change than chemical change or any known kind of material change, and until the discovery of radioactivity such changes certainly had never been observed. If the energy of radium comes from within, radium must be suffering a spontaneous kind of transmutation into other elements. So that, if we would avoid the necessity of believing in the process of transmutation, not as a vague possibility, for example, in the sun and stars, under some unattainable transcendental condition, but as actually going on imperturbably around us, which the first alternative demands, we must seek a way of escape on the second alternative which requires none of these bewildering heresies, but simply transfers the mystery from the radium to the great external unknown, and leaves it there in good company with many of a similar kind.

The Internal Energy of Matter.

At this stage it is well to ask the question, Is there anything opposed either to reason or to probability in the view that the energy evolved from radium is actually derived from an existing previously unsuspected internal store within the atom, and that in this process the element suffers a transformation into other elements? How is it that such enormous stores of energy in matter have remained so long unknown?

One of the most elusive features of energy is that you cannot say by mere observation, or by the use of any instrument, how much or how little is stored up in any kind of matter. For example, this flask contains a large quantity of an oily yellow liquid. We cannot tell by simple inspection the amount of energy stored up in this fluid. It may be some quiet and harmless oil, which can be shaken vigorously with impunity, or it may be nitroglycerine, one of the most dangerous and powerful explosives. Something more than observation is necessary to tell us the amount of energy that may be stored within this substance, possibly only awaiting a slight shock to be evolved. The only way to find out is to try to explode it as thoroughly as we can, and then if it will not explode we may conclude that, *as far as we know*, it has no latent store of energy waiting to be loosed from prison.

Explosion is merely a very rapid and violent type of chemical change, and the same general idea holds good for all the changes it is possible for matter to undergo. We may determine the energy evolved or absorbed in any *change*, that is, in the passage from one kind of matter to another kind. We have no means of telling the absolute amount of energy in any kind of matter. But the one thing of which the chemist is positive is that in all the material changes matter undergoes—radioactivity being excepted—the elements do not change into one another, but remain in their various compounds essentially unaltered. If transmutation were possible, and one element could be changed into another, it would be easy to measure the difference in the amount of energy of the two elements.

As it is, the internal energy of the elements remains always unaffected by previously known material changes, and therefore till recently quite unknowable.

Before we can find out how much or how little energy is internally associated with the atoms we must be able to study a case of transmutation. The great stability of all elements under all conditions—even in the sun the identical elements which we know here persist, if we can rely on the evidence of the spectroscope—is well in accord with the view that all the elements contain a very large store of internal energy, which is never released in ordinary changes, but which makes them indifferent to changes in their environment. Thus the internal kinetic energy of a torpedo containing a revolving gyrostat makes it successfully resist deflection from its course by the wind and waves. The internal energy of the solar system, taken as a whole, is the sole reason why it continues to exist as a system and does not drift apart.

So far then from there being anything opposed to reason or probability in the view that the atom of the element contains a great and hitherto unknown store of internal energy, we see that if it possessed such a store we could not know of it until it changed, while the greater the store the more would it resist change from without, and therefore the less likely should we be to suspect its existence. From this point forward we shall find that the more the apparent objections to the first alternative of internal energy are faced the less serious they appear, while with the second alternative of external energy the contrary is the case.

Radium a Changing Element.

Having with these preliminaries somewhat cleared the ground, I now wish to attempt to explain a series of experimental investigations which have thrown a flood of light upon the nature of radioactivity. Though by a superficial or merely external observation of radium, even over the period of a whole lifetime, it would hardly be possible to detect the least change of any kind in the matter itself or any exhaustion of its output of energy, these investigations have proved that radium, and every element that is radioactive, is actually changing in a very peculiar and definite way. These new changes in radioactivity are always excessively minute as regards the actual quantities of matter undergoing change in any period of time. Except in very special circumstances they are quite beyond the range of the most delicate methods of investigation previously known to the chemist. The methods employed in their investigation are in the first place wholly novel, but they are none the less trustworthy or definite on that account.

Disintegration in Cascade.

They depend on the important fact that when a radioactive element changes *it does not as a rule do so once only*, producing in a single step the final product of its change. Usually there are several successive changes following one another, so to speak, *in cascade*. Just as a waterfall, instead of taking one plunge into a lake, may cascade in a series of successive leaps from pool to pool on the way down, so a radioactive element like radium passes in its change through a long series of intermediate bodies, each produced from the one preceding and producing the one following. Whereas, however, the first change is and must be slow, the subsequent changes may be, and usually are, relatively far more rapid. But for the existence of these ephemeral, rapidly changing, intermediate substances, continually being produced and as continually changing, it is safe to say the mystery of radium would to-day be still unsolved.

Picture to yourselves exactly what this problem involves. Out of a remote, and so far as we know unlimited, past this world has gradually come into the state we find it to-day, and what we find is that there is a process known as radioactivity still spontaneously going on in matter in its natural state as it is dug out of the earth, which we cannot in any way stop or retard, and which we recognise as the intrinsic property of certain chemical elements. We must conclude, until we have evidence to the contrary, that radioactivity is not a process which has started recently, or that it is confined to the particular epoch of the earth's history we are now living in. So long as the radioactive elements have existed this process must have been going on, and, if we are forced to the conclusion that the radioactive elements are changing, is it not obvious that the changes must be excessively slow for any of the radioactive elements to have survived ? What could the methods of chemistry avail in such a search ? Delicate as these are to-day, beyond the limit of what was even conceivable a hundred years ago, infinitely finer and more sensitive methods are required.

The geologists tell us, and we shall find in radioactivity only confirmation, that the earth has existed in much the same physical condition as it exists to-day for hundreds if not thousands of millions of years. A chemist could probably in many cases detect the change of one thousandth part of one element into another, whereas we shall come to see that for even such a small fraction of a primary radioactive element to change a period of the order of a million years would almost certainly be necessary.

You all know the stride that chemistry took forwards when it impressed into its service the spectroscope, and was able to detect with certainty quantities of new elements absolutely imperceptible in any other way. For example, Bunsen and Kirchoff detected by the spectroscope the unknown element *cæsium* in the natural waters of the Durkheim spring in the Palatinate, but to obtain enough cæsium for their chemical investigations they had to boil down forty tons of this water. Coming nearer the present day, Mme. Curie made an equal or even greater step forward when she impressed into the service of chemistry the property of radioactivity and discovered the new element radium in pitchblende, though a ton of pitchblende contains only two grains of radium. But we must improve even on this. We have to detect the change in a minute amount of radium which is changing so slowly that it appears not to be changing at all. The actual amount of new matter which this half-grain of radium bromide would produce by its change in, say, a month or a year, is a quantity so small that one has only to attempt to conceive it to be ready to give up the search in despair. Yet in a moment I hope to show it to everyone in this large room, and to demonstrate to you a few of its most striking properties in the clearest way.

Were radium to change in one single step into, say, lead, which we believe to be the ultimate product in the main line of descent, this would be impossible. Those of you in the back could hardly see a quantity of lead equal in quantity to the whole of this radium. How much less then could you hope to be shown the infinitesimal fraction of this small quantity which is produced in a month or a year? No chemist has yet detected lead as the final product of radium, and our evidence on this point is at present only indirect, but it is now quite conclusive. But radium does not change all at once in one step. At least eight intermediate bodies intervene, each one of which is formed from the one preceding it *with an outburst of energy*, and changes into the next *with another outburst of energy*.

The Successive Outbursts of Energy.

A soldier on a battlefield knows without any doubt when he is being fired at, but it would take him a long and patient examination to find out, and it would be a matter of only secondary interest, whether the bullets are made, say, of lead or of nickel. The energy possessed by the flying bullets are their, to him, practically important feature. After the energy is all spent the bullet ceases to make its presence felt. So it is with radium. The energy possessed by the changing intermediate substances and evolved from them is the sole but sufficient evidence of their existence. After the energy is all spent and the change is complete, only a most minute and patient examination, which has still to be made complete, will reveal the chemical nature of the minute amount of dead products formed. But before this stage is reached, in the long succession of energy outbursts which accompany the change of one intermediate form into the next, we have a succession of most remarkable and obvious phenomena which enable us to detect the separate changes and to discover the whole nature and the periods of average life of all the intermediate bodies, although these all exist only in absolutely infinitesimal quantity, and not one of them is known, or probably ever can become known, to the chemist in the ordinary way. It is one of the most wonderful triumphs in the whole history of physical science that such changes should have ever been detected. Let us turn to the main evidence on which the view that radium is changing was first based.

The Radium Emanation.

If this specimen of radium bromide was dissolved in water and the liquid evaporated down to dryness in order to get back the solid compound, it would be found that as the result of this very simple operation the radium had lost the greater part of its radioactivity in the process. The penetrating β- and γ-rays would have completely disappeared, and the non-penetrating α-rays would only be one quarter as powerful as initially. Then a strange thing would happen. Left to itself the radium would spontaneously *recover* its lost activity, little by little from day to day, and at the end of a month it would be not appreciably less active than it at first was, or as it now is.

This appears to be in direct conflict with the statement previously made that the radioactivity of radium cannot be affected by any known process, but it is only apparently so. If we study the process carefully we shall find that when the radium is dissolved in water "something" escapes into the air, and this "something" is intensely radioactive. It diffuses about in the air, but remains contained within a closed vessel, if it is gas-tight. In short, this "something" is a new *gas* possessing the property of radioactivity to a very intense degree.

We owe the greater part of our knowledge of this new

radioactive gas to Sir Ernest Rutherford, who has given to it a special name. He called it the *emanation of radium*, or, for short, simply *the emanation*. The vague term " emanation " is, with our present exact knowledge of its real nature, apt to mislead. Some, unfortunately, have used the term " emanation " or " emanations " in speaking of the various *radiations* which radium emits, and which we have already considered in some detail. Sir William Ramsay has proposed the name " Niton " for this new gas, in order to emphasise its relationship to the other argon gases. However, as similar new gases or emanations are given by two other of the radioactive elements, thorium and actinium, the original term has been generally retained. The term " emanation," qualified when necessary by the name of the radioactive element producing it, denotes one of these new gaseous bodies, and it is necessary not to confuse this particular use with its older and more general uses.

Experiments with the Emanation.

In the laboratory, half a mile from this lecture-room, I have a further quantity of about half a grain of pure radium bromide which has been dissolved in water. The solution is kept in a closed vessel. This morning I extracted the emanation from the vessel, and I have brought it here to show you. The radium from which it was derived is not in the room, it is still in the laboratory half a mile away. The emanation is contained, mixed with air, in a little glass tube (Fig. 20) provided with taps for its admission and extraction, and inside this tube are some fragments of the mineral willemite, a silicate of zinc. This mineral has the appearance of an ordinary cold greenish-grey stone, quite undistinguished and not very different from many of the common pebbles of the road or seashore. It, however, possesses the power of fluorescing, under the action of X-rays and the rays from radium, with a brilliant

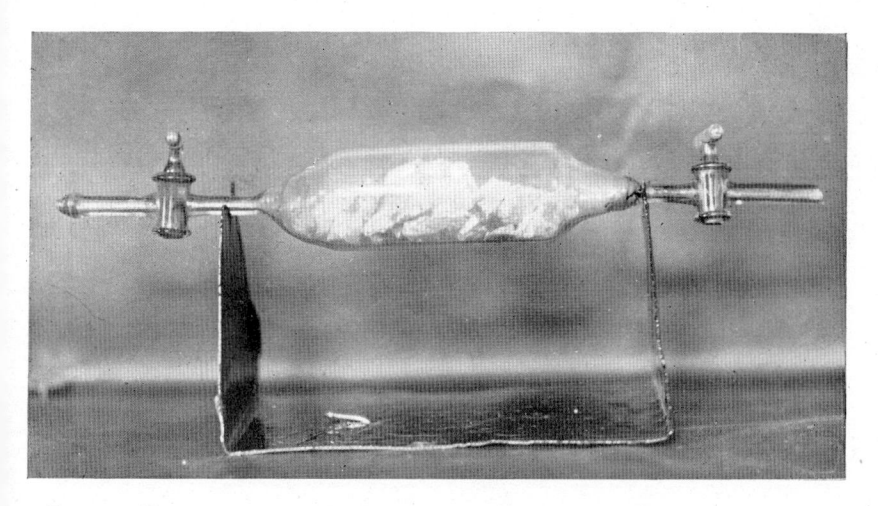

Fig. 20.—Tube containing Willemite used to exhibit the Radium Emanation.

Fig. 21.—The Same Tube photographed in the Dark by its Own Phosphorescent Light.

To face page 78

greenish light, as you may see when I bring my capsule containing half a grain of solid radium bromide near to a block of the mineral in the dark. Let us now in the dark examine the tube containing the emanation and willemite together. We find the willemite glowing with a most remarkable light. Even in ordinary lamp-light or weak daylight the glow of the willemite is clearly visible. Fig. 21 shows the tube (Fig. 20), which has been placed in front of the camera in the dark room, and, as you can see, the pieces of glowing willemite have photographed themselves by their own light. In the negative the walls of the glass tube, which also are rendered feebly fluorescent by the emanation, are faintly visible. The photograph proved somewhat difficult to obtain, as the light, consisting almost wholly of green and yellow, is almost non-actinic to the photographic plate. An isochromatic plate must be employed and a long exposure given. Under these circumstances the β- and γ-rays from the tube, as they are not refracted by the lens, themselves fog the plate uniformly to a considerable extent. The photograph gives no idea of the beauty of the original tube. Willemite glowing in the emanation of radium is one of the most beautiful sights I know, and considered with reference to the origin of its light and all that the phenomenon foreshadows for humanity, it raises feelings which only a poet adequately could express.

What is the emanation of radium? I shall treat this question to-night solely as though the emanation was a body with no connection whatever with radium, because a knowledge of its own nature is necessary before its real relation to radium can be appreciated. In the first place, it is intensely radioactive on its own account—that is to say, it gives out the new kinds of rays very similar in character to those given by other radioactive bodies and capable of producing the same effects. What I am about to say refers only to a tube in which the radium emanation has been confined for some hours. At first the emanation gives only α- but no β- or γ-rays, as we shall consider more nearly later (Chapter IX.).

This tube, in which the emanation is confined, glows in the dark because the phosphorescent willemite it contains is being bombarded by the rays from the emanation. Some of these rays penetrate the glass walls of the tube, as you may see if I bring the X-ray screen between your eyes and the tube. Moreover, if a very thin plate of metal is interposed at the back of the screen it does not perceptibly diminish the effect, for the rays from a tube containing the emanation, like the radium-rays themselves, are capable of penetrating a considerable thickness of metal. They consist, in fact, of α-, β- and γ-rays together. Any of the other phosphorescent bodies—for example, zinc sulphide—would, if placed inside this vessel with the emanation, glow in its characteristic way just as if exposed to radium itself. Similarly, a photographic plate would be fogged almost instantly, and an electrified silk tassel would be discharged at once by the rays proceeding from the emanation confined in this tube. The similarity between the α-rays from the emanation and those from radium itself have been proved by exact physical experiments.

The Condensation of the Emanation by Cold.

The next point is that the emanation is not a solid form of matter dispersed like fine particles of smoke in the air which carries it. It is *a true gas*. This has been proved by innumerable experiments; but I wish to show you one which is particularly beautiful, and which has, I think, convinced everyone who has ever seen it performed that the emanation of radium is a true gas with the property of radioactivity. It was first performed by Professor Rutherford and myself in Montreal in November, 1902. If the emanation is a gas there ought to be some temperature, though, perhaps a very low one, at which it loses its gaseous form and is condensed or frozen. All our attempts to effect such a condensa-

CONDENSATION OF THE EMANATION 81

tion at temperatures down to −100° Centigrade had proved futile, and we had no means of obtaining the very low temperatures now daily employed in a modern laboratory But a liquid air machine was given to the laboratory by its generous founder, and on its first run the emanation of radium was successfully condensed. Exact experiments showed that the emanation is condensed quite sharply when the temperature falls below −150° Centigrade (or −238° Fahrenheit), and it volatilises and again resumes its gaseous state quite

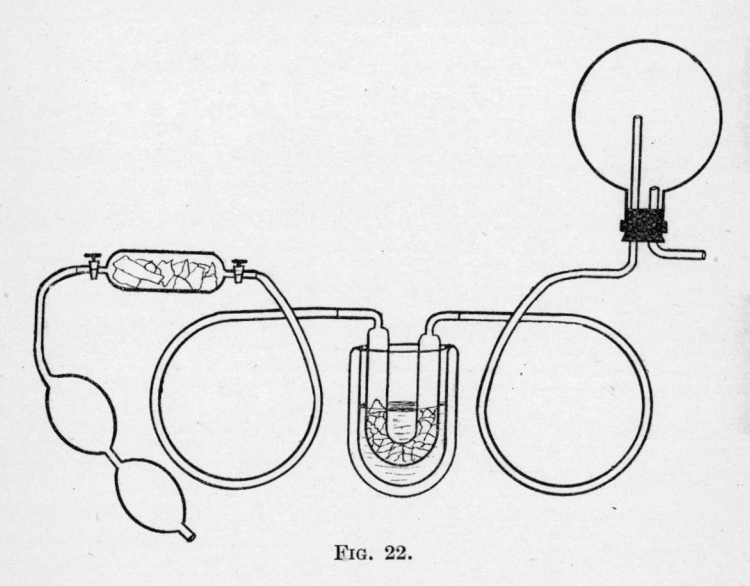

FIG. 22.

sharply when the temperature rises above this. We shall perform the experiment in the following manner (Fig. 22). To one of the tubes of the vessel containing the emanation is attached a rubber blowing-ball, for blowing out the emanation. The other tube is connected with a U-tube of glass containing some fragments of willemite, immersed in a vessel of liquid air and so kept at the very low temperature of about −183° Centigrade or −300° Fahrenheit, into which the emanation is blown. Exposed to this extreme cold the emanation instantly loses its gaseous state and condenses in the tube. To make the experiment more striking, between the tube containing the emanation and the cooled U-tube I have interposed several yards of narrow tubing which the emanation has to traverse before reaching the tube in which it condenses. As you see, when I open the taps and gently blow a blast of air to sweep out the emanation into the cold U-tube, the willemite in the cold tube suddenly shines out brilliantly, at the point where the emanation condenses.

So long as the U-tube is kept in the liquid air the emanation will remain there, though I continue to send a gentle blast of air from the bellows. But a few moments after taking the tube out of the liquid air, it warms up to the point ($-150°$ Centigrade) at which the emanation again resumes its gaseous form, and now we can blow it out with a single puff of air. See! I blow it out through the narrow tubing, which I have connected to the U-tube, into a large flask dusted over its inside surface with the phosphorescent sulphide of zinc. In the dark the globe shines out with a soft white light like some fairy lantern, and I can see to read my watch by its light. The physiological effects of the radium emanation are imperfectly investigated and may be potent. This is a field of investigation I personally have no desire to explore, so that we must not forget to cork the globe and so prevent the emanation from diffusing out into the air of the room.

The Infinitesimal Quantity of the Emanation.

After this demonstration you may have some difficulty in really believing that the actual amount of gaseous emanation which has produced these beautiful effects is almost infinitesimal. By making use of the same property—its condensation by liquid air—the actual volume occupied by the radium emanation freed by freezing from all other gases was measured by Sir William Ramsay and myself. Imagine a bubble of air the volume of a

THE QUANTITY OF THE EMANATION

good-sized pin's head, say, one cubic millimetre, or one fifteen-thousandth part of a cubic inch. It would require thirty times more emanation than was actually employed in the last experiment to fill a bubble of this size. Of course, in the experiments this small quantity of emanation was mixed with a considerable volume of air for convenience in manipulation. The actual quantity of emanation accumulating in a radium preparation is known with accuracy to be 0·6 cubic millimetre per gram of radium (element).

It requires a distinct step for the mind to assimilate the important fact that the property of radioactivity, which so far has been studied only in solid substances and minerals, could be shown equally by a gas, and this fact accounted for the true nature of the emanation remaining largely unrecognised even after the conclusive experiment I have shown you. There is, of course, nothing contrary to the nature of radioactivity in the fact that it is shown by a gas. When we apply Mme. Curie's theory that radioactivity is an intrinsic property of the atom, and of the element in question, the difficulty is not that the emanation is a gas, for many elements are gases, but how it is that a new radioactive element, such as the emanation undoubtedly is, should result when radium compounds are dissolved in water, and this question we have purposely deferred.

The Radioactivity of the Emanation.

The emanation, as we have employed it in our experiments, is mixed with ordinary air, and in this way it can be dealt with and treated like any other gas. We have blown it through tubes from one end of the lecture table to the other. If it had been an ordinary gas, like air, no one could have seen it, or known what became of it. But being intensely radioactive, although its actual quantity is almost inconceivably small, the radioactivity serves as a sufficient evidence of its presence or absence, making it, as a matter of fact, far easier to work with and to investigate than an ordinary gas in ordinary quantity. If a mining engineer wished to know how the air he pumped into his mine got distributed among the various shafts and pits, he could not do better than to put a little radium emanation into the entering air, and then subsequently to take samples at various parts of the mine, and have them tested for content of radium emanation by a gold-leaf electroscope. Many other practical problems in the flow of gases, which are difficult to solve by ordinary methods, might be readily solved by the help of this new gas.

The Chemical Character of the Emanation.

It has even been found possible to settle the chemical nature of this new gas, and to place it in its proper family of elements in the periodic table. Almost all gases, according to their various natures, are absorbed when subjected to the action of various chemical reagents. Thus oxygen is absorbed by phosphorus, hydrogen by heated copper oxide, nitrogen by heated magnesium, and so on. The exceptions, namely, gases which are not absorbed by any reagents and which will not combine with anything, are the newly discovered gases of Lord Rayleigh and Sir William Ramsay—argon, helium, neon, etc.—which exist in atmospheric air. The quantity in the air of these gases is extremely minute except in the single case of argon, which is present to the extent of one per cent. The radium emanation, like argon, is not absorbed by any known reagent, and does not appear to possess any power of chemical combination. It may be passed unchanged through absorbents, or subjected to drastic chemical treatment which would suffice to absorb every known gas except those of the argon type, and the conclusion has been arrived at that the emanation is an element of the same family nature as the argon gases. Like them, it exists in the form of single atoms—that is, its molecule is monatomic. Radium, on the other hand,

AN ARGON TYPE OF GAS

in its chemical nature is extremely similar to barium, strontium, and calcium, a family known as the alkaline-earth elements. None other of the argon elements or the alkaline-earth elements are radioactive, and yet the radioactive elements are quite normal in their chemical properties, closely resembling ordinary elements, and being associated in the clearest and closest way with one or other of the old well-known types or families. More recently, by using quantities of radium about fifteen times as great as those used to-night in our experiments, it has been possible to obtain enough of the emanation for it to be possible to photograph its spectrum. This proves to be a new and characteristic bright-line spectrum, resembling in general character the spectra of the other argon gases, but absolutely distinct.

It has been found possible to obtain some idea of the density of the emanation of radium, and therefore of the weight of its atom, from experiments on the rate of its diffusion from one place to another. These indicate that the gas is extremely dense—denser probably than mercury vapour—and therefore that it has a very heavy atom. Finally, by means of a new special micro-balance thousands of times more sensitive than the most delicately constructed chemist's balance, the emanation has actually been weighed by Sir William Ramsay and Mr. Whytlaw-Gray. These experiments and the whole of the available evidence agree in indicating that the atomic weight of the emanation is 222, which is four units below that of radium, and therefore is the fourth heaviest known.

The Heat evolved by the Emanation.

The heat given out by a gram of radium, as we have seen, is 133 calories per hour, but it must be understood that this refers to radium in its normal condition containing its full quota of emanation. After solution in water, that is, after the emanation is extracted, the radium gives out heat to the extent of only thirty-three calories per hour, while the emanation produces one hundred calories per hour. That is to say, the emanation of radium gives three times as much energy as the radium from which it is derived, although the actual amount of matter in the emanation is itself practically imperceptible.

Now, perhaps it is easy to understand how it is that the minuteness of the quantities of material offers no barrier in the investigation of radioactivity. Mass is not the only consideration. A very small bullet suffices to work terrible havoc, in spite of its smallness, by means of the kinetic energy with which it is impelled. A little torpedo, stuffed full of imprisoned energy in the form of explosives, suffices to sink an enormous battleship. A quantity of emanation, which certainly does not weigh a hundred-thousandth part of a grain, gives out enough energy to produce effects plainly visible to you all at the very back of the room.

If, instead of the thirtieth part of a pin's head full, we could obtain a pint of this gas—and to obtain such a quantity half a ton of pure radium would be required—it would radiate the energy of a hundred powerful arc-lamps. Indeed, as Rutherford has said, no vessel would hold it. Such a quantity would instantly melt and dispel in vapour any material known.

The Decay of the Emanation.

These new facts, which transpire the moment we begin to make a systematic investigation of the radioactivity of radium, make the second alternative, that the energy of radium is derived from outside, well-nigh incredible. For to account for the energy *evolved from the emanation* we must suppose all space to be everywhere traversed by new and mysterious forms of radiant energy of such tremendous and incredible power that the explanation is harder to believe than the fact it is supposed to explain. To avoid the necessity of supposing that the energy resides within the comparatively

THE DECAY OF THE EMANATION

small amounts of radioactive matter in existence, we must fill the whole of external space with radiant energy of a similar order of magnitude. This is straining at a gnat and swallowing a camel.

Fortunately there is a crucial test by which we are now in a position to decide between the two alternative views. Let us apply the theorem we have already deduced (p. 70) from general principles. If the energy comes from within the radioactive matter, its radioactivity must in course of time diminish and decay—the more rapidly the more powerfully radioactive it is. Whereas, if the energy comes from the outside, however powerful the radioactivity may be, there is no reason why it should not continue indefinitely with undiminished power.

We have seen that the emanation is, mass for mass, far more intensely radioactive even than radium, and, if the energy comes from within, it is to be expected that the activity of the emanation will be short-lived in comparison with that of radium, whereas, if the energy is derived from outside, no such decay is to be anticipated. Does the radioactivity of the radium emanation diminish or decay, or does it continue permanently?

The answer to this question is that the radioactivity of the emanation rapidly decays away from day to day. Four days hence the activity will be but one-half of what it now is. In eight days the activity will be reduced to one-fourth, in twelve days to one-eighth, in sixteen days to one-sixteenth, and so on, diminishing practically to zero at the end of a month in a descending geometrical progression with the lapse of time.

The light from the glowing willemite in this tube, when it is left entirely to itself, will gradually fade, and at the end of a month will have died almost completely. Vast as is the store of energy in matter which is released in the radioactive process, it is not infinite, and in the radium emanation we have an example of a change proceeding so rapidly that only a few weeks are necessary for its completion.

The Reproduction of the Emanation by Radium.

Half a mystery is usually greater than the whole, and in science when mysteries begin to appear on all sides, the explanation is often near at hand. We dissolved a compound of radium in water, and the greater part of its activity disappeared in the process. Then little by little the lost activity was spontaneously recovered, and at the end of a month the radium was not appreciably less active than at first. The disappearance of the greater part of the activity after solution was explained by the fact that an extremely radioactive gas —the emanation—was liberated during the act of solution, and this carried away with it the whole of the radioactivity which the radium had lost. But, lo! while the radium slowly recovered its original radioactivity, the emanation lost what it had at first possessed. A quantitative examination of these two processes of decay and recovery at once showed that the total radioactivity had not been affected, but had remained constant in spite of the treatment to which the radium had been subjected. This is a fundamental law of universal application to all radioactive bodies, and it has been called the Law of the Conservation of Radioactivity. Whatever you do to any radioactive substance you cannot artificially alter the total radioactivity, though you may frequently, as in this example, divide it into several parts, for reasons that will soon be clear.

It is easy enough on the first alternative to account for the comparatively rapid decay of the activity of the emanation of radium. It is dissipating its internal store of energy so rapidly that it is soon exhausted. It is a clear case of a short life and a merry one. But how is the gradual *recovery* of the radioactivity of the radium in the course of time to be explained? This is the key to the whole problem, and on the second alternative no answer whatever can be given. The explanation that the energy of radioactive substances is derived from outside is not merely incredible. It is altogether insufficient.

Imagine that a month has elapsed, and that the radium, which has now recovered completely its lost activity, is again dissolved in water and evaporated down to dryness exactly as before. Again you would find that in the process the radium had lost the same large proportion of its radioactivity, and again you would obtain from it *a new amount of emanation* no less than that which is on the table to-night. Repeat the experiment as often as you please and you will find the result always the same. While the emanation you separate from the radium is decaying away from day to day, *a fresh crop is being spontaneously manufactured by the radium.* The change of the radium into the emanation is, as a matter of fact, only the first of a long series of successive changes of a similar character. The gaseous emanation in turn rapidly changes into a third body, not a gas, called radium A; this into a fourth, called radium B; and so on. Nine successive changes are at present known, which we shall have to give some account of later.

Atomic Disintegration.

This explanation of radioactivity, which has come to be known as the theory of atomic disintegration, was put forward by Professor Rutherford and myself as the result of a long series of experimental investigations carried out in the Macdonald Physical and Chemical Laboratories at McGill University, Montreal. It has, since, not only shown itself capable of interpreting all the very complicated known facts of radioactivity, but also of predicting and accounting for many new ones. Although on the surface a revolutionary addition to the theories of physical science, it must be remembered that it is the *facts* of radioactivity which are really revolutionary. While accommodating these strange new facts the disintegration theory conserves in a truly remarkable way the older established principles of physical science. Without such a guiding hypothesis, reconciling the old and the new, it is safe to say that the *facts* of radioactivity would ultimately have wrought a far greater change in scientific theory than has actually taken place. Although the emanation of radium is not and, as we shall come to see, never can be obtained in palpable quantities—it is changing too rapidly for that—we know almost as much about its nature and properties as we do about any of the older gases.

Radioactive Equilibrium.

A very important point is that just as we cannot really alter the radioactivity of a body artificially in any way, we cannot and do not in any process influence the rate at which the emanation is being formed from radium or the rate at which it in turn spontaneously changes. The same amount is always in existence whether you separate it or not. The apparent constancy of the radioactivity of radium is not the real constancy to be expected of a transforming mechanism. It is the apparent constancy produced by the *equilibrium* between continuous and opposing changes, on the one hand the rapid decay of the part of the radioactivity due to the emanation, and on the other the regeneration of fresh emanation as fast as the old disappears. This process of regeneration is always going on at a perfectly definite and unalterable rate, and the property of producing a certain definite amount of emanation in a given time is as much a part and parcel of the very nature of radium—and indeed the best and most easily applied qualitative and quantitative test for the presence of radium in the minutest quantity that we possess—as is its power of giving the rays which lit up the X-ray screen and discharged the silk tassel, or as its power of generating heat.

Energy of Radioactive Change.

All of these properties are but the various aspects of a single primary cause. The element radium is changing, so slowly it is true, that at first sight it appears not to be changing at all, and yet with so tremendous and unparalleled an evolution of energy that the transformation of an otherwise imperceptible part of its mass is accompanied by an amount of energy so great that the change could not by any possibility have remained unknown. The emanation is the first main product of the change of radium. If the emanation were like lead or any ordinary element it would take years of accumulation and the most minute and patient investigation to detect its production. But it is not. The emanation changes again into a third type of matter we have not yet considered (the nature of which does not yet concern us), but whereas it would take hundreds of years for any appreciable fraction of the radium itself to change, the change of the emanation is rapid and goes to practical completion within a single month. It is precisely on this account that we can work with and detect such almost infinitesimal quantities. What may be termed the material evidence of radioactive change, the detection, by purely chemical or spectroscopic methods, of the materials formed in the changes, is still scanty, although not altogether lacking. But the radioactive evidence, which depends not on the material produced, but upon the energy evolved, and on the way in which the energy is manifested, is abundant and sufficient. So long as the energy evolved is sufficient in quantity, and of a kind suitable for detection in any of the various ways I have illustrated, the actual quantity of matter producing the energy is of no consequence.

All Radioactive Changes Equally Detectable.

But the amount of energy produced by any change depends not only on the quantity of matter changing, but also on *the time the change lasts*, that is, on the period of life of the changing matter. Chemical and spectroscopic methods of detecting matter depend on quantity, whereas radioactive methods depend on *quantity divided by life*. The shorter the life of the changing substance the less of it is necessary for its detection by means of radioactivity. This is a merely preliminary and tentative indication of the operation of an exactly compensating principle of great importance, which later it will be possible to formulate as a general law. Its result in the long run is this. Each of the ephemeral intermediate substances in the cascade of changes comes equally within our powers of investigation, whether it changes slowly or rapidly, whether it lasts long enough to accumulate in ponderable quantity, or whether it is changing so rapidly that it

anon,
Like snow upon the desert's dusty face,
Lighting a little hour or two, is gone.

CHAPTER VI

HELIUM AND RADIUM

THE CONNECTION OF THE a-PARTICLE WITH RADIOACTIVE CHANGES.

LAST week we studied the first step in the evidence that radium is changing, and considered in some detail the chief practical reason why such changes have proved within our powers of discovery, namely, that the change is not single but proceeds in cascade from stage to stage, producing ephemeral intermediate transition-forms, of which the radium emanation is one, almost inconceivably minute in their actual quantity but evolving in their next change very large amounts of energy, by means of which it is possible to trace them and study their nature with ease. We considered the first product of the change of radium, namely, the emanation of radium, its nature and properties, and its continual production from radium. We reserved purposely the examination of the connection between radium and the emanation it produces. Now I wish to combine with the knowledge we have gained of the nature of the radium emanation that already considered (Chapters III. and IV.) with reference to the nature of the a-particle.

A radium salt is dissolved in water, and the imprisoned emanation, which was formed but stored during the previous month throughout the whole mass of the substance, is thereby liberated and escapes. The radium left to itself continues to produce fresh emanation at a steady rate. The released stores of emanation begin to lose their radioactivity. We shall confine our attention at first solely to the case of the radium.

When radium in this way is freed from all previously formed emanation *it still gives out α-particles*, although only now one-fourth as many as it gives out when it contains its full quota of emanation and other products.

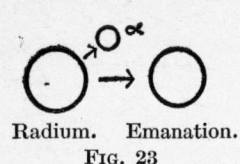

These α-particles we regard as produced from the radium atom in the same change as that in which the emanation is produced. The emanation is regarded, in fact, as radium that has lost one α-particle.

Radium.   Emanation.
FIG. 23

This, which is a perfectly general point of view, was proved from the first by the consideration of a mass of evidence accumulated with reference to the similar changes going on in the element thorium, but much of this may be left for later treatment. The evidence that has since been accumulated enables the same deduction to be more simply made, and this alone need be considered. Henceforth the original reasoning as to the nature of atomic disintegration, although it was, when first put forward, very complete and convincing to those acquainted with the whole of the experimental facts, will be largely replaced by the more direct evidence since obtained.

Helium and the α-Particle.

We have seen in considering the nature of the α-rays that they are now regarded as due to the flight of swarms of helium atoms expelled from the radioactive substance with an almost inconceivable speed of from 8,000 to 12,000 miles per second. Long before the real nature of the α-particle was known, helium had been first predicted to be and then proved experimentally to be a product of the radioactive changes of radium, and this chapter in the development of the subject has something more than an historical interest.

Before proceeding, one underlying consideration

RADIOACTIVE EQUILIBRIUM

governing the view that an atom of helium and an atom of emanation are simultaneously formed when an atom of radium disintegrates, must be made clear. It refers to the relative quantities of each product, helium and emanation, which it may be expected will be formed by the continuous operation of the process. Helium we know is not radioactive, and therefore there is no evidence that helium is changing in any way, and we may in this sense refer to it as one of the ultimate products of the change. The emanation, on the other hand, is changing so rapidly that the change may be regarded as complete in the course of a single month. The bodies it is changing into we have not yet dealt with, and they do not immediately concern us.

Now a changing substance, like the emanation, cannot possibly accumulate in quantity with lapse of time beyond a certain very small extent. It is true it is constantly being formed from radium in the same way as helium, but whereas the helium, being a stable substance, may be expected to accumulate in a quantity that is proportional to the time that elapses, the quantity of emanation will not increase beyond a certain point. For in a very short time after the process of accumulation of emanation from the radium begins, as much emanation will itself change as is formed, and the quantity from that time on will remain constant. This condition is known generally as "radioactive equilibrium," and when we speak of the emanation being in equilibrium with the radium we mean that the quantity of emanation has reached a maximum and does not further appreciably increase with lapse of time. In the case of the emanation practical equilibrium results in the comparatively short time of a few weeks. That is to say, however long radium is left undisturbed to accumulate its emanation, the quantity of the latter never exceeds a practically almost infinitesimal one, for it is a quantity which is produced from the change of the radium in quite a short period of time. Its quantity is therefore excessively minute. It is so very minute that *were it not changing* and evolving energy it would not be detectable by any ordinary method.

You will see that it follows at once from this point of view that if any element were produced in the disintegration of radium, which itself did not change but was permanent, then on the one hand, owing to the extreme smallness of the amount formed, it would not be easy in a short period to obtain evidence of its production, by means of ordinary chemical tests, but, on the other hand, the quantity would go on accumulating indefinitely with lapse of time.

The Ultimate Products.

As we saw last week, the first evidence of atomic disintegration was dynamical and due solely to the energy which is evolved in the process. The answer to the question as to what are the ultimate products of atomic disintegration must be looked for on quite different lines. The ultimate products formed will be too small for detection in the ordinary way by the statical methods of chemistry and physics, but they will accumulate indefinitely.

Since the processes go on steadily, so far as we know, in the *minerals* in which the radioactive elements are found, the ultimate products, formed through past ages of disintegration, must accumulate therein from one geological epoch to the next. So that at the present day one ought to find in the radioactive minerals the ultimate products of the disintegration process, accumulated in sufficient quantity to be capable of detection by the ordinary methods of chemistry.

Now the radioactive minerals are always very complex, and contain a very large proportion of the total number of elements known, so that in most cases it is impossible to deduce very much from this evidence. Nevertheless, there was one clear definite exception, and that was the element *helium*. Another definite but less unequivocal exception was the element *lead*.

DISCOVERY OF HELIUM, SOLAR AND TERRESTRIAL.

The history of our knowledge of helium is unsurpassed by that of any other in interest. Its very name (from ἥλιος, the sun) stands witness to the fact that it was known to exist in the sun as an element before it was known to exist on the earth at all. It was discovered in 1868 by the spectroscope in the sun's chromosphere, by means of the characteristic bright yellow line in its spectrum, which is technically known as "D_3". Then, in 1895, Sir William Ramsay discovered it in certain minerals found in the earth's crust, and made a systematic investigation of its physical and chemical nature. It is a gas, the second lightest known, only twice as dense as hydrogen, and for long was the only gas which successfully resisted all efforts made to liquefy it by extreme cold and pressure. In 1908, however, Kammerlingh Onnes succeeded by the exercise of wonderful experimental skill and persistence in reducing helium to the liquid state, attaining thereby a far lower temperature (270° Centigrade, or only 3° from the absolute zero of temperature) than has ever before been reached. It is readily evolved from the minerals in which it is found, either by heating them or by dissolving them, but once evolved it cannot again be absorbed by the minerals or by any other substance known. Indeed, helium resembles argon perfectly in chemical nature, in that it is quite without any combining power, and exists free as single atoms without being known to form compounds of any kind whatever. Its atomic weight is four (hydrogen=1). Sir William Ramsay drew attention to the fact that all the minerals in which he found helium contained either uranium or thorium. This was before the days of radioactivity, and for long the origin of the helium—a non-condensable, non-combining gas—in minerals containing uranium and thorium was a matter for comment and speculation. In certain cases the volume of helium evolved is nearly a hundred times as great as the volume of the mineral in which it is contained.

Prediction of the Production of Helium.

The disintegration theory enabled Professor Rutherford and myself at once to give a probable explanation which has since proved to be correct. We regarded helium as one of the ultimate products of the disintegration of the radioactive elements, radium, uranium, and thorium. Forming during the long ages of the past throughout the mass of the mineral, which is often of a glassy nature, it is unable to escape until the mineral is heated or dissolved, and it steadily accumulates with the passage of geological time. We ventured to predict that helium was one of the ultimate products of radioactive changes, being formed in Nature from radium, uranium, and thorium, excessively slowly, but still fast enough to ensure that all minerals containing these elements must contain helium also. This has since been proved to be the case. It is true that in certain uranium minerals—*e.g.*, autunite and carnotite, the amount present is often excessively minute, but these also are just the minerals which it is believed are of extremely recent geological formation. Indeed, the ratio between helium and uranium or thorium in minerals is now one of the recognised methods of estimating their age.

From this point the work proceeded along two separate lines. Rutherford, in an exhaustive examination of the nature of the α-rays, which we have already considered, proved first that they consisted of positively charged atoms expelled with great velocity. At first their mass was given as twice that of hydrogen, on the assumption they carried one atomic charge. Then, as the sequel to the beautiful counting experiments we have considered, it was proved in 1908 that each α-particle carries two atomic charges of positive electricity. Therefore the mass of the α-particle is four, that is to

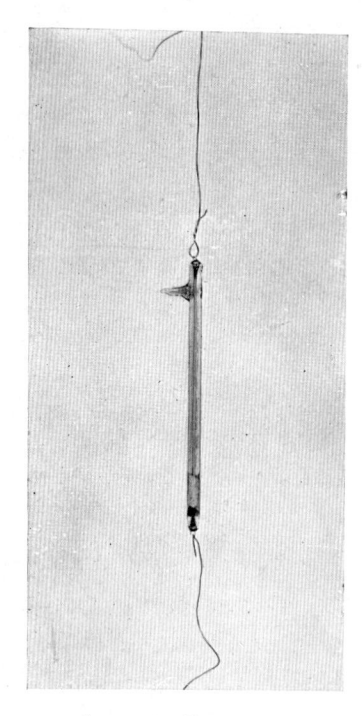

FIG. 24.—Original Spectrum-Tube in which the Formation of Helium from Radium was first observed.

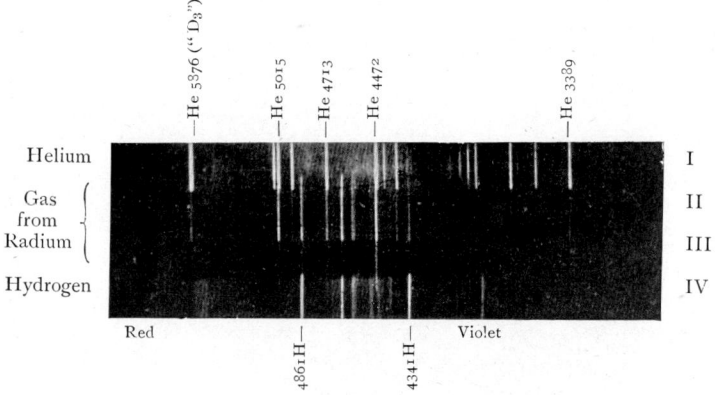

FIG. 25.—Dr. Giesel's Photograph of the Spectrum of the Gas from Radium.

II 20 minutes', III 5 minutes' exposure. I is the Spectrum of Helium, IV that of Hydrogen, for comparison.

To face p. 99

PRODUCTION OF HELIUM FROM RADIUM

say, it is the same as that of the atom of helium. This made it very probable, therefore, that the α-particle is an atom of helium.

Production of Helium from Radium.

The prediction that helium was a product of radioactive changes was proved directly by Sir William Ramsay and myself in 1903. We chose for the particular case of radioactive change studied that of the emanation of radium, since it is rapid, and the emanation can readily be obtained, free from other gases, first by the action of suitable absorbents, and finally by condensing it with liquid air and removing the gases not condensed with a pump. So purified, it was sealed up in a small spectrum tube, so that the spectrum of the gas could be examined at will, and then it was left to itself. At first no helium was present. Helium, not being condensable by liquid air, could not have been present in the tube as first prepared. But in the course of three or four days, as the emanation disintegrated, the spectrum of helium gradually made its appearance, and finally the whole characteristic spectrum of helium was given by the tube. Fig. 24 shows a photograph of one of the original spectrum tubes in which the production of helium from radium was proved. This observation of the production of the element helium from the radium emanation, and therefore (since the emanation in turn is produced from radium) from the element radium, has since been verified and confirmed by numerous investigators in various parts of the world. It has also been found by Debierne in a similar manner by the spectroscope that actinium, a radioactive substance found by him in pitchblende, produces helium. Dr. Giesel has actually succeeded in photographing the spectrum of the gases generated by radium, and one of his photographs is reproduced in Fig. 25. It represents four separate spectra, one below the other in parallel strips. The uppermost (I) is ordinary helium. The second and third (II and III) are two photographs obtained from the gas generated by radium. In the second an exposure of twenty minutes, and in the third one of five minutes were given. The lowest spectrum (IV) is that of hydrogen. It will be seen that many of the helium lines are present in the spectrum of the gas from radium. The other lines are those of hydrogen, due, no doubt, to the presence of a trace of moisture. The figures above and below the plate refer to the stronger lines of helium and hydrogen respectively clearly visible in photograph II. They refer to the wave-lengths in Ångstrom units (10^{-10} metre). It must be remembered that the (visually) brilliant yellow line D_3, owing to its colour, appears far less intense in the photograph than the blue and violet lines.

Production of Helium from Uranium and Thorium.

I was engaged for four years in an attempt to detect the production of helium from the primary radio-elements uranium and thorium, and succeeded in proving in both cases that helium is produced, and, moreover, that the rate of production is almost exactly what is to be expected from the theory of atomic disintegration. This quantity is about one five-hundred-thousand-millionth of the mass of the uranium or thorium per annum! A photograph of the apparatus employed, as it stood in the Physical Chemistry Laboratory, is shown in Fig. 26. These are seven exactly similar arrangements side by side, each of which is quite separate and unconnected with the others. Each consists essentially of a large flask, capable of holding a considerable quantity of the material experimented upon in the form of solution. Each is provided with a peculiar form of mercury tap, which, while it serves perfectly to keep out the atmosphere from the flask for an indefinite time, can at any moment be opened by sucking down the mercury in the barometer tubes, so that the

FIG. 26.—Photograph of the Apparatus employed to detect the Production of Helium from Uranium and Thorium.

To face p. 100

PRODUCTION OF HELIUM FROM URANIUM

accumulated gases from the flask can be extracted and tested for helium without admitting air. Air has been the great trouble. A pin's-head-full of air left in the whole of the large flask or in the solution, or leaking in during the periods of accumulation, would completely ruin the experiment. Most of the elaborations of the apparatus have to do with the preliminary thorough removal of the air from the apparatus before the experiments are commenced. The methods of testing for helium are also entirely new. They depend on the power I found was possessed by the metal calcium, when heated to a very high temperature in a vacuum, of absorbing the last traces of all gases except the gases of the helium and argon type. In this way the minute amount of helium produced (usually not more than a thousandth part of a cubic millimetre) is freed perfectly from every other trace of gas and water vapour. Finally, it is compressed by means of mercury into the smallest-sized spectrum tube that can be made and its spectrum examined. As shown in numerous special experiments, the D_3 line of the helium spectrum can be detected with certainty if one millionth part of a cubic centimetre, or one five-thousand-millionth part of a gram of helium is present. This is certainly the smallest quantity of any element that has ever been detected by the spectroscope.

By frequently repeated experiments one can find for each flask a period of accumulation that must be allowed before helium can be detected in the expelled gases, and so one can obtain a measure of the rate of production of helium. In this way I have obtained helium repeatedly from both uranium and thorium salts, and the rate of production has been found to be of the same order as that previously calculated from the disintegration theory. For the case of uranium the rate of production is about two milligrams of helium from a thousand tons of uranium per year.

Identity of the α-Particle and Helium.

The position is then this: helium has actually been found to be produced from the various radioactive substances—radium, thorium, uranium, actinium—which have in common the fact that they all expel α-particles. The mass of these particles has been measured and found to agree with the mass of the helium atom. All α-particles have been proved to have the same mass and to differ only in the initial velocity of expulsion, whether expelled from radium itself, from the emanation, from actinium, uranium, thorium, or any other of the bodies which expel them. Hence we are justified in concluding that the α-particle is an atom of helium, or at least becomes one after the velocity with which it is expelled is lost and it is brought to comparative rest.

One further step in this long converging series of experiments clinches the argument. We have seen that the α-particle, though but feebly penetrating, has a very definite small penetrating power. Now glass is a substance that can be blown to an excessive degree of thinness and yet retain to the full its air-tight properties. I have succeeded in blowing small windows of glass thin enough to allow the α-particle to get through, and yet strong enough and tight enough to stand the pressure of the air on one side when there was an almost perfect vacuum on the other. So that it ought to be possible, if the α-particle is an atom of helium, by storing the radioactive substance in a very thin-walled air-tight glass vessel, to get helium produced *outside* the vessel, although no helium or other gas in the ordinary state confined inside the vessel could escape. This experiment has been performed by Rutherford and Royds with a large quantity of radium loaned by the Austrian Government. The emanation from the radium, which gives α-particles and has been shown to give helium, was stored in an excessively thin-walled but still perfectly gas-tight capillary tube, enclosed within a wider vessel. After some days the gas in the outer vessel was found to contain helium. It was proved that when helium was stored in the inner tube, none got through into the outer vessel. This final experiment clinches the proof that the α-particle is an atom of helium.

The First Change of Radium.

So we are justified in writing the first disintegration suffered by radium:

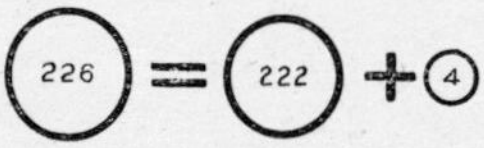

$$(226) = (222) + (4)$$

Radium.   Emanation.   Helium.

Fig. 27.

There is a great deal of evidence which proves that one atom of a radioactive body expels but one α-particle at each disintegration. Hence, since the atomic weight of radium is 226, and that of helium 4, the atomic weight of the emanation is presumably 222. This is the value obtained by direct experiment (Chapter V.).

The above diagram is typical of no less than nineteen different radioactive changes, in all of which an atom of mass between 240 and 206 expels an α-particle, or helium atom, of mass 50 or 60 times less. By the usual dynamical law it is to be expected that the heavy residue of the original atom, whatever it is, should *recoil* in the direction opposite to that in which the α-particle is expelled with a velocity between 50 and 60 times less than the α-particle, that is to say, with a velocity between 150 and 250 miles a second. The kinetic energy of this recoiling atom, since it depends upon the mass multiplied by the square of the velocity, will also be between 50 and 60 times less than that of the α-particle. The velocity and kinetic energy possessed by a recoiling atom, though greatly inferior to that of an α-particle, are nevertheless greatly superior to that possessed by an ordinary gas molecule at any attainable temperature.

Radioactive Recoil.

The phenomenon of radioactive recoil comes into evidence in a very curious and interesting manner, which at the same time has proved of very great practical utility. Very many of the products resulting from the expulsion of α-rays, although *after* their formation they are either not at all volatile or can only be volatilised at a high temperature, yet at the moment of production behave like volatile substances, and are carried away under suitable circumstances from the preparation in which they are produced, and deposited on the nearest available surface. The best conditions are obtained by working in a good vacuum, and charging the preparation positively, and the surface, on which it is required to deposit the recoil product, negatively. The residual atom, after the α-particle is expelled, carries a positive charge, and so is attracted to the negatively charged surface. It is essential that the preparation should be in the form of a very thin layer in order to give the recoiling product a chance of escaping from it. In this way many products, of period of life too short to allow of their being separated by any other method, have been isolated and identified with ease.

CHAPTER VII

THEORY OF ATOMIC DISINTEGRATION

QUESTIONS OF NOMENCLATURE.

THE question, How *can* an element or the atom of an element change? has given rise to many arguments, of etymological rather than scientific importance. What we now certainly know, and what radioactivity has given us for the first time the opportunity of learning is, first, that some elements *do* change, and secondly, *how* they change. The element radium changes, by the loss of an atom of helium, into the emanation, which is about as different from radium in its chemical or material nature as two elements well could be. The one is a member of the group of alkaline-earth, the other of the argon family of elements.

After all, is not this rather to be anticipated? When we arrange the elements in order of their atomic weights —an arrangement which led to the recognition of what is known as the Periodic Law (Fig. 43, p. 214)—the most sudden and surprising differences appear between *succeeding* elements. Chlorine, potassium, and argon are three succeeding elements in such an arrangement, and there is no resemblance whatever between them. In the nine successive transformations radium undergoes, the atom suffers, in most but not in all, a disintegration in which a helium atom is expelled. The heavy residues of the original atom remaining after the successive loss of one, two, three and so on of these helium atoms constitute the intermediate bodies—the emanation, radium A, radium B, and radium C—successively produced, each from the preceding. It is therefore rather to be expected that the succeeding transition-substances produced one after the other should differ entirely from one another in their material characteristics. Further discoveries on this important question are dealt with in Chapter XV.

Definition of the Atom.

Let us from the point we have gained now face the question, which has proved a difficulty to so many, of how it is we find that the elements and the atoms are actually changing. The word *atom* is, of course, derived from the Greek, and at first meant the indivisible or the undivided. For a long time it had a subjective meaning only, being the smallest particle imaginable, rather than the smallest particle obtainable, and as such it belongs to metaphysics, not to physical science. The idea of the atom was first given an objective meaning by Dalton. He showed that chemical change between two elements occurs in definite proportions by weight of the two elements. If unit weight of one is taken, the weight of the other will have a definite fixed value. But often the same two elements unite to form more than one compound in different proportions. Then, if unit weight of the one is still taken for reference throughout, the ratio of the weights of the other in various compounds will be simple multiples or submultiples of one another, indicating that elements do not combine in haphazard proportions, but " atom for atom " by fixed increments or units of combination having definite relative weight. Thus, one atom of carbon combines with either one or two atoms of oxygen, and for iron and oxygen the ratio is either one to one or two to three. These units of chemical combination of definite relative weight are the *atoms of the chemist*. In all the various changes of matter which *chemistry* has investigated it has sufficed to regard all combination as taking place atom by atom, and fractions of an atom or the subdivision of atoms has not been necessary.

In compounds the component atoms preserve their individuality and identity, because compounds can always be decomposed to give back the same elements out of which they are formed and not new ones. In none of these changes does any deep change of the component atoms themselves take place. As chemical changes till recently were the most fundamental material changes known, the chemist's atom fulfilled in a derived sense the ancient meaning of the smallest particle that exists. It did not suffer subdivision in the most fundamental changes known. But in this sense its meaning was coupled with that of the particular element to which it referred. Thus the atom of uranium is about 240 times as massive as the atom of hydrogen. An atom of uranium is the smallest particle of *uranium* which exists. An atom 240 times lighter than this is known, but it is not uranium, it is hydrogen.

Elements and Chemical Compounds.

The discoveries in radioactivity have left this meaning of the word *atom* unchanged. The atom of radium is the smallest particle of *radium* that exists, and is the unit of all the chemical changes radium undergoes. When, by new and more fundamental changes than those before known, it changes, it is no longer an atom *of radium*. The matter formed is as unlike radium as any body well could be. You may, if you like, regard the radium atom as a compound of the atom of emanation, and of the helium atom which result on its disintegration, as it certainly is such a compound, but you must make it quite clear that you do not mean a mere *chemical* compound, which may at will be formed from and decomposed into its constituents. Were radium a chemical compound of helium it would, as Sir William Huggins has pointed out, show the spectrum of helium. Instead, it shows an entirely new spectrum, clearly analogous to but distinct from that shown by barium, its nearest chemical relative. The spectrum of helium is not shown

108 THEORY OF ATOMIC DISINTEGRATION

until after the radium has disintegrated. The radium spectrum does not contain a single helium line.

The most vital distinction, however, between an element and a compound in the chemical sense is this: both are ultimately compound. Of that there can be now no doubt. But the energy change which attends the resolution of an element into its constituent parts is of an order of a million times greater than in the case of the resolution of any chemical compound. Although this is a question of degree, it is of a degree of so entirely different an order of magnitude that it completely differentiates the two types of complexes, and nothing but confusion can result from giving to each the same name. Radium is as much an element as any of the other eighty. If radium is complex, so, almost certainly, are all to greater or less degree. If radium changes, so may (perhaps even so do) all. Their complexity is of a completely different character from that of chemical compounds, and it is best in the end to retain the old words "atom" and "element" in the sense they have had since the time of Dalton rather than attempt to meddle with this traditional, and to scientific men, well-understood nomenclature. The atom of the chemist remains exactly what it was. Why, therefore, alter its name? If you call it a molecule, how are you to distinguish it from the chemical molecule, which has also its own definite meaning distinct from the chemical atom?

The Experimental Facts.

These questions of nomenclature at first diverted attention from the experimental *facts*, and gave rise to much more or less random criticism of the younger workers in radioactivity. Another source of confusion has been the tendency to associate the discoveries in radioactivity with other entirely distinct discoveries made somewhat earlier with reference to the nature of the negative electron.

It was thought at one time that it would be possible

NATURE OF ATOMIC DISINTEGRATION

to explain the atoms of matter as being built up entirely of electrons or atoms of electricity, which turned out to be as little in accord with actual evidence as it would be to regard the solar system as composed entirely of planets and to neglect the central sun. The problem of the real nature of the atoms of matter has not been completely solved by either of these independent scientific advances.

Another objection to the validity of radioactive evidence has been the minuteness of the amounts of matter on which the evidence is based.

It has been stated that it is impossible to come to any settled conclusions in regard to radioactivity, until enough of the materials can be obtained to suffice for the requirements of chemical investigation. But surely, this criticism puts weight on mere familiarity with the older methods rather than on their real intrinsic value. The tests by which we can recognise and identify with ease, and measure with accuracy the amount of, say, one billionth of a milligram of the radium emanation, possess a philosophical foundation which would challenge comparison with any of the tests of the chemist on any kind of matter, in any quantity great or small.

The Nature of Atomic Disintegration.

It is my intention to give you, so far as I am able with accuracy, broad general mental pictures of radio-active processes, rather than the detailed technical investigations on which these pictures are based. Bear in mind exactly the relation of such mental pictures to the discovered facts. The pictures may not be true, but they are not demonstrably false at the present time. That is to say, you may in any case, without fear of being led into error, apply the picture you have to what is taking place, and the view will lead you to expect certain consequences, and these consequences in every known case agree with the facts. Without such mental pictures, or generalising hypotheses, no man could encompass even a small part of one science. So long as the deductions from the hypothesis are in agreement with facts and can be used to predict them accurately, even when they are still unknown, thus saving the memory, the hypothesis or mental picture is not even supposed or expected to be the absolute truth. So long as all the known facts occur as though the hypothesis were true, the latter serves a very useful purpose, although at any time it may be replaced by a deeper view, one step nearer to absolute truth.

In the early history of the subject two possible alternatives had to be taken into account with reference to the exact nature of radioactive changes. Radioactivity is an atomic phenomenon, and the radio-elements are slowly undergoing changes. What do we mean by "slowly" in this connection? Two possibilities arise. Either the slow changes may result from a slow gradual alteration, through all the atoms of a radioactive substance gradually evolving their stores of internal energy and changing by slow degrees into new kinds of matter. This point of view it was never possible to entertain for a moment. Or, the change is slow and gradual with regard only to the mass of the substance as a whole, but sudden and explosive in character with regard to each individual atom as its turn to disintegrate arrives. This, from the first, the only possible point of view, is in accordance with all that has since been discovered with regard to the nature of the successive disintegrations and of the α-rays expelled. Radioactive changes proceed in cascade, from step to step, the accomplishment of each successive step taking on the average a definite time. But as regards the individual atom disintegrating, the change is sudden in time and of the nature of an explosive disruption, in which an α-particle is expelled with enormous speed, and the old atom becomes *ipso facto* a new one, of atomic weight four units less. Regarding the individual radium atom, for example, there is no gradual change into the emanation and helium atoms. Regarding the whole mass of radium, there is a very gradual change in the sense that some definite small proportion of the whole suffers disintegration in each unit of time.

The Chance of Disintegration.

This, then, is the very vivid mental picture of atomic disintegration which the detailed researches in radio-activity have established. Any one radio-element like radium being considered at any instant, among its innumerable host of atoms, most of which are destined to last for hundreds, some for thousands of years, a comparatively very small proportion every second fly apart, expelling α-particles and becoming emanation atoms. Next second the lot falls to a fresh set to disintegrate, and so the process goes on, α-particles being expelled as a continuous swarm, and yet so small a fraction of the whole changing that the main part of the radium will remain unchanged even after hundreds of years. Now consider the emanation atoms formed. These are much less stable than the atoms of radium. A much larger *fraction* of these disintegrate every second, producing more α-particles and a new body not yet considered.

It is now necessary to consider briefly the exact nature of radioactive change and the laws it follows. The deduction of these laws is a matter for the mathematician. We are chiefly concerned with the general conclusions which have transpired. I will first state the most important of these in words divested of mathematical symbols. The chance at any instant whether any atom disintegrates or not in any particular second is *fixed*. It has nothing to do with any external or internal consideration we know of, and in particular it is *not* increased by the fact that the atom has already survived any period of past time. The events of the past in radioactive change have, so far as we can tell, no influence whatever on the progress of events in the future. This follows from the consideration of the one general mathematical law which all known cases of atomic disintegration so far investigated have been found to follow. Fortunately the law itself is simple. Its application in individual cases is often complicated, but I shall confine myself to the simplest, which are at the same time the most generally important, consequences. The chemist has to do with many types of change all following different laws. In some the rate of change— that is, the quantity of the substance changing in the unit of time—is proportional to the quantity present of the substance which is changing, in others to some power of this quantity. Now, in radioactive change the rate of change is invariably simply proportional to the quantity of changing substance. This seems easy enough, but I would warn the uninitiated that they must not overlook the important fact that since the quantity of a changing substance itself changes as time goes on, owing to the progress of the change, the rate of change being proportional to the quantity also continuously changes, and at no time has a constant value. Hence you cannot get much further by simple arithmetic and algebra. Of course, in the case of a slow change like that of radium itself, when even in a lifetime the quantity of radium is not very appreciably reduced by the operation of the change, it is allowable to neglect the slow alteration of the rate of change with the time and to consider the rate of change as constant, since for short periods of time it essentially is so. In most cases some knowledge, withal a slight one, of the mathematics of continuously varying quantities is essential for the complete deduction of the laws of radioactive change. However, as my intention is to avoid mathematics, I shall simply state these consequences *ex cathedrâ*.

The Period of Average Life of a Disintegrating Atom.

The rate of change in any single case of atomic disintegration is proportional to the quantity of the substance which is changing. The usual plan is to let the symbol λ represent the *fraction* of the total changing per second, and to this symbol λ is given the special name "the radioactive constant." λ may represent a small or a large fraction, according to the particular case, according as the disintegration process is slow or rapid. The important point is that it is a real constant of nature in every case, independent of the past and future history of the substance, its actual amount whether large or small, and of every other consideration whatever. Thus for the emanation of radium, λ, the radioactive constant, has the value $1/481,250$, which signifies that in this case $1/481,250$th of the total amount of emanation in existence changes per second. The next step, skipping the mathematics,[1] is that the average period of life of the atom of a radioactive substance—that is to say, the period of time in seconds it exists on the average before its turn comes to disintegrate—is simply the reciprocal of the radioactive constant, or $1/\lambda$. Thus the average life of the radium emanation is $481,250$ seconds, or $5\cdot 57$ days.

Now as radioactive change proceeds during every instant at the rate proportional only to the total quantity of substance undergoing the change, which is present and remains unchanged at that instant, and as in this method of looking at the changes we do not consider at all the absolute quantities, only the fraction of the whole changing, it follows that λ is always of the same value throughout the process from start to finish. It also follows that $1/\lambda$, the period of average life of the remaining atoms, does not, as you might be inclined to suppose, tend to lessen as time goes on. The atoms disintegrating first have a far shorter period of life, and those disintegrating last have a far longer total period than the average. But at *any* instant throughout, considering only the atoms still remaining unchanged at that instant, then from that instant the average period of life is always $1/\lambda$.

[1] So far as I know, the period of average life was first deduced by Mr. J. K. H. Inglis, to whom I put the problem.

Our own period of average life, of course, follows very different and far more complicated laws. The expectation of life at any age is a practical problem for the actuary. But every one knows, owing to the mortality among infants, that the expectation of life at birth is less than shortly afterwards, when it reaches a maximum and then gets less and less with increasing age. The "expectation of life" of a radioactive atom is independent of its age—as it happens the simplest possible law and one lending itself, as will appear, to some most beautiful deductions. That this is so can be directly proved in the simplest way, by comparing, for example, the rate of change of newly-born radium emanation, not in existence a few minutes before, with that of the residue of an originally much larger quantity that has survived a period several times greater than the period of average life.

The Unknown Cause of Disintegration.

This answers fully the general question, How does an element change? You will probably wish to know why it changes in this particular way. That cannot be said, although the true answer would undoubtedly take us far. All that can be stated is that the immediate cause of atomic disintegration appears to be due to *chance*. If the destroying angel selected out of all those alive on the world a fixed proportion to die every minute, independently of their age, whether young or old, if he regarded nothing but the number of victims and chose purely at random one here, and one there, to make up the required number, then our expectation of life would be that of the radioactive atoms. This, of course, is all that is meant by the statement that the course of atomic disintegration appears to be due to the operation of "chance."

It is natural to inquire why this particular law is followed. On this fundamental question no light is yet forthcoming. There is always "a cause of the

THE PERIOD OF HALF-CHANGE

ultimate cause." Atomic disintegration is assuredly the ultimate cause of radioactivity. It does not weaken this deduction that as yet we have not found the ultimate cause of atomic disintegration. Various possible causes have been discussed. Most of them, so far from helping the elucidation of the " why," do not conform even to the " how." The law of radioactive changes shows clearly that the past history of an atom does not increase its chances of undergoing disintegration in the future, which is a fundamental step gained, although it leaves the ultimate problem unsolved.

There is another way of stating the law of radioactive changes, and that is by saying that as the time increases in arithmetical progression the amount of substance remaining decreases in geometrical progression. Suppose in a time of τ seconds one-half of the total amount changes and one-half remains unchanged. In the next period of τ seconds, 2τ altogether, one-half of what is left—that is, one-quarter—changes, and one-quarter of the total remains unchanged. In 2τ the quantity is reduced to $1/2^2$. In any period of time represented by $N\tau$ seconds, where N is any multiple or submultiple, the quantity of substance remaining is $1/2^n$. It remains to state what relation the time τ required for the half-change to occur, bears to the period of average life $1/\lambda$ of the former way of considering the change. There is a fixed ratio between these two periods, the latter being always 1·45 times the former. In a time equal to the period of average life $1/\lambda$, the quantity of substance present is reduced to $1/\epsilon = 0.368$ of the initial quantity.

Determination of the Period of Average Life.

These considerations would have little interest to us but for the fact that they afford the means whereby the period of average life of any radioactive element can by their aid be exactly determined, not only for those transition-bodies like the emanation, which change so rapidly that we can watch their complete transformation in the course of a few days or weeks, but also for the primary radio-elements, some of which we know require thousands of millions of years to run their course of change. The average life of a radioactive element, representing as it does a fundamental constant of nature, is one of its most important attributes. Our own period of average life being strictly limited, it naturally affects very much our way of looking at the various radioactive bodies. If, for example, the average life is a matter of a few days, as in the case of the radium emanation, we regard the body as an ephemeral transition-form. If it is, as in the case of radium, a few thousand years we are inclined to look upon the substance as a permanent and primary radio-element. There is really not this sharp difference. But it is convenient to divide radioactive bodies into two classes, and in the one to put those for which the periods of average life are short compared to our own, and in the other to put those for which the periods are long. The method employed to determine the value of this fundamental and all-important constant is naturally quite different in the two cases. In the first, simple direct observation suffices. Thus if we measure the decay of the activity of any separated quantity of the emanation of radium with time, we shall find that it decays in a geometrical progression with the time to half its initial value in the course of 3·84 days. The period of average life is 1·45 times greater, or 5·57 days. But in the case of a body, of which one thousandth, or one thousand-millionth as the case may be, changes annually, simple direct observation does not help much. How are we to proceed?

In the first place, let us consider the cases of uranium and radium. We may determine how many times more powerfully radioactive radium is than uranium. The radioactivity of radium is several million times that of uranium when the α-rays of equal quantities of the two elements are compared. From this it may be concluded that the period of uranium is several million times longer than that of radium, and if the latter is known, that of uranium may be roughly estimated, although it is a period of some thousands of millions of years.

As a matter of fact, there is a very beautiful generalisation, I have already referred to briefly, and which later on I shall try to develop further by the aid of an analogy, by means of which the periods of average life of the radio-elements of the second class, those, that is, which are long-lived compared with ourselves, have come into the region of exactly knowable quantities. If the period of average life of a single member of a series of successive atomic disintegrations is known the others can be calculated, provided certain data, not entirely impossible to obtain, are known. It will clear the ground considerably if I attempt to give you the main idea succinctly in the case of radium itself and of the first product of its disintegration, the emanation of radium. I have already alluded to the fact that owing to the very rapid disintegration of the emanation its quantity does not continuously accumulate, but reaches an equilibrium ratio with respect to the radium producing it, in which the amount of already formed emanation disappearing is exactly counterbalanced by the amount of new emanation formed.

The Period of Average Life of Radium.

This state of things is known generally by the name of radioactive equilibrium. The importance of the existence of this state of *radioactive equilibrium* it is impossible to overrate. Many problems, as we shall come to see, which, to us with our limited period of life, might well appear absolutely insoluble, connected as they are with periods of time so vast that our little life by comparison appears a mere moment, are solved directly by the proper application of this principle. Now I am only giving you the main idea and one specific illustration of what is in fact a law of great generality.

118 THEORY OF ATOMIC DISINTEGRATION

By the law of radioactive change, if λ_1 is the radioactive constant of radium—*i.e.*, the fraction of the whole changing per second—and N is the total number of radium atoms dealt with, then the number of radium atoms changing into the emanation per second, and therefore also the number of atoms of fresh emanation produced per second, is $\lambda_1 N$. But in equilibrium this equals the number of emanation atoms disappearing. If the radioactive constant of the emanation is λ_2, and the number of atoms of emanation present during equilibrium is denoted by X, the number of emanation atoms disappearing per second is $\lambda_2 X$. Hence we have

$$\lambda_1 N = \lambda_2 X \text{ and } \frac{X}{N} = \frac{\lambda_1}{\lambda_2}.$$

This law, the most important in radioactivity, thus states that in successive disintegrations the product accumulates in quantity until a fixed ratio with respect to the parent body is attained, and this ratio is inversely proportional to their respective radioactive constants or directly proportional to their respective average lives. It is necessary for the law to hold true that the period of the parent body should be much longer than the periods of any of its products, and in this case the product selected need not necessarily be the first product, but may be any one of the successive products formed in the series.

λ_2 is well known by direct observation. Now if X/N, the ratio between the number of atoms of emanation and of radium in equilibrium together, can be found, then λ_1, the radioactive constant and therefore $1/\lambda_1$, the period of average life of radium can be deduced. That is the important thing—the period of the average life of radium, the rate at which it is changing, and a host of vitally important consequences, can be deduced. For a slowly changing body like radium the second is an inconveniently short unit of time to employ, and it is better to take a year. What is wanted is the fraction of any quantity of radium which changes

AVERAGE LIFE OF RADIUM

in a year. The quantity X/N, which is the ratio of the number of atoms of emanation and of radium in equilibrium together, can be deduced by ordinary physico-chemical laws if the actual volume of emanation in equilibrium with a given quantity of radium can be determined. As already mentioned (p. 82), this volume was first approximately measured by Sir William Ramsay and myself in 1904. The actual volume of emanation is excessively minute, but it is just within the range of measurement. From our results we concluded about 1/1150th part of the radium changes annually, so that the period of average life on this estimate is 1,150 years. Owing to the excessive minuteness of the volume, the method is not an accurate one, tending, since the volume of emanation is likely to be too great unless every trace of other gas is absent, to give too short a period. Later experiments by the same method with much larger quantities of radium have shown that the correct value is about double that first found. With the growth of the subject other methods, less direct but more accurate, have become available. Professor Rutherford recently, from a consideration of a large number of separate data accumulated by himself and others bearing on this question, came to the conclusion that the period of average life of radium is not very far removed from 2,500 years, and we shall take this value as the most probable. It may suffer slight further alteration as fresh data are accumulated, but it is very improbable that it is seriously in error. Within narrow limits the average life of radium may be taken to be 2,500 years.

THE TOTAL ENERGY EVOLVED IN THE COMPLETE DISINTEGRATION OF RADIUM.

A knowledge of this important constant enables us at once to say how much energy any quantity of radium would evolve in the course of its complete

120 THEORY OF ATOMIC DISINTEGRATION

change—that is, during a period of some thousands of years. We saw (p. 22) that a gram of pure radium evolved about 133 calories of heat per hour. There are 8,760 hours in the year, so that in a year a gram of radium evolves about 1,160,000 calories. In a year 1/2500th part changes. Therefore in the complete change of one gram of radium no less than 2,900,000,000 calories would be evolved. The energy evolved in the change of radium is nearly a million times greater than that evolved from a similar weight of matter undergoing any change known previously to the discovery of radio-activity. By the burning of a gram of coal, for example, only about 8,000 calories are obtained. In this change, however, $2\frac{2}{3}$ grams of oxygen are also consumed, so that per gram of the two substances taken together the heat evolved is only 2,200 calories. On this basis of calculation the energy of radium is well over a million times that furnished from the combustion of coal. No wonder then that to account for the boundless energy displayed everywhere in the starry heavens proved a difficult problem for physicists, acquainted with no more energetic chemical process than the burning of coal !

CHAPTER VIII

THE ORIGIN OF RADIUM

Why has Radium Survived?

ONE of our chief duties will be to follow out this theory of the disintegration of atoms in radioactivity. The bare idea of elements spontaneously changing raises so many obvious and apparently insurmountable difficulties that it will be interesting to consider them as they arise and to consider what answer can be made to them. To-night we must concentrate on one of the chief of these—a difficulty which no doubt has already presented itself in many of your minds. If radium is changing at the rate of nearly one two-thousandth part every year, how is it that there is any radium left at the present time? Even at the beginning of the time recorded in past history there must have existed several times as much radium as there is now, if the rate of disintegration has been constant over that period, while a hundred thousand years ago it can be calculated that there must have existed a thousand billion times as much as to-day, had the steady disintegration been going on at its present rate. That is to say, even if the whole world were originally pure radium, in a period of time brief compared to that which we know from geological evidence it has actually been in existence, there would be practically none left, and certainly not as much as actually exists to-day. Or, looking forward instead of backward, if we put this half-grain of radium bromide in a safe place, and then could revisit the earth say twenty-five thousand years hence, we should find less than one-thousandth part of it remaining. The slow disintegration would have done its work and changed the radium into the non-radioactive elements which are being formed from it. This question, apparently so insoluble, in reality admits of the most direct and satisfactory answer on the disintegration theory and serves as a good example of how a theory, if it is worth the name, must be able to predict future discovery as well as to explain the existing facts.

An analogy to facts we have already discussed will help us to find the solution of this difficulty. In the emanation of radium we have become acquainted with a body changing so rapidly that at the end of a month none of the original quantity remains. How is it there is any emanation in existence at all? Because it is being reproduced as fast as it disappears. Is there any reproduction of radium going on, balancing the effect of its disintegration and maintaining its quantity from age to age? Radium is the direct parent of the emanation. Itself changing more than a hundred thousand times slower than its product, it maintains the quantity of emanation in existence over a period a hundred thousand times longer than would otherwise be the case. Is there then a parent of radium? Does there exist any other element producing radium by its own disintegration as fast as that already in existence disappears?

The Reproduction of Radium.

Do not regard this thirty milligrams of radium bromide as something merely by itself. Consider its history. By infinite labour and patience this tiny quantity of radium has been separated from several hundredweights of the mineral pitchblende. Suppose in this operation all the rest of the mineral, after the extraction of the radium, were preserved and put in a safe place. When we revisited our specimen of radium twenty-five thousand years hence, and found practically none of it remaining, should we find that the mineral from which it was extracted had in the meantime grown a fresh crop of radium? The answer is that we should.

This was one of the first predictions made from the theory of atomic disintegration and one of the most recent to be confirmed by experiment. Long before the data were available which enabled an exact estimate of the life of radium to be calculated, it was recognised that radium, though at first sight a permanent and primary radio-element, is changing so rapidly that, had there existed no process in which fresh radium is supplied to replace that changing, none could possibly have survived till the present day, and from general principles it was possible to make a shrewd prediction as to which element was the parent of radium. We have already considered the general principles which enabled the prediction that helium was one of the ultimate products of radioactive changes to be made. Ultimate products must co-exist with the radio-elements producing them in all the natural minerals in which the latter are found. Something of the same reasoning applies to the parent of radium, only in this case it is far more definite and elegant. The parent of radium must co-exist with radium in all minerals in which radium is present. Now it is at once obvious, if this explanation of the parent of radium is to meet the case, that such a body must be changing very much more slowly than radium, otherwise there would arise the same necessity to assume the existence of a parent of the parent as there is of a parent of radium. The original first parent of radium must be changing excessively slowly to maintain a steady supply of radium over long epochs of geological time.

The Ratio between the Quantities of Uranium and Radium in All Minerals.

By the law already formulated on p. 118, in two successive, not necessarily consecutive, disintegrations of which the second is much more rapid than the first, the more rapidly changing body accumulates in quantity until a fixed ratio with respect to the parent body is attained, and this ratio is inversely proportional to the ratio of their respective rates of change, or directly proportional to the ratio of their respective periods of average life. Let us apply this law. The parent body is the parent of radium. The quantity of radium in minerals *must therefore attain a fixed ratio* with respect to the quantity of the parent of radium, and this ratio is the ratio of the parent of average life of radium to that of its parent. The quantity of helium that accumulates in a mineral continually increases as time goes on, assuming the helium does not succeed in escaping, and no definite proportion between helium and radium is to be expected. But the case is different with radium and its parent. There must be a fixed ratio, independent of the age of the mineral examined. As the original first parent of radium must be changing excessively slowly to survive geological epochs of past time, there must be always a very large quantity of it in the mineral. As the radium is changing, from the standpoint of geological epochs of time, very rapidly, there must always be a very small quantity of radium. Between these quantities great and small there must exist the same ratio as between the respective periods of average life of the two bodies.

A very cursory examination of the minerals in which Mme. Curie found radium was sufficient to point strongly to the probability that uranium is the primary parent of radium. Uranium was, as we have seen, the original element for which the property of radioactivity was discovered, and its radioactivity is several million times more feeble than that of radium. Now the radioactivity depends only on the atoms actually breaking up, and therefore in comparing uranium with radium it follows that uranium must be disintegrating several million times more slowly even than radium, so that if uranium produces radium the quantity of uranium must be several million times greater than the quantity of radium in minerals. But this is exactly what Mme. Curie found to be the case in the minerals she worked

QUANTITY OF RADIUM IN MINERALS

up for radium. So that from the very first there existed a strong presumption that uranium is the original parent of radium. The evidence in support of this view at the present time is complete and satisfactory. We owe it to the careful work of McCoy, Strutt and Boltwood that the genetic relation between uranium and radium has been established. They determined the ratio between the quantities of uranium and of radium in a large number of minerals. In every mineral examined containing uranium there was found to exist a direct proportionality between the quantity of uranium and that of radium. To Rutherford and Boltwood together we owe the exact determinations of this important constant of proportionality. They found that for every one part of radium there always exists 3,200,000 parts of uranium. This constant gives directly, unless other undetermined factors interfere, the ratio of the average lives of the two elements. As we have seen, that of radium is 2,500 years. Hence it follows that that of uranium is 8,000,000,000 years. Enormous as this period is, it is not now merely a deduced or calculated value. I obtained the same result by direct experiment from the rate of production of helium from uranium.

Hydraulic Analogy to Radioactive Change.

It will help us considerably if we try to find some analogy to the important and intricate relations that exist between uranium and radium. We may take for illustration the magnificent system of waterworks which supply this city, which we will suppose have been given over to us by the Corporation to control for the purposes of our illustration. As you know, we in Glasgow are supplied ultimately from Loch Katrine through an intermediate reservoir at Milngavie. We shall first cut off Loch Katrine from all fresh sources of supply of water, and from all outlets except to the intermediate reservoir at Milngavie, and we shall see to it also that the latter receives no water except from Loch Katrine, and delivers none except to Glasgow. We shall then issue to our engineers the instructions that there must be delivered every hour at Milngavie from Loch Katrine approximately one eight-millionth part of the total store of water in Loch Katrine, and from Milngavie to Glasgow every hour one two-thousand-five-hundredth part of the total store of water at Milngavie. Then, if instead of hours we read years, the quantity of water in Loch Katrine represents the quantity of uranium, and the quantity of water in Milngavie that of radium. For the sake of brevity we shall term Loch Katrine the source and Milngavie the reservoir.

First we shall suppose that our regulations have been in operation already a considerable number of hours, as this is the condition in which, reading years for hours, we find uranium and radium together in minerals in Nature, for example, in a piece of pitchblende. What relation will the quantity of water in the source bear to the quantity in the reservoir—that is, the quantity of uranium to the quantity of radium ? The amount of water the reservoir receives is quite independent of the amount it contains, but the amount it delivers is proportional to the amount it contains. Similarly the amount of radium produced from uranium does not depend at all on the amount of radium already present, while the amount that itself changes depends *only* on and is proportional to the amount present. Nevertheless, we shall find that there is about three million times more water in the source than in the reservoir. Because only under this condition is the intake of the reservoir equal to the outflow from the reservoir—that is, the production of new radium equal to the disappearance of the old. Imagine, for example, that there was just twice as much water as this ratio in the reservoir, then twice as much would flow out as flows in, and the supply in the reservoir would be rapidly depleted. Or, if there were but one half as much in the reservoir, twice as much would flow in as out, and the supply in the reservoir would increase. In either case, intake and outflow would ultimately become equal, and no further change would then occur until both the source and the reservoir were empty. But let us now disconnect Loch Katrine from Milngavie reservoir, which is equivalent to separating, as Mme. Curie did, the radium from the uranium in pitchblende. Obviously the reservoir by itself will now be able to supply water for a very much shorter time than it did before, and, in general, with the conditions stated, source and reservoir together will last three million times longer than the source alone. The radium on the table will have half disintegrated, so that only half will remain, in about 1,700 years. Whereas had it remained in the mineral associated with its parent uranium, the quantity of radium in the mineral will not be reduced to one half what it is now until 5,000,000,000 years have elapsed.

The Age of Pitchblende.

Thus we can say, following a cautious reservation once made by Professor Tait, provided the causes that are now at work have always been in continuous operation in the past as they are now, and that we know of all the causes that have been at work, 5,000,000,000 years ago there must have been about twice as much uranium and radium in this piece of pitchblende as there is to-night. Since, however, there is actually in this pitchblende now over 50 per cent. of uranium, it is not possible that it can have been in existence in its present form more than 5,000,000,000 years. But, even from a geological point of view, this is a very long period of time indeed; longer, perhaps, than it would be profitable in the present state of science to push back our inquiries. That, then, is the position with regard to the maintenance of radium in Nature. Even when we deliberately leave out of account the possibility there may exist in Nature entirely unknown processes replenishing the supplies of uranium, just as there are replenishing Loch Katrine, there is no difficulty in accounting for the continuous maintenance of radium over a period of the past as great as, or greater than, there is any reason to believe the earth has been in existence in its present condition. This is as far as we need pursue our analogy for the moment, but we shall again find it useful at a later period. We must pass on to another aspect of the question.

Uranium X.

At this stage it will be well to make a short digression into the radioactivity of uranium itself, and how it is explained on the theory of atomic disintegration. Uranium and its compounds in their normal state give out both α- and β-rays. As in all other cases, the β-rays, being photographically the most active and being the more penetrating, were the first chiefly studied. Sir William Crookes and also M. Becquerel found that by certain chemical processes a new substance in minute quantity could be separated from uranium, to which Crookes gave the name uranium X, and this new body produced the whole of the photographic activity of uranium. The uranium after this treatment no longer affected a photographic plate. Crookes concluded that the radioactivity was due in reality to the presence of the foreign substance in minute amount, which he called uranium X, and that pure uranium was not radioactive. I repeated these experiments, and found that only the β-rays of uranium belonged to the uranium X. Uranium freed from uranium X gave its normal amount of α-rays. Then it was found that the β-radiation of uranium X decayed steadily in a geometrical progression with the time, whereas the uranium that had been freed from uranium X and at first gave no β-rays, gradually and completely recovered its power of producing β-rays. Uranium *grows* uranium X, in exactly the same way as radium grows the emanation. The activity of uranium X after separation from uranium, consisting entirely of β-rays, steadily decays in a geometrical progression with the time, falling to one half the initial value in 24·6 days. The average life of uranium X is thus 35·5 days.

The disintegration of uranium up to the point so far discussed is represented on the following scheme:

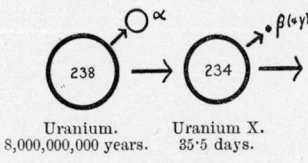

Uranium.   Uranium X.
8,000,000,000 years.   35·5 days.

FIG. 28.

This is as far as the methods of radioactivity enable us directly to trace the disintegration of uranium at the present time. The substance produced—uranium X—is only an ephemeral transition-form, lasting on the average 35·5 days, and when it disintegrates, the process appears to come to a stop so far as our experimental methods have yet been able to disclose.

Now, on the view that has been developed that uranium is the parent of radium, it is natural to suppose that uranium X in the course of time turns into radium. A little consideration will show that if this were the case it might easily be overlooked at first on account of the very long period of life of radium compared with that of uranium X. As already explained (p. 92), chemical and spectroscopic methods of detecting matter depend only on quantity, but radioactive methods depend upon quantity divided by life. Assuming equal effects produced in the disintegration of an atom of uranium X and of an atom of radium, since the life of the latter is 30,000 times that of the former, it will be necessary to have 30,000 times as much radium as of uranium X to produce equal radioactive effects.

ATTEMPTS TO DETECT THE GROWTH OF RADIUM.

In 1903 I started a series of special experiments which have been continued ever since, partly in conjunction with Mr. T. D. Mackenzie and more lately with Miss A. F. Hitchins, to see whether uranium does, in fact, produce radium. The uranium, after being purified as completely as possible by chemical methods from radium, is left sealed up in a flask and is periodically tested to see if a growth of radium has occurred. The method of testing for minute traces of radium is a very simple and accurate one, allowing quantities of radium of only a few million-millionths part of a gram to be detected with certainty and measured with exactitude. Use is made of the characteristic emanation generated by radium. Uranium does not generate any emanation. The uranium solution to be tested for radium, after standing sealed up in a glass flask for a period of at least a month to allow the equilibrium quantity of emanation to accumulate, is boiled in a vacuum, and the gases expelled are collected and introduced into a sensitive gold-leaf electroscope. If radium is present in the solution, its emanation causes the leaf to lose its charge, and the rate at which the discharge occurs under defined conditions can be used accurately as a measure of the amount of radium present. The test is qualitative as well as quantitative, and there is no possibility of making a mistake as to the identity of the emanation and of the radium from which it is formed.

The first result of these experiments, while they furnished the first evidence of a growth of radium, withal in very minute amount, showed that this growth is not due to uranium. In the first experiments the uranium salt was only specially purified from radium, not from any other impurities that might have been present, derived from the minerals from which uranium is obtained, and a very slow growth of radium from the preparation was actually observed.

In later experiments more perfect methods of purifying the uranium initially were adopted, with the result that the growth now of radium occurred chiefly in the impurities separated, whilst the growth in the purified

FIRST EXPERIMENTS

radium was reduced to an excessively minute amount. In these the greatest growth recorded was only one fifty-millionth of a milligram of radium after six years. At this rate, even at the present enormous price of radium, it would require sixty thousand years to produce one pennyworth.

Now if uranium X, when it disintegrates, produced radium directly, then with the quantities of materials used in these later experiments, the amount formed in a single hour would be greater than has actually been formed in six years. In the earlier experiments, with not specially purified uranium, the growth of radium, although quite detectable, was still only one thousandth part of what would have occurred had uranium X changed directly into radium. In spite of this apparently conclusive negative result, it was practically certain that uranium is the original parent of radium, and that in the course of years our preparations would begin to grow radium.

Existence of Intermediate Products.

The natural explanation of this failure to detect a growth of radium from uranium is, that one or more intermediate bodies of long life exist in the disintegration series between uranium and radium. On the analogy proposed, this means that between Loch Katrine and Milngavie reservoir one or more large intermediate reservoirs exist, which have to fill up before the water reaches Milngavie. Uranium X represents the first of such a series of intermediate reservoirs, it is true, but owing to its short period of life and the large fraction of the total quantity always passing through on the way to the next, such a reservoir would be an extremely small one, and for periods such as we are considering its effect on the flow would be practically negligible.

It would be quite otherwise if one or more reservoirs as large as Milngavie—if one or more intermediate substances as long-lived as radium—existed in the series.

I well remember one fact told me by the engineer in charge of the magnificent scheme of waterworks, supplying the mines at Kalgurli, in Western Australia, from a source near the coast across three hundred miles of desert. There are several intermediate reservoirs on the way. The plant installed is capable of pumping five million gallons of water daily, and yet it took a period of many weeks since pumping operations began before the water appeared in Kalgurli. When uranium is carefully purified from all other substances one can be sure that one starts with all the intermediate reservoirs empty—that is, with none of the intermediate substances present. Water is flowing steadily from the source all the time, as the disintegration of uranium is always going on. We watched and waited seven years at the radium reservoir—strictly speaking, at the one beyond radium, since the emanation of radium, not radium itself, is actually employed for the test. But the flow had not reached there yet and the radium reservoir remained practically as empty as at the start. But there was no doubt it would come, and there was good reason to expect that some of us, at least, would be still alive when it arrived.

It is not beyond the resources of mathematics to find out a good deal about these intermediate reservoirs. The present results indicate that if there is but one long-lived intermediate body between uranium and radium, then its period of average life must be at least 100,000 years, that is, forty times that of radium itself. Also, that the radium, in this case, must be produced at a rate proportional to the square of the time from purification, the growth in a century being a hundred times as great as that in the first decade. On our analogy, then, between Loch Katrine and Milngavie, there must exist a reservoir of forty times the capacity of Milngavie, provided there is only one. Since the equilibrium quantity to which an intermediate body accumulates is proportional to its period of average life, then if there is only one intermediate parent of radium between radium and uranium, there must be forty times as much of it in minerals containing radium as there is of radium itself.

IONIUM.

This leads me to the next step. The failure to detect a production of radium from uranium merely foreshadowed the actual discovery of an intermediate substance of long period of life. Boltwood in America succeeded in isolating it from minerals containing radium, and it proves to be the direct parent of radium. It possesses the property of producing radium directly from itself by disintegration, and it has been called *ionium*. It expels α-rays during its disintegration into radium, and these α-rays possess a relatively low velocity. Their range is very little more than one inch of air. Chemically, ionium resembles thorium so completely that the two substances, if mixed, cannot be separated. This gives the means of separating the new body from minerals. Some thorium is added and separated by the well-known methods of chemical analysis. It is then purified as completely as possible. The parent of radium is not separated from the thorium by this treatment, although all other substances are. The chemical resemblance between these two different elements is complete. Later we shall come to recognise many other cases of the same kind. Ionium and thorium are what are now called *isotopes*.

The disintegration series thus reads:

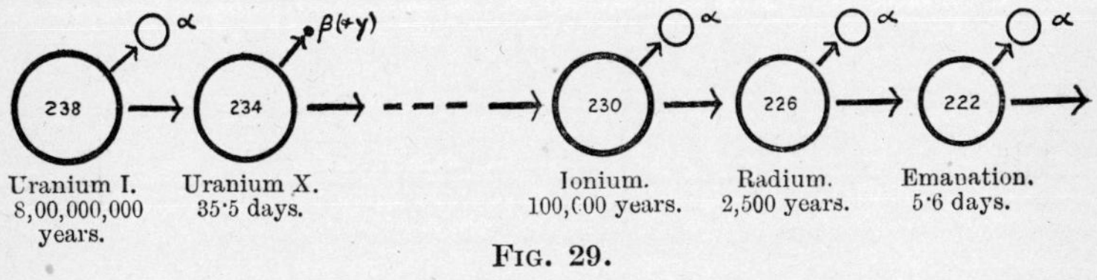

238	234		230	226	222	
Uranium I. 8,00,000,000 years.	Uranium X. 35·5 days.		Ionium. 100,000 years.	Radium. 2,500 years.	Emanation. 5·6 days.	

FIG. 29.

as far as we have yet considered it. In the centre is placed the known or presumed atomic weights of the various bodies.

Production of Radium by Uranium.

Going back to the purified uranium preparations, in 1915 with the help of Miss Hitchins, the measurements of the quantity of radium present first clearly established that there was a steady growth of radium, and, moreover, that it was proceeding proportionally to the square of the time, as the theory requires. This growth has continued regularly up to the present time (1919). The period of average life of ionium calculated from it is almost exactly 100,000 years. The amount of radium in some of the preparations is (1919) about ten times as great as initially. But the problem has taxed to the uttermost even the extraordinarily delicate tests for radium. For the preparation containing the largest quantity of uranium—namely, three kilograms calculated as the element—the growth of radium after ten years has been only one five millionth of a milligram—*i.e.*, one part of radium from fifteen *billion* of uranium.

The Stately Procession of Element Evolution.

So far, then, as we have inquired, uranium, uranium X, ionium, radium, and the emanation represent respectively the starting-point and the four successive stopping-stations in the long journey of continuous devolution from the heaviest and most complex atom known into less heavy and complex atoms which is going on around us, or, to preserve our original analogy, the source and four successive intermediate reservoirs in the flow of elementary evolution. " All things flow " was one of the dogmas of ancient philosophy, and in this, as in many others, the ancients guessed truer than they knew. Instead of four stopping-stations or intermediate reservoirs in this stately procession of elements disclosed by radioactivity, there are now known no less than thirteen, starting from the element uranium, but for our present purposes of illustration these four will suffice. But this new transformation scene on which the curtain of the twentieth century has been rung up, beginning as it has done with the transformation of the most fundamental and permanent of the existences which physical science has recognised in the past, extends beyond physical science and transfigures with new light some of the most fundamental and permanent ideas which in one form or another are deep-rooted in the world's philosophies.

CHAPTER IX

THE SUCCESSIVE CHANGES OF RADIUM

The Later Changes of Radium.

We have attempted to trace radium to its source. It remains to follow through its disintegration briefly to the end. This was a task to which Rutherford particularly devoted himself, after the main principles of atomic disintegration had become familiar, with the consequence that, with the exception of a lacuna here and there still to be supplied, our knowledge of the whole process from the start to finish is now tolerably complete. In addition, some new considerations have transpired which concern us nearly in the broad general application of the principles of atomic disintegration, so that for this reason, if for no other, the work claims our attention.

Most of you who have read at all in the subject will be aware of one mysterious and extraordinary power possessed by radium, which I have hitherto carefully avoided all mention of, not wanting to have too many irons in the fire at once. Radium possesses the power of endowing with some of its own radioactivity neighbouring objects. Thorium, which is very like radium in many ways, particularly in giving a gaseous emanation (which, however, has the very short period of average life of only a little over a minute), also possesses a similar power. The phenomenon was discovered by the Curies for radium and termed "induced radioactivity," and for thorium simultaneously by Rutherford and termed "excited radioactivity." With the explanation of the property the original names have largely fallen into disuse. We shall now confine ourselves to the case

THE ACTIVE DEPOSIT

of radium. Any object left in the immediate neighbourhood of a radium salt becomes radioactive, but after it is removed the radioactivity decays away rapidly and almost completely, abnormally at first, but subsequently more regularly, with a half-value period approaching thirty minutes. The temporary activity so "induced" consists of α-, β-, and γ-rays. The activity exists as an invisible film or deposit over the surface of the object rendered radioactive, for, by sandpapering, the activity can be rubbed off and then is found on the sand-paper. It is now customary in consequence to refer to it as the " active deposit of radium."

This power is, strictly speaking, not a property of radium itself, for if the radium is contained in a completely closed vessel—it does not matter how thin-walled so long as it is air-tight—no radioactivity whatever is produced outside. The first step in understanding the nature of the phenomenon consisted in tracing it to the action of the emanation of radium. In the ordinary condition the emanation is always diffusing away to some extent from radium salts unless they are contained in air-tight vessels. The " active deposit " is the product of the disintegration of the emanation. Just as radium cannot exist without continuously producing the emanation, so in turn the emanation cannot exist without continuously producing this active deposit. In any vessel containing radium emanation this body is being continuously deposited on the walls of the vessel, so that if the emanation is at any time blown out, the active deposit remains behind. Radium expels one α-particle and changes into the emanation. The emanation expels a second α-particle and changes back again into a solid, or at least into a non-gaseous form of matter, the first of the " active deposit " group. The latter in turn expels more α- and also β-particles, and so the course of successive disintegrations goes on. In the active deposit itself at least three changes follow one another with great rapidity, so that the analysis of them proved a complicated task.

The Active Deposit of Radium.

You know that if a moisture-laden atmosphere is sufficiently chilled, the vapour of water condenses directly into the solid form, and a snowstorm results. Something of this kind is always happening in an atmosphere containing the radium emanation. Every second two out of every million of the atoms of emanation disintegrate, expelling α-particles and leaving a solid residue, so that there is a sort of continuous snowstorm silently going on covering every available surface with this invisible, unweighable, but intensely radioactive deposit. Unlike snow, however, the particles of this active deposit are charged with positive electricity, so that if two surfaces are provided, one charged negatively and the other positively, the deposit is attracted almost entirely to the negatively charged surface. The other surface repels the particles and so does not get coated. By making the negatively charged surface very small the active deposit can be almost entirely concentrated upon it. This enables me to show you more effectively the production of the active deposit from the emanation and some of its chief properties. The separation of the non-volatile product of a volatile parent or emanation by this use of a negatively charged surface is a very simple operation, much more so than when the parent substance is non-volatile and the recoil of the product is used to effect its separation and concentration on a negatively charged surface, as discussed on p. 104.

It would take us too long and too far if we attempted first to study these properties, and then tried from them to deduce their explanation. It must suffice if I give you first the explanation of the facts according to the theory of atomic disintegration and then illustrate as many of the points in it as possible experimentally. I have said that after the disintegration of the emanation at least three successive disintegrations, following one another rapidly, occur. The bodies produced are

RADIUM A, B AND C

referred to as radium A, radium B, radium C, in order to avoid the necessity of inventing a host of new names for bodies having such fleeting existence (Fig. 30)

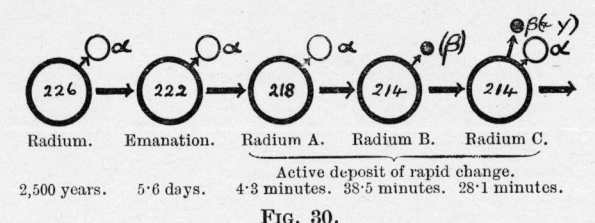

Radium.	Emanation.	Radium A.	Radium B.	Radium C.
		Active deposit of rapid change.		
2,500 years.	5·6 days.	4·3 minutes.	38·5 minutes.	28·1 minutes.

FIG. 30.

As before, the presumed atomic weights are placed inside the circles corresponding with the successive products. The periods of average life are placed below. The symbol (β) here and throughout indicates that β-rays are expelled, but that they are not the normal penetrating β-rays, but rays akin to the cathode-rays in their low penetrating power and low velocity. They only come into evidence in special experiments, and are not of great general importance. The first body produced from the emanation, radium A, changes with great rapidity with a period of average life of 4·3 minutes, expelling an α-particle. The body radium B resulting undergoes a change which was at first thought to be entirely " rayless." Neither α- nor β-rays of the ordinary kind can be detected, although a very feebly penetrating β-ray is produced, which we need not further consider. The period of this substance is 38·5 minutes. The body produced, radium C, changes, expelling both α- and β-particles and γ-rays also. The period is 28·1 minutes. It is probable that this change is complex and that the β- and γ-rays are given off in a separate change to that in which the α-rays result. This point will be dealt with later.

THE RADIATIONS FROM THE ACTIVE DEPOSIT.

We started our description of the rays of radium with the statement that they consisted of α-, β-, and γ-rays. One of the most interesting points of the above scheme is to show that the β- and γ-rays do not come from radium itself, any more than they do from uranium itself, but from the later products. It is loose, but convenient, to talk of the β- and γ-rays of radium. Really we mean the β- and γ-rays of radium C. The emanation, like radium itself, gives only α-rays. The whole of the β-rays result in the later changes of the active deposit. We have seen that, freshly prepared from solution, radium salts give only α-rays. The β- and γ-rays make their appearance only after the subsequent products have accumulated.

Experiments with the Active Deposit.

On the table there is a small glass vessel silvered internally (Figs. 31 and 32) containing the emanation from half a grain of radium bromide. It is arranged so that steel knitting-needles can be inserted into the emanation and withdrawn through a glass tube held in a cork. The needle is connected to the negative pole of the electric supply and the silver coating to the positive pole. If only the point of the needle is made to project beyond the glass tube, the whole of the active deposit can be concentrated on the point. Some hours before this lecture a needle—we will call it No. 1—was so inserted, and by now its point should be coated to its maximum degree of radioactivity with the products of the disintegration of the emanation. After some hours the products all arrive at the state of radioactive equilibrium, in which the quantity is at its maximum for all the products, radium A, radium B, and radium C, as much of each changing as is produced from the emanation. The disintegrations all going on together, the wire should give α-, β-, and γ-rays, the β- and γ-rays being as intense as those given from the half-grain of radium bromide from which the emanation was derived. Now I withdraw No. 1 needle from the emanation, and with the room darkened we will examine its active deposit.

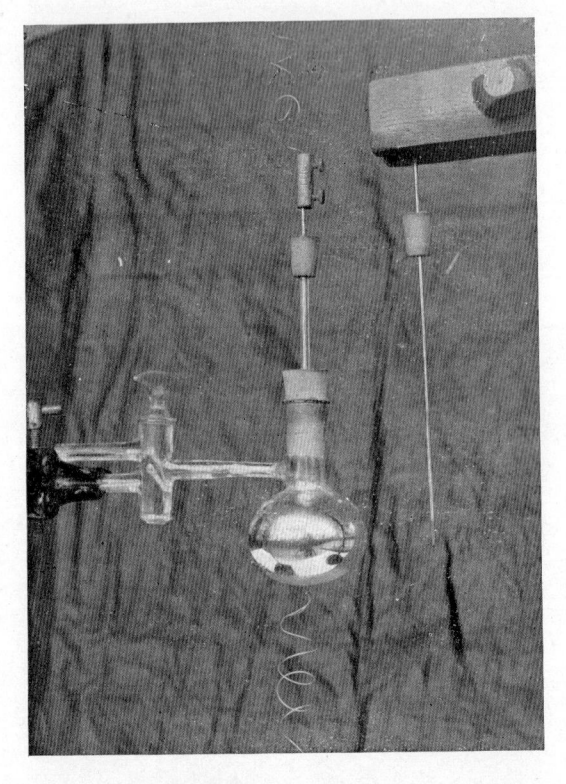

FIG. 32.—APPARATUS FOR OBTAINING THE ACTIVE DEPOSIT OF RADIUM.

EXPERIMENTS WITH ACTIVE DEPOSIT 141

To detect the α-rays we will use a glass translucent screen, thinly coated with phosphorescent zinc sulphide on one side. I bring the point of the needle gradually near the coated side of the screen. As soon as it comes within a distance of three inches the screen lights up, and when the point is only a little distance removed from the screen a most brilliant phosphorescence is produced. Now if I interpose between the wire and the screen a single sheet of paper, the effect practically

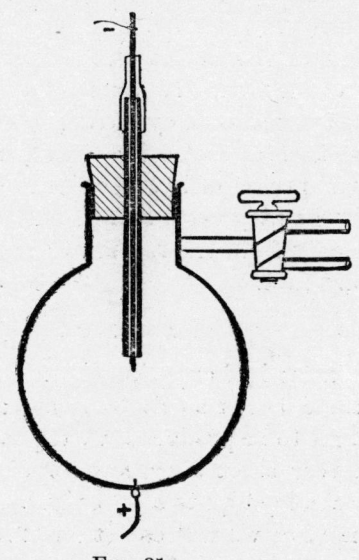

FIG. 31.

entirely ceases. The α-radiations producing this effect come both from radium A and from radium C.

To detect the β-rays we will use an ordinary cardboard X-ray screen of barium platinocyanide. Bringing the needle behind the screen, so that the rays have to penetrate the cardboard, you observe the screen lights up as brightly as with half a grain of radium bromide itself. In the dark I happened actually to touch the back of the screen with the active needle-point, and in so doing some of the active deposit has been transferred to the back of the screen. You can see where the back of the screen was touched, because this spot still glows though the needle has been removed.

If now the needle is again presented to the back of the X-ray screen with thin pieces of metal foil interposed, you see that the rays are only slightly stopped by having to traverse the foil. When a piece of thick lead sheet is interposed, a faint luminosity on the screen still remains produced by the γ-rays. In fact the active needle-point gives all the penetrating rays given by half a grain of radium bromide.

It is now several minutes since the needle was removed from the emanation. If we now again examine the α-rays you will notice they already are very perceptibly less intense than at first. Practically all the radium A, of which the period of average life is only 4·3 minutes, has already disintegrated, and in consequence the α-rays now come only from the radium C, and are only half as intense as at first.

Radium A.

Now if, instead of exposing the needle to the emanation for some hours so as to allow all the successive products time to be produced, we expose it to the emanation for a very short time, say for five minutes by the watch, we shall get quite a different set of effects. Here is a new needle; we will call it No. 2. Before putting it in I will test it with the screen to show you that at present it is an ordinary needle, not at all radioactive. We will let it stay in the emanation, connected to the negative pole as before, for five minutes and withdraw it, and test its α-rays immediately, exactly as before. You observe that it is already giving α-rays abundantly. Comparing it with No. 1, the two are now very similar in their α-ray-giving power, No. 1 being only slightly the better. The α-rays from No. 2 come almost entirely from radium A, for there has not yet been time for any appreciable quantity of radium C to be formed. The α-rays from No. 1 come entirely from radium C, and this

EXPERIMENTS WITH ACTIVE DEPOSIT

radiation has not yet had time appreciably to decay. Let us, however, test their β-rays. You observe that No. 2 gives no β-rays worth considering, whereas No. 1 still gives β-rays in practically undiminished intensity. Radium A gives no β-rays, and as there is no appreciable quantity of radium C formed there yet, the consequence is that No. 2 wire gives no β-rays.

I can show you at this stage a very striking experiment with another needle, No. 3, which has been in the emanation a few minutes. I take it out and draw the point once through a piece of emery-cloth and expose the latter to the zinc sulphide screen. You observe that a single rub has removed a large part of the active deposit from the needle and transferred it to the emery-cloth, so that the latter makes the screen glow almost as brilliantly as the needles themselves.

Radium B and C.

Now we will contrast the decay of the activity of the needles Nos. 1 and 2. The activity due to radium A by itself decays very rapidly, half disappearing every three minutes. The consequence is, if we now again test the α-rays of No. 2, we shall find they have already nearly disappeared, whereas No. 1 still continues to give α-rays at about the same strength as it did when last examined. In ten minutes the α-rays of No. 2 practically disappear.

It is thus not difficult to give you a certain amount of experimental evidence in favour of the conclusion that the first change of the active deposit is a very rapid one in which α-, but no β-rays are expelled, and that this is followed by a less rapid change in which both α- and β-rays are expelled. It is more difficult to give you in a lecture satisfactory evidence of the existence of radium B, a body not itself giving rays, intermediate between the first and second changes in which rays are expelled. If we examine carefully the decay of the α- and β-rays of wire No. 1, in which at first all these products co-existed in equilibrium, we shall find, as already shown, that for the first half-hour after removal from the emanation the β-rays suffer very little change and then the regular decay begins. In the next half-hour the β-rays decay approximately to one-half their original intensity, and the decay then goes on at this rate regularly and continuously to the end. After two hours they are only a few per cent. of what they originally were, and in three or four hours they can no longer be detected. The initial pause before decay begins is due to the quantity of radium C being maintained, in spite of the fact that it is disintegrating all the time, expelling α- and β-rays, by the disintegration of radium B. The latter continues to supply new radium C to replace that disappearing for the first half-hour or so after the needle is removed from the emanation. Exactly the same pause occurs in the decay of the α-rays. As we saw with No. 1, within a very few minutes after the needle was removed from the emanation the α-rays had decayed to about one-half, owing to the disappearance of the α-ray-giving radium A. Then, however, little further change occurred. It is now about half an hour since No. 1 was first tested, and the α-activity is similar to what it was when last tested twenty minutes ago. The α-rays of No. 2 have now almost completely disappeared. If we continued to examine No. 1, we should find, from now on, a rapid decay of both α- and β-rays at the same rate, so that at the end of the lecture both will be much enfeebled, and by midnight both will have ceased so far as we could tell by these rough methods.

The Radiation from the Emanation.

Now that we have finished with the emanation used in the preceding experiments, it is an interesting experiment to show that itself it gives no β-rays. If we blow the emanation out into a U-tube of thin glass cooled in liquid air, it is condensed in the cold tube.

THE RAYS OF THE EMANATION

The tube can then be sealed up to prevent the emanation from escaping. The tube contains some phosphorescent zinc sulphide and glows brightly owing to the α-rays from the emanation inside. But if we hold the tube against the X-ray screen, you can see that no penetrating rays come from the tube. The emanation itself gives no β-rays, only α-rays. By the end of the lecture, however, sufficient radium C will probably have been formed inside the tube to give an appreciable β-radiation. Owing to the existence of the intermediate body radium B, there occurs a similar pause in the growth of β-rays from the emanation to that which, as we have seen, occurs in their decay, after the emanation is taken away. But in two or three hours the β-rays from all the needles will have decayed, and that from the sealed U-tube will have reached a maximum.

The Later Slow Changes of Radium— Radium D, E, and F.

This finishes this subject and brings us to the next. What happens to radium C when it disintegrates? Is this the real or only the apparent end of the process? It is, in fact, a very long way from the end. Madame Curie discovered that the rapid and almost complete decay of the active deposit, at the end of a few hours after removal from the emanation, is not in fact quite complete. A very small residual radioactivity remains and persists for years. The series of changes have now entered on a stage which is as slow as the previous ones were rapid. The next change requires almost as many years as the last required minutes for completion. The effect of these further changes is in consequence extremely small, but they last a very long time. Continuing our diagram where it last ended at radium C, the next stage is represented in Fig. 33.

The body produced from radium C, radium D, has a period of many years. It is too early yet to state it exactly. One recent estimate makes it twenty-four years. No very important rays are given in its change. β-rays, however, result from the body produced from it, which changes rapidly again with a period of only a

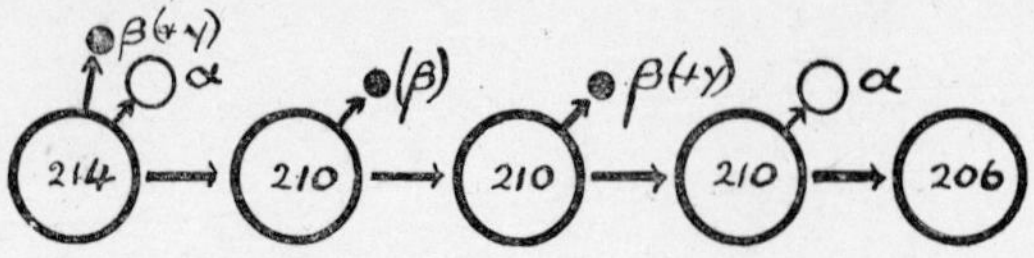

β(+γ)   (β)   β(+γ)   α

214 → 210 → 210 → 210 → 206

Radium C.   Radium D.   Radium E.   Radium F.   Radium G.
(Polonium.)   (Lead ?)

Active deposit of slow change,
28·1 minutes. 24 years (?) 7·5 days. 202 days.

FIG. 33.

few days. We shall pass over these intermediate changes and consider the last known change of the series, that of radium F, which has a period of average life of 202 days, in which an α-particle is expelled. Radium F is the *polonium* of Madame Curie, having been separated by her from pitchblende first before she discovered radium.

POLONIUM.

A digression may here conveniently be made on what is known about polonium, before its connection with radium is considered. Chemically it resembles bismuth, and was separated first from pitchblende in association with the bismuth contained in the mineral. Its radio-activity, which consists entirely of α-rays, slowly and completely decays, so that a few years after it has been prepared, the most intensely active preparations of it lose practically all their activity. The work was carried on by Marckwald in Germany, who discovered new and simple methods of extracting polonium from the mineral and worked up many tons of pitchblende for this substance. His careful chemical investigations of the nature of the body made it clear that it was quite as nearly allied in chemical nature to the element tellurium as to bismuth, and he first proposed the name " radio-tellurium " for it, which, however, with the elucidation of its identity with polonium, has fallen into disuse. He proved that there is far less polonium in the mineral even than radium. In a ton of mineral there is less than a thousandth part of a grain of polonium, but the radio-activity is correspondingly intense, and greatly exceeds, so far as the α-radiation is concerned, that of pure radium itself. The period of average life, 202 days, is deduced by direct observation from the rate of decay of the radio-activity.

Returning now to the consideration of radium C, we saw that after its activity had decayed there existed still a residual activity which is very feeble. This steadily *increases* with time, and consists both of α- and β-rays, which, however, increase at different rates. The α-rays are due to polonium, or radium F. These go on increasing for the first two years and then a maximum is reached, the amount of the radium F formed being in equilibrium. The β-rays, however, reach a maximum much more quickly. The β-ray product (radium E) having a much shorter period, equilibrium is reached in a few weeks. If at any time the active matter is subjected to the chemical processes worked out by Marckwald for the separation of polonium, the α-ray body radium F can be separated from the other products, and its activity then decays away completely at exactly the same rate as in the case of polonium. Moreover, it shows the property of being volatile at a temperature of a bright red heat, which is the basis of one of the methods originally used by Madame Curie in separating polonium from the bismuth in pitchblende. This is merely a sketch of the evidence in favour of regarding polonium as the last radioactive substance produced in the disintegration of uranium.

The Ultimate Product of Radium.

One more step remains to be discussed, and then this long story of continuous transformation is at an end. What is the ultimate product? When radium F or polonium expels its α-particle, what is produced? The estimated atomic weight of polonium is 210, which is deduced by subtracting from the atomic weight of radium (226) the weight of the four atoms of helium known to be expelled in the form of α-particles. This agrees well with its chemical nature, for there is a vacant place in the periodic table for an element, the next heavier than bismuth (atomic weight, 208·5), and this element would be chemically analogous to tellurium. The expulsion of an α-particle would further reduce the atomic weight four units, leaving a residue of atomic weight 206. What is it?

Now, if this is really the final product and not merely a very slowly changing substance, the formation of which in proportion to the degree of slowness of the change would be difficult experimentally to detect, then it follows that the ultimate product must accumulate in quantity indefinitely with time in the minerals containing the elements of the uranium-radium series, and must therefore be a well-known common element. Lead has the atomic weight of 207·2, and bismuth, 208·0. The next known element is thallium (204), and then comes mercury (200).

Lead is found in all the common minerals containing uranium in considerable quantity, and there is also evidence that the older the geological formation from which the mineral is obtained, the greater the percentage of lead present. Recently a uranium mineral, autunite, has been found containing no chemically detectable quantity of lead. But then the same mineral contains only an excessively minute trace of helium, and less than its full equilibrium amount of radium. There is every reason to believe that its formation as a mineral has occurred in quite recent times.

This question has now been settled by indirect means, and there is no longer room for doubt that lead is the ultimate product of uranium. This evidence, however, may be deferred. The method of settling it directly is to study the change of polonium, separated from enormous quantities of pitchblende, by the aid of the spectroscope, and on this task Mme. Curie and her colleagues have for long been engaged, but as yet without definite proof that lead is the product.

Uranium I and Uranium II.

A variety of evidence, some of which may be dealt with more profitably later, has lately established the conclusion that the change suffered by the uranium atoms when the α-particles are expelled, is not, as first supposed, a single change. The substance uranium, which chemists have hitherto considered an element, differs from every other known substance expelling α-rays, in that, per atom disintegrating, two α-particles are expelled instead of one. Moreover, these two α-particles are expelled at slightly different initial velocities, with the result that the " ranges " of the two sets of α-rays in air are slightly different (see p. 164). Most probably the two α-particles are not expelled from the uranium atom simultaneously but *successively*. In consequence, what chemists hitherto have accepted as a single element is, in reality, a mixture of two, chemically so much alike that they have not yet been separated, the first having the atomic weight 238·5, and which has been termed provisionally uranium I; the second, resulting after the expulsion of the first α-particle, having the atomic weight 234·5. It has been termed uranium II. It is probable that this uranium II is present in relatively very insignificant proportion by weight, although it contributes one-half of the total α-radiation. Its period of life can only be estimated from very indirect and incomplete data at the present time. The more slowly a radioactive substance changes the shorter the range of the α-particles it expels, and so from the range of the rays an estimate of the period of average life may be formed. This estimate, such as it is, attributes a period to uranium II of about two million years.

150   THE SUCCESSIVE CHANGES OF RADIUM

Numerous similar examples of elements identical chemically, but differing in radioactivity, are now known. These are called *isotopes* or *isotopic* elements.

Uranium X and Uranium X$_2$ (Brevium).

Even more recently it was first predicted and then shown that uranium X is not a single substance. Uranium X gives two kinds of β-rays, one of low velocity and comparatively non-penetrating—*i.e.*, (β-) rays (compare p. 139) and ordinary high velocity β-rays.

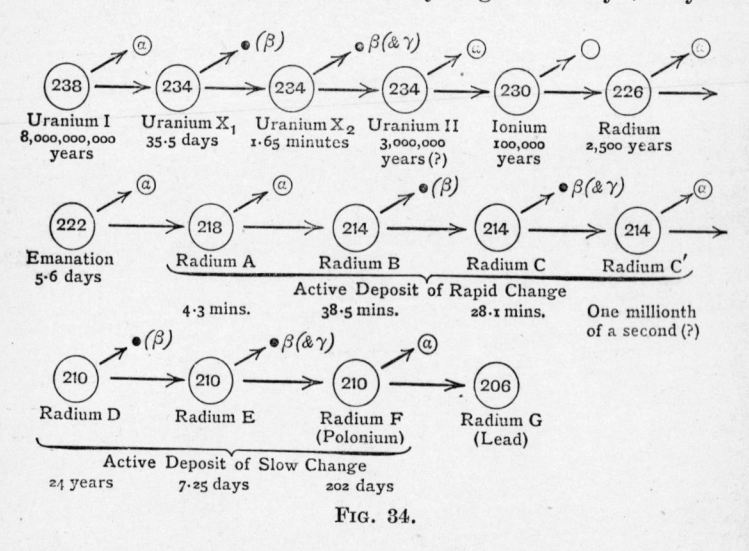

Fig. 34.

These have been shown to originate from two distinct substances successively produced, and which are called uranium X$_1$ and uranium X$_2$. Uranium I expels an α-particle and changes into uranium X$_1$, which has a period of average life of 35·5 days, and expels, not the penetrating β-rays of "uranium X," but the feeble and unimportant (β)-radiation. Its product, uranium X$_2$, sometimes called brevium, has the very short period of average life of only 100 seconds, and, in its change, the powerful penetrating β-rays are expelled. Uranium X$_2$, after its change, is believed to become uranium II.

COMPLETE URANIUM SERIES

The latter in its change expels an α-particle and is believed to produce ionium. Uranium X_1 and uranium X_2, unlike uranium I and uranium II, can be separated from one another by chemical methods. These new discoveries, although of highest theoretical importance, make very little practical difference to the results, which for almost all ordinary purposes are precisely what they would be were the simple scheme, shown in Fig. 29, actually the one followed.

Radium C and Radium C'.

Lastly, there is indirect evidence that radium C consists of two successive products, distinguished as radium C and radium C', the first giving the β- and γ-rays in its disintegration, and producing the second, which has a period of average life of only a millionth of a second, and changes, emitting an α-particle, into radium D (see p. 202).

Fig. 34 shows so far as it is at present known the complete disintegration series of uranium.

CHAPTER X

RADIOACTIVITY AND THE NATURE OF MATTER

RATIO OF QUANTITIES OF POLONIUM AND RADIUM IN MINERALS.

FROM the law, which has already been found so useful, we can calculate the ratio of the quantities of radium and polonium that exist together in a mineral from their periods of average life. The period of average life of radium is 4,500 times that of polonium, so that there must be 4,500 times more radium than polonium in minerals. A good pitchblende with 50 or 60 per cent. of uranium in it contains about an ounce of radium in 150 tons. The same quantity of polonium would therefore be contained in about 700,000 tons. The whole output of the Joachimsthal mine per annum, reckoned as 15 tons, contains about one hundredth of a grain of polonium. This is borne out by Marckwald's experiments, already referred to.

Let us apply the law not only to radium and polonium, but to the whole list of known transition-forms existing as products of uranium. In the table this has been done. The first column gives the name of the substance, the second its period of average life, and the third its relative quantity in minerals, the quantity of uranium being considered 1,000,000,000. If these numbers are taken to refer throughout to milligrams (1 milligram is about $\frac{1}{70}$ of a grain), then since 1,000,000,000 milligrams is roughly a ton, the quantities refer to an amount of mineral containing one ton of the element uranium.

COMPOSITION OF A URANIUM MINERAL

TABLE.

Period.	Quantity.
Uranium I, 8,000,000,000 years.	1,000,000,000 mg. (=1 ton).
Uranium X .. 35·5 days.	One eightieth mg.
Uranium X_2 .. 1·6 minutes.	1/250,000th mg.
Uranium II, 3,000,000 years (?).	400 grams (?).
Ionium .. 100,000 years.	12·5 grams.
Radium .. 2,500 years.	312·5 mg.
Emanation .. 5·6 days.	One five-hundredth mg.
Radium A .. 4·3 minutes.	One millionth mg.
Radium B .. 38·5 minutes.	Nine millionths mg.
Radium C .. 28·1 minutes.	Seven millionths mg.
Radium D .. 24 years (?).	3 mg. (?).
Radium E .. 7·5 days.	One four-thousandth mg.
Radium F .. 202 days.	One fourteenth mg.
(Polonium)	

These respective quantities in the last column emit a similar number of α-particles per second in the eight cases where α-particles are expelled at all, and so produce similar radioactive effects. This is an illustration of the compensating principle I spoke of earlier, that the quantity of a radioactive substance divided by its life, not the quantity only, gives a measure of its radioactive effects. It can readily be calculated that the actual amount of radium A used in our experiments, which produced powerful and striking effects on the phosphorescent screen, was much below one ten-millionth of a milligram, or below one thousand-millionth of a grain. For it was derived from 30 mg.—*i.e.*, half a grain of radium bromide. Yet while it lasts it comes into evidence through the energy of the α-particles expelled in its rapid disintegration no less than any of the other products.

IMPOSSIBILITY OF CONCENTRATING MANY OF THE PRODUCTS OF DISINTEGRATION.

The table brings out clearly that radium is but one of many radioactive substances in uranium minerals, which would be of value if they could be extracted. Uranium II, ionium and radium D, all possess sufficiently extended periods of life to repay recovery. Ionium gives only very feebly penetrating α-rays, and so would not be so generally useful as radium, whereas uranium II and radium D both, being followed by short-lived products which give β-rays, would be of great general utility. The reason which has precluded the practical separation of these substances in the past is a general one, which has proved to be of the highest philosophical significance in the chemistry of these new ephemeral elements. They all so closely resemble one or other of the known elements that the separation is impossible. The resemblance between radium and barium is of great practical utility, because these two elements, though very closely alike in chemical nature, can be separated from each other after they have first been separated from every other element. Taking them in order, uranium II cannot yet be separated from uranium I, ionium cannot be separated from thorium, nor radium D from lead. Lead, as has been stated, is almost always present in considerable quantity in uranium minerals, and so usually is thorium, but to a much more variable extent. Hence, though it is easy to separate radium D from the mineral with the lead, it is at present useless practically, as it cannot be concentrated from the lead. By choosing suitable minerals like secondary pitchblendes, which do not contain ponderable quantities of thorium, intensely active preparations of ionium can however be separated. It is at present the only one in the uranium series likely to become useful, and its lack of penetrating rays is a serious drawback. Polonium, with its period of less than a year and its absence of penetrating rays, hardly repays extraction, except for purely scientific investigations. There is, however, another disintegration series, that of thorium, which offers a better chance of providing an efficient substitute for radium, and this series will therefore be briefly considered in a later chapter.

Increase of Radioactivity of Radium with Time.

The increase of the radioactivity of radium after it is prepared is due to the steady growth of the products undergoing further disintegration. As we know, when freshly prepared from solution, the activity of radium is due solely to its own disintegration and consists of α-rays. After four weeks the first four products accumulate to their equilibrium, and the activity now consists of α-, β-, and γ-rays, the α-rays being four times as great as initially. It is not difficult to see that the later slow changes must also cause a very slow further continuous increase of all these types of rays, due to the growth of radium E and polonium from radium D. These considerations are embodied in the following table giving an analysis of the total radioactivity of a radium preparation, kept in a sealed vessel so that none of the products escape, at different periods since preparation:

	α-PARTICLES.	β-PARTICLES.
I. Freshly prepared.	1 (due to radium itself)	0
II. After one month.	4 (1 due to radium) (1 due to emanation) (1 due to radium A) (1 due to radium C)	1 or 2 (due to Ra C)
III. After a century.	5 (as in II and 1 due to radium F)	2 or 3 (1 due to Ra E_2)

The Rarity of Elements.

The idea, which is a necessary consequence of the atomic disintegration theory, that fixed definite relationships must exist between the quantities of elements formed from one another—for example, between uranium, radium, and polonium—forms the first indication that physical laws may exist regulating the relative abundance and scarcity of elements in Nature. Gold and platinum, for example, are valuable or rare metals, and we do not know why. Radioactive bodies like radium are rare *because* of the rapidity with which they are changing. The degree of radioactivity of an element being proportional to the rate at which it is changing, it follows that radioactive elements are scarce and valuable in proportion to their radioactivity. In this case degree of radioactivity is a physical measure of value or rarity. It is, for example, so far as we can see, an impossibility that an element like radium will ever be found in greater abundance in any minerals than in those already known.

Naturally, in the consideration of some of these questions of general interest upon which we are now entering, we are, be it said, in sharp contrast to almost everything we have dealt with in the subject up to now, frankly speculating. But it is helpful and legitimate to speculate upon how far, if at all, the process of atomic disintegration, discovered for the radio-elements, applies to the case of elements not radioactive, of which there is as yet no positive evidence that they are changing at all. The workers in radioactivity have within their province explored thoroughly the process of atomic disintegration. They have made clear the laws it follows, they have measured the rates at which it occurs, and they have established what may be termed its inevitableness or independence from all known influences. But there is no reason why the process should be limited in its scope to the somewhat special phenomena which led to its discovery.

The Currency Metals.

It is, for example, natural to inquire whether the scarcity of elements like gold is fixed by the operation of similar physical laws to those which regulate the rarity of radium. The race has grown used from the earliest times to the idea that gold is a metal possessing a certain fixed degree of value, enabling it to be used safely for the purposes of currency and exchange. It is no exaggeration to say that the whole social machinery of the Western world would be dislocated if gold altered violently in its degree of rarity—if, for example, in some hitherto unpenetrated fastness of the globe a mountain of gold came to be discovered.[1] Is there not at least a strong presumption that this is really as contrary to the operation of natural law as the discovery of a mountain of pure radium would be?

It may, I think, be taken for granted that an element changing more rapidly than uranium, for example—that is, with a period of average life of less than 8,000,000,000 years—is not likely to be much more plentiful in nature than uranium, and therefore that all the common elements—lead, copper, iron, oxygen, silicon, etc., etc.—have periods of average life of many thousands of millions of years. So far, the traditional view that the elements are permanent and unchanging is substantially correct. At the same time, we cannot but recognise that inevitably the effects of atomic disintegration, too slow to be otherwise detectable, would result in the accumulation of the more stable and longest-lived elements at the expense of the others, resulting in some sort of equilibrium in which the relative abundance of the elements was proportional to their respective periods of average life. For example, the ratio between the relative abundance of gold and silver is roughly but pretty certainly known, owing to these metals being employed for currency purposes from the earliest times. It is at least a possible view to take that the elements gold and silver belong to the same disintegration series, both changing very slowly, but the gold many times more rapidly than the silver. Obviously we are only at the beginning. But already it cannot be gainsaid that the interest and importance of this process of atomic disintegration is not confined to radioactivity only or even to physical science. It extends into almost every region of thought.

[1] Since these words were first written the whole social machinery of the Western World has been dislocated by violent alterations in the purchasing power of gold, and it has been shown to be no longer a safe medium for currency. (Compare *A Fraudulent Standard*, A. T. Kitson. London: P. S. King and Son, Ltd., 1917.)

The Nature of Atoms.

I now propose considering briefly another question of general philosophical interest in connection with the recent advances of physical science. Naturally the discoveries in radioactivity have not been made without influencing considerably our ideas on the ultimate nature of atoms. In some points older conceptions have had to be modified, while in others these conceptions have been strangely confirmed. It has always been a matter for remark, considering the myriads of individual atoms which go to make up the smallest perceptible quantity of matter, that there are so few different kinds. The number of atoms which go to make up this world, for example, would run into at least fifty-four figures, yet among them all there are less than a hundred different varieties. Moreover, it has come to be regarded as one of the greatest philosophical generalisations of physical science that all the atoms of one kind, that is to say of one element, are, at least as far as was known up to the beginning of the present century, completely similar in character. There is, for example, not the shadow of distinction between gold found in the Klondyke, in Australia, or in S. Africa. Not only so, but we have learned from the spectroscope that this similarity of nature extends throughout the whole universe. In this connection, both to set forth the idea and to illustrate the deductions which have been drawn from it, I cannot do better than to quote a celebrated utterance of Clerk Maxwell to the British Association in 1873. I may remark that Clerk Maxwell throughout used the word molecule in the sense of " atom " as this word is employed by the chemist, and throughout these lectures.

" In the heavens we discover by their light, and by their light alone, stars so far distant from each other that no material thing can ever have passed from one to another; and yet this light, which is to us the sole evidence of the existence of these distant worlds, tells

A QUOTATION FROM CLERK MAXWELL

us also that each of them is built up of molecules of the same kinds as those which we find on earth. A molecule of hydrogen, for example, whether in Sirius or in Arcturus, executes its vibrations in precisely the same time.

"Each molecule therefore throughout the universe bears impressed upon it the stamp of a metric system as distinctly as does the metre of the Archives at Paris, or the double royal cubit of the temple of Karnac.

"No theory of evolution can be formed to account for the similarity of molecules, for evolution necessarily implies continuous change, and the molecule is incapable of growth or decay, of generation or destruction.

"None of the processes of Nature, since the time when Nature began, have produced the slightest difference in the properties of any molecule. We are therefore unable to ascribe either the existence of the molecules or the identity of their properties to any of the causes which we call natural.

"On the other hand, the exact equality of each molecule to all the others of the same kind gives it, as Sir John Herschel has well said, the essential character of a manufactured article, and precludes the idea of its being eternal and self-existent.

"Thus we have been led, along a strictly scientific path, very near to the point at which science must stop; not that science is debarred from studying the internal mechanism of a molecule which she cannot take to pieces, any more than from investigating an organism which she cannot put together. But in tracing back the history of matter, Science is arrested when she assures herself, on the one hand, that the molecule has been made, and on the other, that it has not been made by any of the processes we call natural.

"Science is incompetent to reason upon the creation of matter itself out of nothing. We have reached the utmost limits of our thinking faculties when we have admitted that because matter cannot be eternal and self-existent it must have been created."

You will admit that, in the light of all that has transpired in the forty-five years since Maxwell used these words, science has advanced far. The concluding words of the address are even more striking from this point of view.

"Natural causes, as we know, are at work, which tend to modify, if they do not at length destroy, all the arrangements and dimensions of the earth and the whole solar system. But though in the course of ages catastrophes have occurred and may yet occur in the heavens, though ancient systems may be dissolved and new systems evolved out of their ruins, the molecules out of which these systems are built—the foundation-stones of the material universe—remain unbroken and unworn."

Before we dwell upon the modifications that have been made in this point of view, let us rather consider the chief basis of the argument, namely, that all the atoms of any one element are exactly alike. On this fundamental question the evidence to-day is far more complete and definite than it was in 1873. Recent developments in connection with isotopes have modified our point of view, but for the moment we may neglect this special advance.

We no longer regard the atom as a simple thing. On the contrary, we now look upon it as an almost infinitely complex piece of mechanism. The late Professor Rowland, of Baltimore, once made the remark that a grand piano must be a very simple piece of mechanism compared with an atom of iron. For in the spectrum of iron there is an almost innumerable wealth of separate bright lines, each one of which corresponds to a sharp definite period of vibration of the iron atom. Instead of the hundred-odd sound vibrations which a grand piano can emit, the single iron atom appears to emit many thousands of definite light vibrations. Two pianos would be regarded as in perfect tune together when there was a comparatively rough approximation of period between the various notes. Whereas by the spectroscope a difference in "tune" or period in the vibra-

THE PERFECTION OF THE ATOMS

tions emitted by different atoms of only one part in many millions would be easily detectable, and no such variation exists. In a similar vein Professor Schuster, referring to the broad teachings of the spectroscope, has compared the atoms of the same element to an innumerable number of clocks all wound and regulated to go at the same period. If all these clocks were set at the same time, not one of them would vary by a single second even after many many days. No clockmaker could make such clocks. Yet these almost infinitely complicated pieces of mechanism we call atoms are turned out by Nature with such undeviating accuracy and fidelity that in all the myriads in existence there are less than a hundred different kinds known.

The Velocity of α-Particles.

We can, however, from the point of view of recent researches in radioactivity, push this idea even one step further, to the case of atoms actually in the condition of breaking up. We have seen that it is a property of the α-rays to possess a very sharp and definite range. In a beam of homogeneous α-rays passing through a homogeneous absorbing medium the number of α-particles suffers little or no diminution until the extreme end of the path is reached, and then they cease altogether. Just without the extreme range, there is absolutely no effect perceptible, while just within this range, the effect, per small element of path, is at the maximum. Every α-particle expelled from the radio-element in the same change travels exactly the same distance before it ceases to be detectable, and, as Rutherford has shown by direct measurement of the magnetic and electric deviation, is expelled at the same velocity.

In the table following, the approximate initial velocities of the α-particles from the changes in the uranium series have been collected, together with their " ranges " or distances in millimetres they will penetrate in air at 15° C. and 760 mm. of mercury pressure.

α-Particle from	Period.	Velocity (miles per second).	Range.
Uranium I,	8,000,000,000 years	8,800	25
Uranium II,	3,000,000 years	9,300	29
Ionium	100,000 years	9,400	30
Radium	2,500 years	9,600	33
Emanation	5·6 days	10,400	42
Radium A	4·3 minutes	10,900	47·5
Radium C'	1/1,000,000th sec. (?)	12,400	69·5
Radium F	202 days	10,200	37·7

The atom thus retains its rôle of a perfect piece of mechanism even up to and during the moment of its dissolution. So exactly alike are all the atoms of the same radioactive element, that when the break-up occurs the velocity with which the fragments of the atom, or α-particles, are expelled is exactly the same in each case. We may liken the disintegration of an element to the bursting of shells, in which the fragments of the different shells all are expelled with the same velocity. Certainly no shells ever constructed would answer this requirement. Truly, in the words of Sir John Herschel, the atom bears the essential character of a manufactured article, but of a degree of perfection humanly unattainable.

But with regard to the process of manufacture and of the cause of this undeviating fidelity to a few types, what a revolution of thought has taken place in the last few years! The evolution, or rather devolution, of matter, its continuous change, the generation and destruction of atoms—all of the things which seemed impossible in Clerk Maxwell's day—we know to be going on before our eyes. It is true the processes call for periods of time so vast, even in the most favourable cases, that the physicist of a generation ago would have dismissed them as physically inconceivable. Yet these periods are to-day actually determined by direct measurement in the laboratory.

STABILITY AND SURVIVAL OF ELEMENTS.

Instead of regarding the hundred or less elements which exist to-day as manufactured, created, once for all time, we rather regard them as existing *because* they have survived. All other forms less stable than those we recognise as elements have been weeded out. Over sufficiently great periods of time the rarity or abundance of an element must be controlled by its degree of instability or stability. Probably for every stable atom many unstable ones could be, even are being, formed. But only the stable forms can accumulate in quantity and become known to us as ordinary chemical elements. We have seen that the rarest of such in all probability must have a period of thousands of millions of years, while for the more common elements, if they are changing at all, periods of billions of years may be anticipated.

At first glance only, the material universe gives the impression of a permanent and finished creation. In reality the now familiar remorseless operation of slow, continuous change moulds even " the foundation-stones " themselves. By this last step the doctrine of evolution has become universal, embracing alike the animate and inanimate worlds. But whereas in the former slight changes of environment effect the profoundest modifications, in the latter the controlling factors still remain absolutely unknown. By the spectroscope a partial material survey of the whole universe has been rendered possible, and what we find is everywhere an essential similarity of composition. For example, there is no evidence that in the sun or stars large quantities of elements unknown to us exist. The reason why some atoms are stable and others are not is a mystery we have not yet begun to probe. Yet this question, to us only of academic interest and possibly somewhat remote at that, will, as we shall soon come to see, be one of life and death to the inheritors of our civilisation.

Connection between Range of α-Rays and Period.

A very interesting development may now be mentioned, which has resulted in a connection being established between the ranges or velocities of the various types of α-rays, and the periods of life of the atoms from which they are derived. As a general rule—not, it is true, entirely without exceptions, but possibly the exceptions may prove to be only apparent—the more rapidly a radioactive substance disintegrates, or the shorter its period of average life, the greater is the velocity with which the α-particle is expelled from the atom, and the greater therefore is the range of the α-particle. Thus, the most stable radio-elements, uranium and thorium, give α-rays having the lowest ranges, and the low range of the α-rays of ionium was for long the only evidence that its period must be very long. The greatest ranges occur in the short-lived " active deposit " products. The very long ranges of the α-rays of radium C (69·5 mm.), and of the corresponding thorium C (86 mm.), is generally explained by the supposition that the real atoms giving these rays have periods of the order of only a millionth of a second, and therefore that it is impossible to separate them from their parents, which thus appear to be giving rays which in reality come from their products. This will be referred to again. Latterly, this generalisation has been put into stricter form by the discovery that if the logarithm of the period is plotted against the logarithm of the range or of the velocity, straight lines result for each of the three known disintegration series. The three straight lines are parallel to but not identical with one another. The reason for this is still obscure. Some mathematical connection exists between the two quantities, and that is all that can yet be said. On the other hand, it has been found possible to calculate approximately some of the unknown periods—like that of ionium, so estimated at 200,000 years, for example, from the ranges of the α-rays by means of this relation before it was directly determined to be 100,000 years.

For long it was known that uranium was exceptional in that it appeared to give out two α-particles per atom disintegrating instead of one, as in all other cases. A very careful investigation revealed the fact that the ranges of these two sets of α-particles were not exactly alike. One set, those from uranium I, presumably, have a range of 25 mm., and the other set, those from its shorter-lived product, uranium II, presumably, a range of 29 mm. The period corresponding with 29 mm. of range is, in the uranium series, two million years, and this is the main evidence for believing that such a product, uranium II as it is called, exists, and that it has so far not been separated from uranium because of the identity of the chemical properties of the two elements.

Pleochroic Halos.

The account given in this chapter and in Chapter III. of the many extraordinary properties of the α-particle would be incomplete if another natural phenomenon in a totally distinct field were omitted. The α-, in common with the other rays from radioactive substances, have the power of darkening glass and other transparent materials such as mica after long exposure. Indeed, the colours of many natural gems have been traced to the effect of such rays from naturally occurring radioactive materials in the earth, operating over immense periods. Sir William Crookes artificially coloured a large colourless diamond an intense green by exposing it for some weeks to the rays from a pure radium compound.

Many other gems, usually found in a colourless state, can similarly be made to assume the most varied colours, the nature of which depend probably upon slight chemical impurities present in the gem. Mica under these circumstances becomes deeply stained and dark.

Now, occurring in various natural micas, there are sometimes found microscopic halos of darkening of perfect circular outline, called pleochroic halos. These have been very exhaustively studied by Professor Joly, and the microphotographs shown in Figs. 35 and 36 are taken from a paper by him and Mr. Fletcher in the *Philosophical Magazine* for 1910. Fig. 35 shows two of these halos in a specimen of mica. Sometimes the halos are made more visible by the use of polarised light, but this is not always necessary. It can be shown, by suitably sectioning the material, that the halos are true spheres, and often at the centre a minute microscopic nucleus is visible. Professor Joly measured exactly with the microscope the diameter of these halos, and found them to correspond perfectly correctly with the "range" of the α-particles from radium C, which in mica is 0·06 mm. He put forward the view that they were due to α-particles, from radioactive material in the central nucleus, darkening the mica over a sphere bounded by the range of the α-rays. This conclusion has been most brilliantly confirmed. It is possible to find halos in various stages of development. Young and incompletely developed halos often show only a central "pupil" of only 0·013 mm. in radius. This corresponds with the range of the shorter α-particles, due to uranium, ionium, and radium itself. In later stages a distinct "corona" appears of the full radius, 0·03 mm., which is the range of the α-particle from radium C in mica. And in particularly favourable cases it is possible to see between them an inner ring of dimensions corresponding with the intermediate range of the α-particles of radium A. A much enlarged micro-photograph of such a halo is shown in Fig. 36.

Uranium and Thorium Halos.

Moreover, a careful search revealed other halos of slightly greater radius than 0·03 mm.—viz., 0·038 mm.— which corresponds with the range of the fastest α-par-

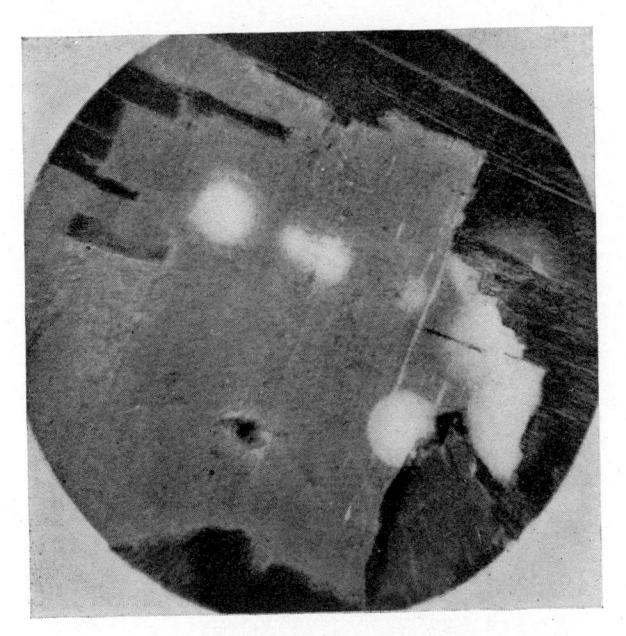

Fig. 35.—Thorium and Radium Halos in Biotite.
(× 150 Diameters.)

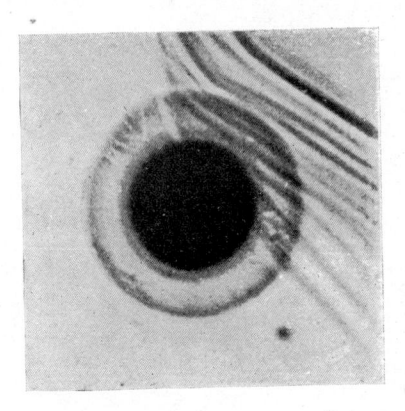

Fig. 36.—Halo in Biotite. (× 450 Diameters.)
Showing ring due to Radium A.

ticle emitted in the thorium series. An examination of them showed a course of development totally different from that of the uranium halos. The successive states in this case correspond with the α-rays of the ranges that are emitted in the thorium series.

As a matter of fact the lower halo in Fig. 35 is due to uranium and the upper one due to thorium. The uranium halo is fully developed, so that the central "pupil," though visible in the microscope, cannot be seen in the reproduction. The thorium halo shows faintly but quite clearly the corona due to the long range rays of thorium C', the longest known. Still other halos attributed to radium emanation without the earlier members of the series have been observed.

It may be concluded that the nucleus at the centre either contains uranium or thorium in minute quantity, or has the power of occluding radium emanation from water that has flowed through uranium minerals. But the actual amounts of radioactive materials so put into evidence are almost inconceivably minute and far beyond the power of detection even by the most sensitive electrical method. It has been estimated that they are due to the expulsion of sometimes less than 100 α-particles per year, continuing for several hundred million years. The mica integrates these infinitesimal effects throughout the ages so that at length they are able to produce consequences visible to the eye. Until this explanation was forthcoming, they had remained a complete puzzle to the petrologist.

CHAPTER XI

RADIOACTIVITY AND THE EVOLUTION OF THE WORLD

THE POTENTIALITIES OF MATTER.

THIS interpretation of radium is drawing to a close, but perhaps the more generally interesting part of it remains to be dealt with. We have steadily followed out the idea of atomic disintegration to its logical conclusions, so far as they can at present be drawn, and we have found it able to account for all the surprising discoveries that have been made in radioactivity, and capable of predicting many, and perhaps even more unexpected, new ones. Let us from the point of vantage we have gained return to the starting-point of our inquiries and see what a profound change has come over it since the riddle has been read. Radium, a new element, giving out light and heat like Aladdin's lamp, apparently defying the law of the conservation of energy, and raising questions in physical science which seemed unanswerable, is no longer the radium we know. But although its mystery has vanished, its significance and importance have vastly gained. At first we were compelled to regard it as unique, dowered with potentialities and exhibiting peculiarities which raised it far above the ordinary run of common matter. The matter was the mere vehicle of ultra-material powers. If we now ask, why is radium so unique among the elements, the answer is not because it is dowered with any exceptional potentialities or because it contains any abnormal store of internal energy which other elements do not possess, but simply and solely because it is changing comparatively rapidly, whereas the elements before known are either changing not at all or so slowly that the change has been unperceived. At first sight this might seem an anti-climax. Yet it is not so. The truer view is that this one element has clothed with its own dignity the whole empire of common matter. The aspect which matter has presented to us in the past is but a consummate disguise, concealing latent energies and hidden activities beneath an hitherto impenetrable mask. The ultra-material potentialities of radium are the common possession of all that world to which in our ignorance we used to refer as mere inanimate matter. This is the weightiest lesson the existence of radium has taught us, and it remains to consider the easy but remorseless reasoning by which the conclusion is arrived at.

Why Radium is Unique.

Two considerations will make the matter clear. In the first place, the radioactivity of radium at any moment is, strictly speaking, not a property of the mass of the radium at all, although it is proportional to the mass. The whole of the new set of properties is contributed by a very small fraction of the whole, namely, the part which is actually disintegrating at the moment of observation. The whole of the rest of the radium is as quiescent and inactive as any other non-radioactive element. In its whole chemical nature it is an ordinary element. The new properties are not contributed at all by the main part of the matter, but only by the minute fraction actually at the moment disintegrating.

Let us next compare and contrast radium with its first product, the emanation, and with its original parent, uranium. Uranium on the one hand, and the emanation on the other, represent, compared with radium, diametrically opposed extremes. Uranium is changing so slowly that it will last for thousands of millions of years, the emanation so rapidly that it lasts only a few weeks, while radium is intermediate with a period of average life of two thousand five hundred years.

We have seen that in many ways the emanation is far more wonderful than radium, as the rate its energy is given out is relatively far greater. But this is compensated for by the far shorter time its activity lasts. Also, if we compared uranium with radium, we should say at once that radium is far more wonderful than the uranium, whereas in reality it is not so, as the uranium, changing almost infinitely more slowly, lasts almost infinitely longer.

The arresting character of radium is to be ascribed solely to the rate at which it happens to be disintegrating. The common element uranium, well known to chemists for a century before its radioactivity was suspected, is in reality even more wonderful. It is only very feebly radioactive, and therefore is changing excessively slowly, but it changes into radium, expelling several α-particles and so evolving large amounts of energy in the process. Uranium is a heavier element than radium, and the relative weights of the two atoms, which is a measure of their complexity, is as 238 is to 226. This bottle contains about a pound of an oxide of uranium which contains about seven-eighths of its weight of the element uranium. In the course of the next few thousand million years, so far as we can tell, it will change, producing over thirteen ounces of radium, and, in that change into radium alone, energy is given out, as radioactive energy, aggregating of itself an enormous total, while the radium produced will also change, giving out a further enormous aggregate quantity of energy.

So that uranium, since it produces radium, contains all the energy contained in a but slightly smaller quantity of radium and more. It may be estimated that uranium evolves during complete disintegration some thirteen per cent. more energy than is evolved from the same weight of radium. But what are we to say about the other heavy elements—lead, bismuth, mercury, gold, platinum, etc.—although their atoms are not quite so heavy as uranium or radium, and although none of them, so far as we yet know, are disintegrating at all ? Is this enormous internal store of energy confined to the radioactive elements, that is to the few which, however slowly, are actually changing ? Not at all, in all probability. Regarded merely as chemical elements between radioactive elements and non-radioactive elements, there exists so complete a parallelism that we cannot regard the radioactive elements as peculiar in possessing this internal store of energy, but only as peculiar in evolving it at a perceptible rate. Radium especially is so completely analogous in its whole chemical nature, and even in the character of its spectrum, to the non-radioactive elements, barium, strontium, and calcium, that chemists at once placed radium in the same family as these latter, and the value of its atomic weight confirms the arrangement in the manner required by the Periodic Law. It appears rather that this internal store of energy we learned of for the first time in connection with radium is possessed to greater or lesser degree by all elements in common, and is part and parcel of their internal structure.

The Total Energy evolved by Uranium.

Let us, however, for the sake of conciseness, leave out of account altogether the non-radioactive elements, of which as yet we know nothing certainly. At least we cannot escape from the conclusion that the particular element uranium has relatively more energy stored up within it even than radium. Uranium is a comparatively common element. The world's output per year is to be reckoned in tens of tons, whereas that of thorium, which we have still to consider, exceeds a thousand tons.

I have already referred to the total amount of energy evolved by radium during the course of its complete change. It is about 360,000 times as much energy as is evolved from the same weight of coal in burning (p. 120). The energy evolved from uranium would be some thirteen per cent. greater than from the same weight of radium. This bottle contains about one pound of uranium oxide, and therefore about fourteen ounces of uranium. Its value is about £1. Is it not wonderful to reflect that in this little bottle there lies asleep and waiting to be evolved the energy of at least one hundred and sixty tons of coal? The energy in a ton of uranium would be sufficient to light London for a year. The store of energy in uranium would be worth a thousand times as much as the uranium itself, if only it were under our control and could be harnessed to do the world's work in the same way as the energy in coal has been harnessed and controlled.

There is, it is true, plenty of energy in the world which is practically valueless. The energy of the tides and of the waste heat from steam fall into this category as useless and low-grade energy. But the internal energy of uranium is not of this kind. The difficulty is of quite another character. As we have seen, we cannot yet artificially accelerate or influence the rate of disintegration of an element, and therefore the energy in uranium, which requires a thousand million years to be evolved, is practically valueless. On the other hand, to increase the natural rate, and to break down uranium or any other element artificially, is simply transmutation. If we could accomplish the one so we could the other. These two great problems, at once the oldest and the newest in science, are one. Transmutation of the elements carries with it the power to unlock the internal energy of matter, and the unlocking of the internal stores of energy in matter would, strangely enough, be infinitely the most important and valuable consequence of transmutation.

The Importance of Transmutation.

Let us consider in the light of present knowledge the problem of transmutation, and see what the attempt of the alchemist involved. To build up an ounce of a heavy element like gold from a lighter element like silver would require in all probability the expenditure of the energy of some hundreds of tons of coal, so that the ounce of gold would be dearly bought. On the other hand, if it were possible artificially to disintegrate an element with a heavier atom than gold and produce gold from it, so great an amount of energy would probably be evolved that the gold in comparison would be of little account. The energy would be far more valuable than the gold. Although we are as ignorant as ever of how to set about transmutation, it cannot be denied that the knowledge recently gained constitutes a very great help towards a proper understanding of the problem and its ultimate accomplishment. We see clearly the magnitude of the task and the insufficiency of even the most powerful of the means at our disposal in a way not before appreciated, and we have now a clear perception of the tremendous issues at stake. Looking backwards at the great things science has already accomplished, and at the steady growth in power and fruitfulness of scientific method, it can scarcely be doubted that one day we shall come to break down and build up elements in the laboratory as we now break down and build up compounds, and the pulses of the world will then throb with a new source of strength as immeasurably removed from any we at present control as they in turn are from the natural resources of the human savage.

Primitive Man and Fire.

It is, indeed, a strange situation we are confronted with. The first step in the long, upward journey out of barbarism to civilisation which man has accomplished appears to have been the art of kindling fire. Those savage races who remain ignorant of this art are regarded as on the very lowest plane. The art of kindling fire is the first step towards the control and utilisation of those natural stores of energy on which civilisation even now absolutely depends. Primitive man existed entirely on the day-to-day supply of sunlight for his vital energy, before he learned how to kindle fire for himself. One can imagine before this occurred that he became acquainted with fire and its properties from naturally occurring conflagrations.

With reference to the newly recognised internal stores of energy in matter we stand to-day where primitive man first stood with regard to the energy liberated by fire. We are aware of its existence solely from the naturally occurring manifestations in radioactivity. At the climax of that civilisation the first step of which was taken in forgotten ages by primitive man, and just when it is becoming apparent that its ever-increasing needs cannot indefinitely be borne by the existing supplies of energy, possibilities of an entirely new material civilisation are dawning with respect to which we find ourselves still on the lowest plane—that of onlookers with no power to interfere. The energy which we require for our very existence, and which Nature supplies us with but grudgingly and in none too generous measure for our needs, is in reality locked up in immense stores in the matter all around us, but the power to control and use it is not yet ours. What sources of energy we can and do use and control, we now regard as but the merest leavings of Nature's primary supplies. The very existence of the latter till now have remained unknown and unsuspected. When we have learned how to transmute the elements at will the one into the other, then, and not till then, will the key to this hidden treasure-house of Nature be in our hands. At present we have no hint of how even to begin the quest.

Source of Cosmical Energy.

The question has frequently been discussed whether transmutation, so impossible to us, is not actually going on under the transcendental conditions obtaining in the sun and the stars. We have seen that it is actually going on in the world under our eyes in a few special cases and at a very slow rate. The possibility now under consideration, however, is rather that it may be going on universally or at least much more generally, and at a much more rapid rate under celestial than under terrestrial conditions. From the new point of view it may be said at once that if it were so, many of the difficulties previously experienced in accounting for the enormous and incessant dissipation of energy throughout the universe would disappear.

Last century has wrought a great change in scientific thought as to the nature of the gigantic forces which have moulded the world to its present form and which regulated the march of events throughout the universe. At one time it was customary to regard the evolution of the globe as the result of a succession in the past times of mighty cataclysms and catastrophes beside which the eruptions of a Krakatoa or Pelée would be insignificant. Now, however, we regard the main process of moulding as due rather to ever-present, continuous, and irresistible actions, which, though operating so slowly that over short periods of time their effect is imperceptible, yet in the epochs of the cosmical calendar effected changes so great and complete that the present features of the globe are but a passing incident of a continually shifting scene. Into the arena of these silent world-creating and destroying influences and processes has entered a new-comer—" Radioactivity "—and it has not required long before it has come to be recognised that in the discovery of radioactivity, or rather of the sub-atomic powers and processes of which radioactivity is merely the outward and visible manifestation, we have penetrated one of Nature's innermost secrets.

Whether or no the processes of continuous atomic disintegration bulk largely in the scheme of cosmical evolution, at least it cannot be gainsaid that these processes are at once powerful enough and slow enough to furnish a sufficient and satisfactory explanation of the origin of those perennial outpourings of energy by virtue of which the universe to-day is a going concern rather than a cold, lifeless collocation of extinct worlds. Slow, irresistible, incessant, unalterable, so apparently feeble that it has been reserved to the generation in which we live to discover, the processes of radioactivity, when translated in terms of a more extended scale of space and time, appear already as though they well may be the ultimate controlling factors of physical evolution. For slow processes of this kind do the effective work of Nature, and the occasional intermittent displays of Plutonic activity correspond merely to the creaking now and again of an otherwise silent mechanism that never stops.

Radium in the Earth's Crust.

It is one of the most pleasing features of this new work that geologists have been among the very first to recognise the applicability and importance of it in their science. I am not competent to deal adequately with or discuss the geological problems that it has raised. But this story would be incomplete if I did not refer, though it must be but briefly, to the labours of Professor Strutt[1] who initiated the movement and to those of Professor Joly who has carried it on. These workers carried out careful analyses of the representative rocks in the earth's crust for the amount of radium they contained. Absolutely, the quantity of radium in common rocks is of course very small, although with the refined methods now at the disposal of investigators it is quite measurable. The important fact which has transpired, however, is that the rocks examined contain on the average much larger quantities of radium, and therefore necessarily of its original parent uranium, than might be expected. The amount of heat which finds its way in a given time from the interior of the globe to the surface and thence outwards into external space by radiation has long been accurately known. Strutt concluded that if there existed only a comparatively

[1] Now Lord Rayleigh.

thin crust of rocks less than fifty miles thick of the same composition, as regards the content of radium, as the average of those he examined, the radium in them would supply the whole of the heat lost by the globe to outer space. He concluded that the surface rocks must form such a thin crust, and that the interior of the globe must be an entirely different kind of material, free from the presence of radium. Otherwise the world would be much hotter inside than is known to be the case. So far then as the earth is concerned, a quantity of radium less than in all probability actually exists would supply all the heat lost to outer space. So that there is no difficulty in accounting for the necessary source of heat to maintain the existing conditions of temperature on the earth over a period of past time as long as the uranium which produces the radium lasts—that is to say, for a period of thousands of millions of years.

Professor Joly in his interesting work, *Radio-activity and Geology*, has considered in detail some of the consequences of the existence of radioactive materials in the earth. One of the specific instances is the effect of the radium in the rocks of the Simplon Tunnel in producing the unexpectedly high temperatures there encountered. From a radioactive analysis of these rocks he came to the conclusion that without undue assumptions it is possible to explain the differences in the temperature of the rocks encountered in boring the tunnel by the differences in their radium content.

Various Possible Fates of the Earth.

The presence in the rock of a proportion amounting to a few million millionths of radium above the normal quantity very nearly wrecked the whole enterprise. From the importance of radioactivity in this instance, of a tunnel a few miles long bored through a mountain, some idea may be obtained of the significance of the new discoveries in the general problem of the thermal condition of the interior of the globe. Since Strutt's original work, it has been established that not only radium, but all the other radioactive materials, including the whole thorium disintegration series, must contribute an important quantity of heat, so that his estimate of a crust only fifty miles thick is in reality too great, and a much thinner crust would suffice. Joly has had the courage to push the argument to its logical conclusion, and has supposed that the radioactive materials are not confined to a thin surface crust, but are equally distributed throughout the globe in much the same proportions as they are in the crust. If this is so, there is no escape from the conclusion that the interior of the earth, so far from gradually parting with its heat and cooling down, must actually be getting steadily hotter. The heat generated within, even after the lapse of hundreds of millions of years, would scarcely appreciably escape from the surface, for, as Lord Kelvin deduced, the central core of the earth must be almost insulated thermally from the surface, owing to the low conductivity of the rocks composing the crust. He assumes throughout an average composition of the globe of two parts of radium per million million, which is considerably below the average he found for the rocks of the crust, and he calculates that in the course of a hundred million years this minute quantity will produce a rise of the temperature of the central core of no less than 1,800° C. Unless, therefore, this heat is utilised in some unknown way, or the disintegration of the radio-elements is prevented by the high temperature and pressure, the ultimate fate of the globe must be very much as depicted in the Biblical tradition. Sooner or later the crust must succumb to the ever-increasing pressure within, and the earth must become again, what it is supposed once to have been, a vastly swollen globe of incandescent gas. As Joly remarks, there is no evidence that this has not already occurred more than once, nor assurance that it will not recur. So far as physical science yet can deduce, the accumulation of thermal energy within a world containing elements undergoing atomic disintegration during the "geological age" must alternate with a state of things which might be termed "the incandescent age," in which this accumulated energy is dissipated by radiation. This periodic cycle of changes must continue until the elements in question have disintegrated—that is, over a period which radioactive measurements indicate is of the order of tens or hundreds of thousands of millions of years. During the incandescent age the loss of heat by radiation, which increases according to the fourth power of the temperature, is immensely greater than could be supplied even by atomic disintegration.

Thus, if the known laws hold, it is certain that the present loss of heat of the sun cannot be supplied by the presence of radium. For this to be the case a very large part of the sun's mass must consist of uranium, and this we know from the spectroscope is very improbable. Still, it is by no means to be concluded that the heat of the sun and stars is not in the first place of inte nal rather than, as has been the custom to regard it, of external origin.

As soon as sufficient of the heat energy of a world has been radiated away for a solid crust to form, the poor thermal conductivity of this crust at once reduces the radiation loss to a negligible figure again, a fresh geological age is inaugurated, and again the heat accumulates within. This view, that the elements contain within themselves the energy from which Nature obtains her primary supplies, and that in cosmical time "geological age" and "incandescent age" alternate as the night and day, however imperfect it may still be, is at least more in harmony with existing knowledge than the older conventional view that the universe was wound up once for all in the beginning like a clock to go for a certain time, for the most part quietly and uneventfully, pursuing its allotted path towards ultimate physical stagnation and death. But what a picture it conjures up of life and of the precariousness of its tenure—from its lowest beginnings to its highest evolution, not a permanent accomplishment, but a process to be inaugurated and consummated afresh, if at all, between the ending and beginning of each new cosmical day!

To escape from this conclusion it is necessary to suppose that atomic disintegration is cosmically not the inevitable uncontrollable process it has hitherto been proved to be under all laboratory conditions, but that under conditions of pressure and temperature, such as exist in the interior of a world, it may either be stopped altogether, or compensated for by unknown complementary processes of atomic synthesis in which energy is taken up.

The Most Probable View.

The balance of probability appears to rest with the view that the radioactivity of the materials comprising the earth is confined to a crust and that the central core is more or less free from radioactive matter. Our knowledge of earthquake phenomena, and particularly of the three distinct routes by which an earthquake wave travels from one point on the surface of the earth to another—(1) and (2) by circular paths clockwise and counter-clockwise through the crust, and (3), the " P3 " route, by a straight line joining the two points—has strongly supported the view that the core of the earth is of a totally different nature from the crust. On the P3 route, once the wave gets below the crust, it travels much faster than it does through the surface. This, especially, confirms the picture of the earth as a metallic sphere of nickel-steel within, surrounded with a thin surface layer of solidified slag, which its high specific gravity and the composition of meteorites first suggested. On this view, it is to be expected that the radioactive materials will be confined to the crust and be absent from the metallic core, and, therefore, that the crust may have reached a steady temperature, at which the loss of heat by radiation is exactly balanced by the heat evolved by its radioactive constituents. If this is so, the present state would continue without much change for hundreds of millions of years.

Be that as it may, our outlook on the physical universe has been permanently altered. We are no longer the inhabitants of a universe slowly dying from the physical exhaustion of its energy, but of a universe which has in the internal energy of its material components the means to rejuvenate itself perennially over immense periods of time, intermittently and catastrophically, which is the first possibility that presents itself, or continuously and in orderly fashion, if there exist compensating phenomena still outside the ken of science.

Radioactivity and Mythology.

The world probably being of much greater antiquity than physical science has thought to be possible, it is interesting and harmless to speculate whether man has shared with the world its more remote history.

In this connection it is curious how strangely some of the old myths and legends about matter and man appear in the light of the recent knowledge. Consider, for example, the ancient mystic symbol of matter, known as Ouroboros—" the tail devourer "—which was a serpent, coiled into a circle with the head devouring the tail, and bearing the central motto, " The whole is one." This symbolises evolution; moreover, it is evolution of matter—the very latest aspect of evolution—the existence of which was strenuously denied by Clerk Maxwell and others of only last century. The idea which arises in one's mind as the most attractive and consistent explanation of the universe in the light of present knowledge is, perhaps, that matter is breaking down and its energy being evolved and degraded in one part of a cycle of evolution, and in another part, still unknown to us, the matter is being again built up with the utilisation of the waste energy. If one wished to symbolise such an idea, in what better way could it be done than by the ancient tail-devouring serpent ?

Some of the beliefs and legends which have come down to us from antiquity are so universal and deep-rooted that we are accustomed to consider them almost as old as the race itself. One is tempted to inquire how far the unsuspected aptness of some of these beliefs and sayings to the point of view so recently disclosed is the result of mere chance or coincidence, and how far it may be evidence of a wholly unknown and unsuspected ancient civilisation of which all other relic has disappeared. It is curious to reflect, for example, upon the remarkable legend of the philosopher's stone, one of the oldest and most universal beliefs, the origin of which, however far back we penetrate into the records of the past, we do not probably trace to its real source. The philosopher's stone was accredited the power not only of transmuting the metals, but of acting *as the elixir of life*. Now, whatever the origin of this apparently meaningless jumble of ideas may have been, it is really a perfect and but very slightly allegorical expression of the actual present views we hold to-day. It does not require much effort of the imagination to see in energy the life of the physical universe, and the key to the primary fountains of the physical life of the universe to-day is known to be transmutation. Is, then, this old association of the power of transmutation with the elixir of life merely a coincidence? I prefer to believe it may be an echo from one of many previous epochs in the unrecorded history of the world, of an age of men which have trod before the road we are treading to-day, in a past possibly so remote that even the very atoms of its civilisation literally have had time to disintegrate.

Let us give the imagination a moment's further free scope in this direction, however, before closing. What if this point of view that has now suggested itself is true, and we may trust ourselves to the slender foundation afforded by the traditions and superstitions which have been handed down to us from a prehistoric time? Can we not read into them some justification for the belief that some former forgotten race of men attained not only to the knowledge we have so recently won, but also to the power that is not yet ours? Science has reconstructed the story of the past as one of a continuous Ascent of Man to the present-day level of his powers. In face of the circumstantial evidence existing of this steady upward progress of the race, the traditional view of the Fall of Man from a higher former state has come to be more and more difficult to understand. From our new standpoint the two points of view are by no means so irreconcilable as they appeared. A race which could transmute matter would have little need to earn its bread by the sweat of its brow. If we can judge from what our engineers accomplish with their comparatively restricted supplies of energy, such a race could transform a desert continent, thaw the frozen poles, and make the whole world one smiling Garden of Eden. Possibly they could explore the outer realms of space, emigrating to more favourable worlds as the superfluous to-day emigrate to more favourable continents. The legend of the Fall of Man, possibly, may be all that has survived of such a time before, for some unknown reason, the whole world was plunged back again under the undisputed sway of Nature, to begin once more its upward toilsome journey through the ages.

The New Prospect.

The vistas of new thought which have opened out in all directions in the physical sciences, to which man is merely incidental and external, must in turn react powerfully upon those departments of thought in which man is central and supreme. We find ourselves in consequence of the progress of physical science at the pinnacle of one ascent of civilisation, taking the first step upwards out on to the lowest plane of the next. Above us still rises indefinitely the ascent to physical power—far beyond the dreams of mortals in any previous system of philosophy. These possibilities of a newer order of things, of a more exalted material destiny than any which have been foretold, are not the promise of another world. They exist in this, to be fought and struggled for in the old familiar way, to be wrung from the grip of Nature, as all our achievements and civilisation have, in the past, been wrung by the labour of the collective brain of mankind guiding, directing, and multiplying the individual's puny power. This is the message of hope and inspiration to the race which radium has contributed to the great problems of existence. No attempt at presentation of this new subject could be considered complete which did not, however imperfectly, suggest something of this side. It is fitting to attempt to see how far purely physical considerations will take us in delimiting the major controlling influences which regulate our existence.

Surveying the long chequered, but on the whole continuous, ascent of man from primeval conditions to the summit of his present-day powers, what has it all been at bottom but a fight with Nature for energy—for that ordinary physical energy of which we have said so much? Physical science sums up accurately in that one generalisation the most fundamental aspect of life in the sense already defined.

Of course life depends also on a continual supply of matter as well as on a continual supply of energy, but the struggle for physical energy is probably the more fundamental and general aspect of existence in all its forms. The same matter, the same chemical elements, serve the purposes of life over and over again, but the supply of fresh energy must be continuous. By the law of the availability of energy, which, whether universal or not, applies universally within our own experience, the transformations of energy which occur in Nature are invariably in the one direction, the more available forms passing into the waste and useless unavailable kind, and this process, so far as we yet know, is never reversed. The same energy is available but once. The struggle for existence is at the bottom a continuous struggle for fresh physical energy.

This is as far as the knowledge available last century went. What is now the case? The aboriginal savage, ignorant of agriculture and of the means of kindling fire, perished from cold and hunger unless he subsisted as a beast of prey and succeeded in plundering and devouring other animals. Although the potentialities of warmth and food existed all round him, and must have been known to him from natural processes, he knew not yet how to use them for his own purposes. It is much the same to-day. With all our civilisation, we still subsist, struggling among ourselves for a sufficiency of the limited supply of physical energy available, while all around are vast potentialities of the means of sustenance, we know of from naturally occurring processes, but do not yet know how to use or control. Radium has taught us that there is no limit to the amount of energy in the world available to support life, save only the limit imposed by the boundaries of knowledge.

It cannot be denied that, so far as the future is concerned, an entirely new prospect has been opened up. By these achievements of experimental science Man's inheritance has increased, his aspirations have been uplifted, and his destiny has been ennobled to an extent beyond our present power to foretell. The real wealth of the world is its energy, and by these discoveries it, for the first time, transpires that the hard struggle for existence on the bare leavings of natural energy in which the race has evolved is no longer the only possible or enduring lot of Man. It is a legitimate aspiration to believe that one day he will attain the power to regulate for his own purposes the primary fountains of energy which Nature now so jealously conserves for the future. The fulfilment of this aspiration is, no doubt, far off, but the possibility alters somewhat the relation of Man to his environment, and adds a dignity of its own to the actualities of existence.

PART II

CHAPTER XII

THE THORIUM AND ACTINIUM DISINTEGRATION SERIES

The Thorium Disintegration Series.

Those who have mastered the intricacies of the uranium disintegration series may wish to know something of the important developments which have taken place since these lectures were first given in 1908, and of the other two great disintegration series known to science, the thorium and the actinium series. Space precludes a description as detailed and non-technical as that before aimed at, and in some of the more difficult sections it will be necessary to assume a considerable knowledge on the part of the reader of physical and chemical science. But the attempt seems worth making for the sake of completeness.

The thorium disintegration series is becoming increasingly important, and its consideration does not involve any new principles. Thorium is an element which was at one time rare and little known even to chemists, but has come into prominence during the last twenty years, because of its use as a constituent of the incandescent gas-mantle, which is composed of about 99 per cent. of thorium oxide, and 1 per cent. of cerium oxide. Fairly abundant sources of thorium have been discovered in the sands of certain coasts in Brazil, North and South Carolina, etc., where a natural concentration has taken place by the action of the sea-waves of the particles of the heavy mineral monazite, which occurs as a minute constituent in many rocks, and in the sands derived from them by the action of weathering agencies. The monazite is concentrated from the sand usually by magnetic methods, until it contains 4 per cent. of thorium oxide. This constitutes the monazite sand of commerce, and from it every year hundreds of tons of pure thorium salts are now manufactured for the gas-mantle industry. More recently the find has been made of a very rich monazite in Central India, containing nearly 10 per cent. of thorium.

Mesothorium and Radiothorium.

As already described, the usual α-radioactivity of commercial thorium compounds is of about the same strength as that of pure uranium compounds, but the β- and γ-, or penetrating activity, is several times less intense. We have seen (p. 153) that in the uranium minerals, although several intermediate products of the disintegration of uranium are present, with periods of life sufficiently long, and radioactivity sufficiently important, to repay extraction, it is practicable to extract only one of these—namely, radium. In the thorium minerals there are two such products, named mesothorium and radiothorium, and though their periods of average life, about eight years and three years respectively, are very much less than that of radium, they are sufficiently long to make their extraction and utilisation practicable. Whereas the sources of radium are costly and comparatively limited in amount, the by-products of the thorium industry, after the extraction of the technically valuable thorium, are the source from which mesothorium and radiothorium are extracted. Much greater quantities of these by-products have to be handled, it is true, than in the extraction even of radium from pitchblende to produce similar results. The new substances must, on this account, always be costly to produce. But in the by-products of a single year's manufacture of thorium the new products capable of being extracted possess as much radioactivity as at least an ounce of pure radium. They thus offer an abundant source of radioactive material, which at present is mostly wasted, and the product, while it lasts, is in every respect the equal of radium in its properties. The only disadvantage it possesses is its relatively much shorter period of life.

The discoveries in the thorium series of these two technically valuable members were made by Otto Hahn, who has worked both with Sir William Ramsay and Sir Ernest Rutherford, comparatively recently, after the rest of the members had become quite well known. The historical development of the subject from the first discovery of the radioactivity of thorium compounds up to the present time is a most interesting chapter to the student, but would unduly complicate the subject if considered here. It is better to proceed in order through the thorium disintegration series as it is at present known, apart from historical considerations as to the order in which they were discovered, though, as in the case of the uranium series, the first members were the last to be separately recognised.

Radioactivity of Thorium.

Unlike pure uranium salts, which, a few months after preparation, have a definite constant radioactivity, consisting of all three types of rays, the α-activity being due to uranium, and the β- and γ-activity to the short-lived uranium X in equilibrium with it, thorium salts, though chemically pure, vary continuously in their whole radioactivity for twenty or thirty years after manufacture. Even after these periods, slight changes must still be going on, and probably fifty years would have to elapse before they became quite inappreciable. But in spite of the great apparent differences between the two elements, there is a very close analogy in their disintegration series, every one of the eleven known members of the thorium series having an analogue in the twelve

RADIOACTIVITY OF THORIUM

members of the uranium series as far as radium D, at which point the thorium disintegration appears to come to an end. One α-ray giving product in the uranium series is not represented in the thorium series. The analogous members in the two series usually give out similar kinds of rays, and although their periods are often widely different, there is a rough correspondence in the two series between the relative periods of the successive members, the periods in the thorium series being, however, usually much less than in the uranium series. Thus uranium I, with its period of 8,000,000 years, gives α-rays, and is followed by uranium X_1, giving (β)-rays, of period 35·5 days, and by uranium X_2, or brevium, of very short period, which gives powerful and penetrating β-rays. Uranium II, which follows, is chemically identical with uranium I, and, like it, is of long period and gives α-rays. This produces ionium, which gives α-rays, and has the period of 100,000 years. Ionium, in turn, produces radium, which gives α-rays, and has a period of 2,500 years. Thorium itself is provisionally estimated to have a period about three times longer than uranium I, and gives only α-rays. It produces by its disintegration " mesothorium I," which does not give any important rays, and has a period of 7·9 years. It is identical in chemical character with radium, and corresponds with uranium X_1, except that no β-rays at all are expelled. Its product is called " mesothorium II," which corresponds very closely with uranium X_2, giving out powerful β- and γ-rays, and having a period of only 8·9 hours. It produces in turn " radiothorium," which corresponds perfectly with ionium, giving α-rays, and having a period of 2·9 years. These last two substances are chemically identical with one another, and also with thorium itself, and cannot be separated by any known method when mixed together. This fact is of considerable importance, as thorium when separated from a mineral, always contains at first all the radiothorium in the mineral and also all the ionium, if uranium was also present, as is almost invariably the case.

THORIUM AND ACTINIUM

The product of radiothorium is thorium X, which corresponds with radium, giving α-rays, but having a period of only 5·6 days. Thorium X is chemically identical with radium, and also with mesothorium I. This chemical identity of radium and mesothorium I is the dominating fact in the separation of these new substances, as will later be more clear. After thorium X, the thorium emanation results, corresponding perfectly in its whole nature as a member of the argon family of gases, with the radium emanation, and giving α-rays, but having the much shorter period of only 76 seconds. Its product is the thorium active deposit, of which the

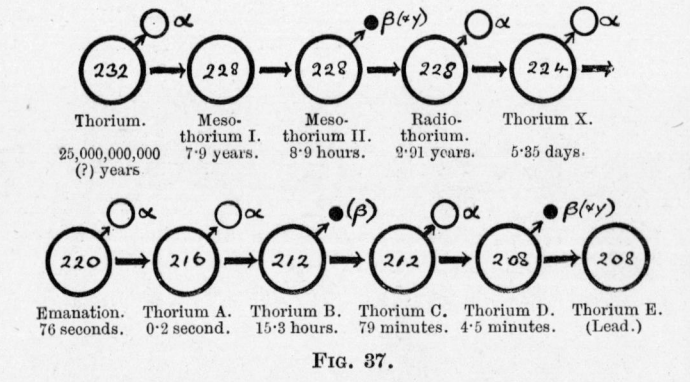

FIG. 37.

first three members, called thorium A, B, C, are almost precisely analogous to the corresponding radium members, except in period. The period of thorium A is only one-fifth of a second. Those of thorium B and C are 15·3 hours and 79 minutes respectively. These last are the only two, except thorium itself, possessing periods longer than the corresponding members of the uranium series. Lastly, there exists, as the product of thorium C, thorium D, the last active member known, which gives β- and γ-rays, and has the short period of 4·5 minutes. It has little analogy to radium D. The ultimate product of thorium was till recently not even guessed. All that could be said is that its atomic weight, calculated from that of thorium and the number of α-particles expelled, is 208, and this is the atomic weight of bismuth! It cannot be bismuth, because in some ancient thorium minerals hardly a trace of bismuth can be found. The discovery of its nature came as a surprise, for in spite of the difference of atomic weight, it proves to be the same element as ends the uranium series—namely, lead. This has raised very deep issues. The complete thorium disintegration series is shown on p. 190 (Fig. 37), so far as we have yet considered it. But thorium C, there shown single, is like radium C complex (see p. 201).

The extraordinary analogies between this series and the uranium series, on the one hand, and the actinium series, on the other, will later receive a very satisfying explanation.

Mesothorium.

It is clear that mesothorium I, with the period of average life of nearly eight years, being both the first and the longest lived of the successive products, is the centre of interest. The radioactivity of the element thorium itself, consisting only of low-range α-rays, of relatively feeble intensity because of the enormous period of the element, is technically and scientifically even of less interest than that of uranium. Mesothorium, however, corresponds to radium in that it can be concentrated, and the greater part of the radioactivity of many tons of minerals can be separated in a preparation weighing less than a few milligrams. Just as when radium is first prepared it gives only the relatively unimportant α-activity proper to itself, but in course of time develops enormously in all its activity due to the growth and accumulation of its products, so it is with mesothorium. Freshly prepared and free from its products, it has practically no activity. In the course of a few hours the strong penetrating activity of its short-lived product, mesothorium II, develops, and in two or three days this reaches a maximum or equilibrium value. This part of the activity then remains, so long as the preparation is not chemically treated, apparently constant, but actually decaying very slowly. This decay is to half the initial value after 5·5 years, to a quarter after 11 years, and so on. But the product of this change is radiothorium, which gives α-rays; and, just as in the case of radium, this is followed by a small host of short-lived products, some of which give α- and others β- and γ-rays. What actually happens, therefore, is that in addition to the initial rapid growth of β- and γ-rays already discussed, a slow steady *increase* of the α-, β-, and γ-activity of a mesothorium preparation takes place for many years after its preparation, due to the growth and accumulation of radiothorium and its products. It is calculated that this increase will go on for about four and a half years, and then the activity of the preparation will reach a maximum, the penetrating activity (β- and γ-rays) being then nearly twice that at two days after preparation. From then onwards the regular slow decay of all the radioactivity will set in, and continue with the half-period of five and a half years, as already considered. Twenty years after preparation the activity will be some 12 per cent., whilst after a century it would be less than 1,000th per cent. of the maximum activity.

In practice, however, the change is even more complicated than this on account of the invariable presence of radium in the mesothorium preparations. Radium and mesothorium form, as already remarked, an example of which now so many exist in radioactivity, of two different elements, having entirely different radioactive, but entirely identical, chemical character. For a long time the nature of the chemical processes used to extract mesothorium from the by-products of monazite was kept secret. It was thought that they were peculiarly difficult and forbidding. I was therefore surprised and interested to find—and the same discovery was made at about the same time by Professor Marckwald in Berlin —that mesothorium and radium behaved in chemical processes identically. In consequence the extraction of mesothorium from monazite residues is entirely similar in principle to that of radium from pitchblende residues. Since monazite always contains a minute amount of uranium, and therefore the corresponding quantity of radium, the mesothorium separated always contains the radium also. No successful separation has as yet been achieved, and it is most improbable that it ever will be. After a lengthy fractional crystallisation of the mixture I found the relative proportions of the two elements entirely unaltered. Technical mesothorium owes about 12 per cent. of what has been termed its maximum activity (that after four and a half years) to radium. This activity will remain when all that due to mesothorium has completely decayed away. In practice, therefore, the decay of the preparations will be appreciably slower than if radium were absent.

These discoveries have thus resulted in the provision of an effective substitute for radium, which for such purposes as medical application, or for general researches in the properties of the new radiations, are, while the activity lasts, its equal in every respect. Indeed, it is possible to obtain mesothorium preparations many times more concentrated in their activity than pure radium salts. There is no dearth of the raw material, which hitherto has been a wasted product.

But, of course, from the strictly scientific point of view, the radioactivity of mesothorium is as distinct from that of radium as copper is from zinc, or as one flower is from another. It will be of interest to concentrate upon some of the chief resemblances and differences in the two disintegration series.

The Thorium Emanation.

The thorium emanation was the first of the three emanations to be discovered, and had been fairly completely investigated by Rutherford before the others were known. It is given off in greater or less degree by all thorium compounds. If the radioactivity of the compound is measured by placing it in a closed electroscope, the activity is found to increase for about ten minutes, owing to the accumulation of the emanation, and then remains constant if the instrument is not disturbed. But if a current of air is blown through the instrument, it sweeps out the emanation, and the activity is correspondingly reduced. On stopping the blast of air, it rises again precisely as at first. Uranium compounds show no trace of this behaviour, as they do not generate an emanation. The products of the disintegration of the thorium emanation are known as the thorium active deposit, and they manifest themselves in much the same way as the radium active deposit, being attracted to the negatively charged surface in an electric field. They last much longer, however, the period of half-decay being about eleven hours instead of about half an hour, and, in consequence, they take longer to accumulate. In a vessel containing a thorium or, better, a radiothorium preparation, which acts as a constant source of the evanescent thorium emanation, the active deposit on the walls of the vessel (or on the negative electrode, if an electric field is used), goes on increasing in amount for about two days, whereas in the radium emanation the active deposit reaches the maximum value in about three hours.

Radiothorium.

Radiothorium is the most powerful and convenient source of the emanation and active deposit of thorium. As already explained, radiothorium is not separable from thorium by any chemical process. Freshly prepared thorium compounds contain practically all the radiothorium of the original mineral, but its parent mesothorium being absent, this radiothorium in the course of a few years decays. Before it decays completely, however, mesothorium has been regenerated by the thorium, and in time begins to produce fresh radiothorium. The consequence is that commercial thorium compounds always contain more or less radiothorium, and always, therefore, furnish more or less of the emanation and active deposit. But the amount is insignificant compared with what can now be obtained from a commercial radiothorium preparation. Mesothorium, after it is separated from the mineral and left to itself, produces, as we have seen, radiothorium. After a year or more of accumulation these two substances may with advantage be separated. A trace of a thorium salt is added to the solution, and then precipitated by adding ammonia as thorium hydroxide, which carries with it the whole of the radiothorium, leaving the mesothorium in solution. This radiothorium preparation in turn generates thorium X, and after a few weeks becomes a powerful source of the thorium emanation during the few years it lasts.

Apart from the intrinsic interest attaching to this method of "growing" radio-elements otherwise not separable from the raw material a point of great philosophical interest is involved. Were it not for the existence of mesothorium intermediate between and chemically distinct from thorium and radiothorium, the separate existence of the latter might not have been suspected, and they certainly could never be obtained as individuals. In the case of uranium I and uranium II, the evidence for the existence of two elements remains indirect, and they have never yet been separated. The intervening member, uranium X, is too short-lived and the product uranium II too long-lived for the quantity of the latter produced from the former to be detectable even by radioactive methods (*vide* pp. 129 and 150). One can hardly help wondering how many of the well-known common so-called elements may not be mixtures of more than one element with chemically identical properties.

Experiments with the Thorium Emanation.

Radiothorium may be used to show, in a striking way, by means of phosphorescent screens, many of the older classical experiments on the growth and decay of radioactive substances on which the existing theory of atomic disintegration has been built up. For example, if a radiothorium preparation or old mesothorium preparation containing radiothorium, is kept in a tube through which a puff of air can be sent from a rubber blower, and the accumulated emanation is thus blown out into a flask internally coated with zinc sulphide, as shown in Figs. 8 and 9, it will cause it to phosphoresce brilliantly in the dark. The decay of the emanation in the flask can then be watched from minute to minute with the eyes, and its concomitant reproduction in the radiothorium tube can easily be demonstrated. For example, the radiothorium tube may first be thoroughly blown out, and then the effect observed of blowing through it into a zinc sulphide flask immediately, before any emanation has had time to accumulate, and then after waiting successive periods of, say, ten, twenty, thirty seconds, one, two, ten, or more minutes. For the shorter intervals the amount of emanation produced is very nearly proportional to the time, but for the longer ones the decay of that produced first during the period of accumulation begins to tell, and the increase with time gets less and less. So that after five or ten minutes no increase results, however long a time is allowed to elapse. The emanation is then in " equilibrium," as much decaying per second as is produced per second.

In this way many of the simple laws of the decay and reproduction of the emanation, on which the whole superstructure of radioactive theory was at first largely based, may now be shown to a large audience. But all the original work was done with delicate electrical instruments long before anyone had ever observed a single visible effect, or had any other than indirect electrical evidence of the existence of the evanescent emanation.

Thorium A.

The most recent member to be added to the thorium disintegration series is thorium A, the direct product of the emanation, which, on account of its short period of average life—about one-fifth of a second only—had hitherto not been separately distinguished from the emanation. It was put in evidence by Rutherford and his colleagues in the following ingenious manner: An endless wire passed along the axis of a cylinder, containing a radiothorium preparation, through holes in ebonite stoppers closing the ends of the cylinder, and over suitable pulleys outside of the cylinder driven by an electric motor. In this way the wire was kept passing through a cylinder filled with thorium emanation. The wire was connected to the negative and the cylinder to the positive pole of a battery, so as to concentrate the active deposit on the wire. It was found that the wire immediately after leaving the cylinder was intensely active, giving out powerful α-rays, and capable of lighting up a zinc sulphide screen brought near to the wire. This activity on the wire lasts only a small fraction of a second, so that after the wire has moved away a little from the cylinder its activity has practically disappeared. Thus, although the wire is being driven at a high speed all the time, it is only the part immediately issuing from the cylinder which is active, and which causes the sulphide screen to glow. Thorium A is a non-volatile product of the gaseous emanation, and is attracted to the negative electrode. But almost as soon as it is deposited it breaks up, giving α-rays. On the principle of a short life and a merry one, the effect of this product is far more marked, for short periods of exposure, than that of the longer-lived products it in turn produces. Though it would be easy to show that the wire, after the large activity due to thorium A is over, still possesses activity due to the products formed, this activity is, for short periods of exposure, far too small to light up a phosphorescent screen. In this way the existence of this almost hopelessly unstable element has been demonstrated. In connection with the thorium active deposit and the complex character of thorium C something has still to be said, but it may be deferred.

The Actinium Disintegration Series.

A few words may be said for the sake of completeness on the third and least important disintegration series, but one which is, however, just as interesting to the student as the others. In addition to the polonium and radium separated from pitchblende by M. and Mme. Curie, a colleague, M. Debierne, was successful in isolating a third new radio-element, to which he gave the name *Actinium*. So far as is known, actinium is at least a fairly long-lived radio-element, for although it was discovered very shortly after radium, the original preparations have retained much, at least, of their activity. Recently it has been established that a slow decay, however, does occur which indicates a period of average life for this substance of only about thirty years.

Actinium is separated with the "rare earths" in uranium minerals, and chemically it resembles most closely the rare-earth element, lanthanum, although it is not completely identical with it in chemical properties. In radioactive properties its disintegration series is very closely analogous to that of thorium, and consists of eight members, in addition to itself, the first of which, known as radioactinium, corresponds with radiothorium. The next is actinium X, corresponding perfectly with thorium X, and after that the actinium emanation, actinium A, B, C, and D, follow in regular order, almost exactly as in the thorium series. The analogous products in the two series in each case give out the same kinds of rays, and are, so far as is known, chemically identical in character. But, almost without exception, the periods in the actinium series are uniformly shorter than in the thorium series, the longest,

ACTINIUM

that of radioactinium, being only twenty-eight days, and the shortest, that of actinium A, being only $\frac{1}{350}$th of a second. The full series is shown in Fig. 38.

Actinium.	Radio-actinium.	Actinium X.	Emanation.	Actinium A.
30 years.	28·1 days.	15 days.	5·6 seconds.	0·003 second

Actinium B.	Actinium C.	Actinium D.	Actinium E.
52·1 minutes.	3·1 minutes.	6·83 minutes.	(unknown).

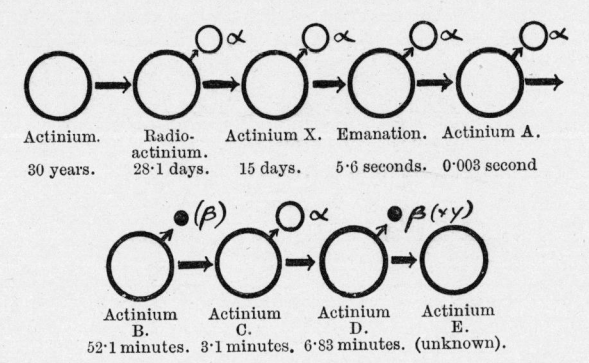

FIG. 38.

THE ORIGIN OF ACTINIUM.

Whereas it is customary to regard the uranium and thorium series each as starting from a primary parent of so long life, that, old as the world is, some still survives unchanged, the problems connected with the real nature and origin of actinium are still not entirely cleared up. Its short period of life, recently established, proves that it cannot itself be a primary radio-element like the other two, and, in fact, its parent is now known. But it is not impossible that it may form part of a third independent primary series, though this has not been the view that has so far gained most support. So far as knowledge has been gained, actinium appears to be found only in the uranium minerals and in all of these which have been examined for it. It is natural to conclude from this that it is a product of uranium. But here a difficulty arises. In the disintegration of actinium at least five α-particles are given out per atom disintegrating, representing a loss in atomic weight of 20 units. There is certainly no room for the actinium series between uranium and polonium, and there is no evidence that it comes after polonium.

Multiple Atomic Disintegration.

The important piece of evidence, however, which shows conclusively that actinium cannot be in the *main* uranium-polonium series, and which at the same time serves to distinguish this series from the others, and to make it practically the most difficult to investigate, is the extraordinarily small relative quantity of actinium in uranium minerals. Although the actinium series gives out at least five α-particles per atom as compared with eight given out by the uranium-radium-polonium series, the α-radiation contributed by the whole actinium series in uranium minerals is only about one-fifteenth or one-sixteenth of that contributed by the uranium series. Whereas, if actinium were in the main line of descent from uranium, the α-activity of its series should be of the order of five-eights of that of the uranium series, in accordance with the principle discussed on p. 153. Two possibilities may be advanced. Either actinium is an entirely separate and independent primary radioelement, and, if so, its occurrence always in uranium minerals, and only in those minerals, is difficult to understand; or actinium may be derived from uranium as a branch, or offshoot, not in the main line of descent. One may suppose that at some stage of the disintegration of the uranium atom a choice of two modes of disintegration presents itself. The large majority of the atoms choose one way—the way leading to polonium—whilst a small minority choose a second way, the way leading through the actinium series. If this is true, it can be calculated that out of every twelve uranium atoms, eleven go through the main line of descent towards polonium, and one goes through the actinium line. This mode of explaining actinium is now supported by much new evidence and by the discovery very recently of actual cases of such a multiple disintegration at the ends of the thorium and radium series, among the active deposit products.

BRANCH SERIES OF THORIUM AND RADIUM.

This may now be briefly dealt with. We have already considered the evidence (p. 164) for supposing that, on account of the very high speed at which the α-particles are expelled from radium C and thorium C, the changes of these substances are complex, and that the α-rays in each case probably result from subsequent products, named radium C′ and thorium C′, of excessively short life-period, which is estimated to be one millionth of a second in the case of the former and one hundred thousand millionth of a second in the case of the latter. In addition, the changes are complicated by branchings of the kind just considered, but especially instructive. Taking the case of thorium C first, it is known that it breaks up in two ways. In the first mode an α-ray is expelled and the product formed then expels a β-ray. In the second mode the order is reversed, the β-ray being expelled first and the α-ray second. This may be represented (see Fig. 39).

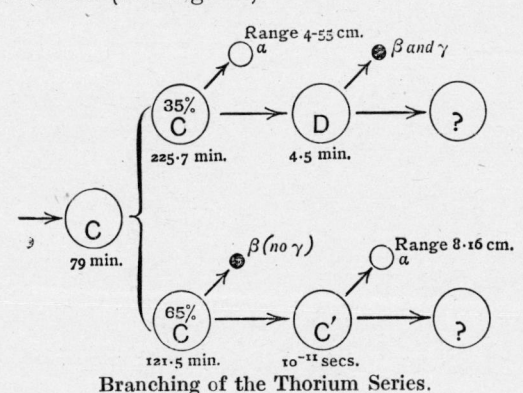

Branching of the Thorium Series.
FIG. 39.

About 35 per cent. of the atoms disintegrating follow the first mode producing thorium D, and give out α-rays of range 4·55 cm.; whereas 65 per cent. give out β-rays in the second mode producing the hypothetical and hopelessly evanescent thorium C′, which gives out

α-rays of range 8·16 cm. The two end products are of the same atomic weight, 208, and whether or not they are really identical cannot yet be said. The two separate periods of average life for thorium C shown in the figure, 225·7 and 121·5 minutes, are those calculated for the two kinds of change separately, assuming that the other did not occur.

In the case of radium C, the same applies with the exception that only 0·03 per cent. of the atoms follow the "α- then β-mode," the overwhelming preponderance, 99·97 per cent., following the "β- then α-mode" (see Fig. 40).

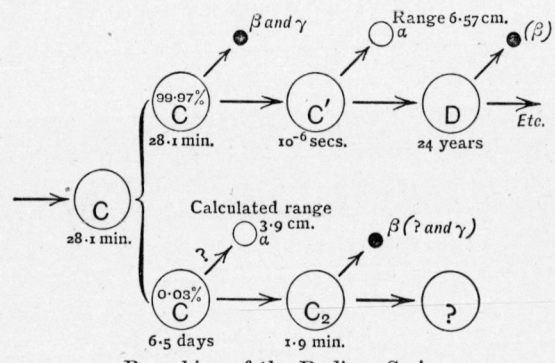

Branching of the Radium Series

FIG. 40.

The product produced in the first mode, called radium C_2 is in such infinitesimal quantity, that little is known about it beyond the value of its period and the fact that it gives β-rays.

THE ACTINIUM BRANCH SERIES.

Reverting now to actinium, the practical consequence of its being formed only in the minor mode of a dual disintegration, claiming only some 8 per cent. of the uranium atoms disintegrating, is that the substance is very much rarer and more difficult to obtain than the members of either of the other two series. If it were more common, it would lend itself to many demonstra-

THE ACTINIUM EMANATION

tions and experiments similar to those detailed under radiothorium, but of an even more striking character. Actinium is relatively poor in penetrating rays, and even the most active preparations it is possible to procure are disappointing in this respect when compared with radium.

THE ACTINIUM EMANATION.

The chief glory of actinium, however, is its emanation, a gaseous disintegration product, precisely analogous in every respect to those of radium and of thorium, but having a period of average life of only 5·6 seconds. The usual principle of a short life and a merry one applies. The dominating characteristic of the radioactivity of actinium preparations is the emanation that is given off. In the dark room, if a preparation is held over a zinc sulphide screen, the emanation diffusing away lights up the screen in patches, which are wafted from one part of the screen to another by draughts or any gentle puffs of air. The rapid decay of the emanation and corresponding rapid regeneration from the actinium preparation makes it quite possible to experiment thus with the emanation in the open-air of the room. Whereas if the radium emanation were dealt with in this way, once it had been dissipated throughout the air of a room, some weeks would have to elapse before a fresh supply was available. Giesel, who rediscovered the substance subsequently to Debierne, actually named it " Emanium " before it was found to be identical with actinium.

ACTINIUM A.

The only other product of actinium which calls for special mention is actinium A, the direct product of the emanation, which, like thorium A, has an extraordinarily short period of life. Indeed, actinium A is the most unstable element directly known, its period being only about $\frac{1}{350}$th of a second. It may be put into evidence by the same device as that described for thorium A (p. 197), but, of course, the endless wire has to be driven considerably more rapidly than is necessary to exhibit the thorium product. As a matter of fact, a forgotten experiment of Giesel, eight years before the discovery of actinium A, clearly puts the existence of that substance into evidence, when rightly interpreted. If a zinc sulphide screen is brought opposite to the open end of a tube containing an actinium preparation, and a little distance away from it, there is a diffuse luminosity produced on the screen in the dark, due to the emanation escaping from the tube. If the screen is now connected with the negative pole of an electrical machine, *instantly* there flashes out on the screen a sharply-defined bright spot of the same geometrical form as the opening of the tube. On discharging the screen this spot *instantly* disappears. Giesel thought, very naturally, that he was dealing with a new kind of radiation, attracted by a negatively charged surface, and called the supposed radiation the "E-ray," in brief for "emanation ray." However, it is not the ray, but the excessively short-lived product giving an ordinary α-ray, which is attracted to the negative surface; but owing to the infinitesimal time this product remains in existence it appears as if it is the ray, rather than the product, which is attracted by the electric field. Another way of showing the same experiment is to coat a wire with zinc sulphide, and to immerse it in a flask containing an actinium preparation. On charging the wire negatively to the flask, the zinc sulphide instantly flashes out and remains brilliantly luminous; but on discharging the wire, the luminosity disappears apparently instantaneously. The same device can be used to show the existence of thorium A, but an appreciable, though small, time-lag occurs before the appearance and the decay of the luminosity.

Eka-tantalum or Proto-actinium.

In 1919 the main problem of the origin of actinium was cleared up by the discovery and isolation of its direct parent in uranium minerals by Cranston and the writer in this country, who named it "eka-tantalum," and by Otto Hahn and Miss Meitner in Germany, who named it "proto-actinium." In each case the search was helped by some wide and far-reaching generalisations, still to be dealt with, from which it was possible to predict the chemical character of the missing parent and its place in the periodic table. This place was the last and still vacant place in the niobium-tantalum family, between uranium on the one side and thorium on the other. Mendelejeff, who was one of the discoverers of the Periodic Law, had called attention to three vacant places in the families of boron, aluminium, and silicon respectively, which he assumed were occupied by three elements still to be discovered, and which he called eka-boron, eka-aluminium and eka-silicon. In each case he was bold enough to predict their chemical character from their position in the table. Shortly afterwards the three missing elements were found, and named scandium, gallium, and germanium, and their properties were found to correspond very closely with what had been predicted.

In the present case "eka-tantalum," a still unknown element, analogous in chemical character to tantalum, had been foreseen to be probably the missing parent of actinium. Beyond the fact that it has been isolated and that it produces actinium slowly and steadily with the lapse of time, just as ionium produces radium, not much work has yet been done on it. It gives α-rays, and from the range of these it is estimated that its period is of the order of from ten to a hundred thousand years.

Uranium Y.

One more member remains to be considered, and that is uranium Y, a radioactive product of short period of average life, 2·2 days, discovered by Antonoff in 1911 to be produced by uranium, and giving (β)-rays somewhat more penetrating than those of uranium X_1. It is probable that this is the immediate parent of eka-tantalum, and the first member of the actinium branch series. The branching is thought to occur either at uranium I or uranium II, probably the latter, and that in both branches an a-ray is expelled. So that the initial changes of the series, represented in Fig. 28 as a single change, has been gradually and with difficulty traced out to be something as follows:

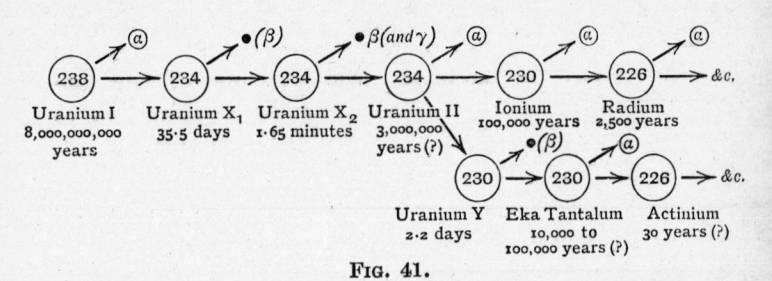

$$238 \xrightarrow{a} 234 \xrightarrow{(\beta)} 234 \xrightarrow{\beta(and\,\gamma)} 234 \xrightarrow{a} 230 \xrightarrow{a} 226 \xrightarrow{a} \&c.$$

Uranium I — Uranium X$_1$ — Uranium X$_2$ — Uranium II — Ionium — Radium
8,000,000,000 years — 35.5 days — 1.65 minutes — 3,000,000 years (?) — 100,000 years — 2,500 years

$$230 \xrightarrow{(\beta)} 230 \xrightarrow{a} 226 \xrightarrow{} \&c.$$

Uranium Y — Eka Tantalum — Actinium
2.2 days — 10,000 to 100,000 years (?) — 30 years (?)

FIG. 41.

Considerations to be now dealt with have shown it to be of extreme importance that every change in the series should be separately and correctly recognised, and when this was sufficiently the case, a very great advance indeed resulted.

Thus, with the discovery of these remaining substances, the science of radioactivity now embraces thirty-six examples of elements in the course of spontaneous change, with periods varying from tens of thousands of millions of years on the one hand, to a few billionths of a second on the other. It is unlikely that any more of these unstable elements remain to be discovered, unless some entirely unknown and unsuspected source of radioactive materials is found. The complete series are set out in detail in the table opposite (Fig. 42).

The Unsolved Riddle of Matter.

There remains unsolved that most fundamental and inaccessible problem, which at the same time appears to be the problem of ultimately the most practical signi-

I. URANIUM, RADIUM, AND ACTINIUM SERIES.

MAIN SERIES.

Element.	Atomic Weight	Radiation	Period of Average Life.	Chemical Character [Isotopic with]
Uranium-I	238	α	8,000,000,000 years	Uranium
Uranium-X_1	234	β	35.5 days	Thorium
Uranium-X_2	234	β	1.65 minutes	Ekatantalum
Uranium-II	234	α	3,000,000 years (?)	Uranium
Ionium	230	α	100,000 years	Thorium
Radium	226	α	2440 years	Radium
Ra. Emanation	222	α	5.55 days	Emanation
Radium-A	218	α	4.3 minutes	Polonium
Radium-B	214	β	38.5 minutes	Lead
Radium-C	214	β (99.97%)	28.1 minutes	Bismuth
Radium-C'	214	α	1/1,000,000th sec. (?)	Polonium
Radium-D	210	β	24 years	Lead
Radium-E	210	β	7.2 days	Bismuth
Radium-F (Polonium)	210	α	196 days	Polonium
End Product	206	...	∞	Lead

BRANCH SERIES.

Element.	Atomic Weight	Radiation	Period of Average Life.	Chemical Character [Isotopic with]
[At either Uranium-I or Uranium-II the series branches, and 8% of the total number of atoms disintegrating, follow the branch Actinium series.]			
Uranium-Y	...	β	2.2 days	Thorium
Ekatantalum	...	α	1000 to 10,000 years (?)	Ekatantalum
Actinium	...	β (?)	?	Actinium
Radioactinium	...	α	28.1 days	Thorium
Actinium-X	...	α	16.4 days	Radium
Ac. Emanation	...	α	5.6 seconds	Emanation
Actinium-A	...	α	0.003 second	Polonium
Actinium-B	...	β	52.1 minutes	Lead
Actinium-C	...	β	3.1 minutes	Bismuth
Actinium-D	...	β	6.83 minutes	Thallium
End Product	[either 206 or 210]	...	∞	Lead
[At Radium-C, 0.03% of the atoms follow the branch series.]			
Radium-C	214	α (0.03%)	28.1 minutes	Bismuth
Radium-C_2	210	β	1.9 minutes	Thallium
End Product	210	...	∞	Lead

II. THORIUM SERIES.

Element.	Atomic Weight	Radiation	Period of Average Life.	Chemical Character [Isotopic with]
Thorium	232	α	25,000,000,000 years	Thorium
Mesothorium-I	228	β	9.67 years	Radium
Mesothorium-II	228	β	8.9 hours	Actinium
Radiothorium	228	α	2.75 years	Thorium
Thorium-X	224	α	5.25 days	Radium
Th. Emanation	220	α	78 seconds	Emanation
Thorium-A	216	α	0.2 second	Polonium
Thorium-B	212	β	15.4 hours	Lead
Thorium-C	212	β (65%)	87 minutes	Bismuth
Thorium-C'	212	...	1/100,000,000,000th sec. (?)	Polonium
End Product	208	...	∞	Lead

BRANCH SERIES (Thorium)

Element.	Atomic Weight	Radiation	Period of Average Life.	Chemical Character [Isotopic with]
[At Thorium-C, 35% of the atoms follow the branch series.]			
Thorium-C	212	α (35%)	87 minutes	Lead
Thorium-D	208	β	4.5 minutes	Thallium
End Product	208	...	∞	Lead

Fig. 42.

ficance—the real internal nature of matter. How is the atom of matter put together, and how can it be pulled apart? These are the practical questions which the discoveries of radioactivity raise in a pressing form without as yet affording a hint of the answer. But in spite of that, our knowledge of the internal structure of the atom continues to grow at a very rapid rate, and some of this more recent work may now be dealt with.

CHAPTER XIII
THE ULTIMATE STRUCTURE OF MATTER

A Flood of Knowledge.

EVER since the recognition of radioactivity, the discovery of radium, the establishment of the theory of atomic disintegration, and the independent proof by the spectroscope that the element helium is actually being produced in a natural transmutation — discoveries which followed one another rapidly as the nineteenth century passed away and the present century succeeded it—it must have seemed to many that such a period of pioneering and fundamental reconstruction in science would soon exhaust itself and be succeeded by one of steady spade-work in the cultivation of the new territory opened up. The development of the new territory and its detailed exploration have gone on steadily and rapidly, but, so far from the wave of original and fertile ideas having exhausted itself, the initial successes above mentioned have proved to be but the first indications of a continuously advancing tide. Already from many totally distinct directions the flood of knowledge has revealed many of the deeper secrets of the constitution of matter. Ignorance and impotence in this field still keeps the human race within its traditional boundaries, and Nature still holds the final citadel against all comers. But now it is being undermined from all sides, and changes its aspect almost from day to day, like an erstwhile impregnable barrier that is crumbling away before our eyes.

The years 1911-13 witnessed a convergence of powerful new methods which, though their simultaneous development must be regarded as largely fortuitous, all bear definite experimental testimony concerning the hidden internal construction of the atom of matter. In fact, we can now distinguish therein three distinct regions, one within the other, between which probably no interchange whatever of constituents occurs, but through which, in succession, the atom makes the particular impression by which we recognise it in the external world, and by which, in turn, it is successively guarded from any direct influence from without. The first, outermost region is that which the older sciences of physics and chemistry have studied so minutely, and which is directly concerned in endowing the atom with most of those properties by which in the past it has been recognised and studied. The second is an intermediate region which can be reached and set into the vibration known to us as X-rays, by the purely artificially generated projectiles, the free-flying electrons or cathode-rays of the Crookes tube, dealt with in Chapter IV. The last and innermost region of the atom, or the nucleus, has never yet been reached save by methods which we owe solely to the study of natural radioactive changes and by the projectiles, of such inimitable swiftness and energy, which are spontaneously expelled during those changes.

The Nature of Mass.

Actually before the coming of radioactivity, the discovery of the electron, a particle more minute than the smallest individual atom of matter, had given, in the hands of Oliver Heaviside and Sir Joseph Thomson, a possible clue to the nature of mass (p. 57). Without any direct evidence that the mass of matter was, in fact, due to this cause, the reasoning indicated that, if the electron were sufficiently small—if the electric charge of which it consists were concentrated into the volume of a sphere of about 2×10^{-13} cm. radius, which is about one-hundred thousandth of the usually accepted value for the radius of an atom—it would possess a mass equal to that found—namely $\frac{1}{1830}$th part of the mass of the hydrogen atom, by virtue of thoroughly well-known and understood electro-magnetic principles. A charge of pure electricity, entirely unassociated with matter, as the negative electron is believed to be, cannot be moved from rest without an expenditure of energy, nor if moving can it be brought to rest without yielding up its energy. It, therefore, must possess inertia or mass. A moving charge of electricity is indistinguishable from a current of electricity. In the case of an ordinary electric current " self-induction " opposes both its starting and stopping. If we trace further the origin of the " self-induction " in the case of a flow of the electric current, or " electro-magnetic inertia " in the case of an individual electron, both terms being technical expressions for an identical action, we find it in a fundamental distinction between electrostatic and electrodynamic phenomena—that is, between a charge at rest and one in motion. The former has no magnetic properties, whereas the latter has. The space surrounding a current of electricity, or a moving charge, is endowed with magnetic properties, and the change in the surrounding space when an electric charge, before at rest, is caused to move, demands the expenditure of energy. This change is believed to be transmitted outward from the electron with the velocity of light. This endows a purely electric charge with inertia or mass. So that a charge of pure electricity must, if sufficiently small and concentrated, simulate matter in its most fundamental attribute. For the same charge concentrated into spheres of different radius, the mass is inversely proportional to the radius. Are there, then, two kinds of inertia or mass, the one " material " and the other " electro-magnetic," the one for matter, still a fundamental, and the other for electricity, a derived conception that can be fully explained by the phenomena known to attend its motion ?

Sir Joseph Thomson's Model Atom.

From this the idea arose naturally and was developed by Sir Joseph Thomson, that atoms of matter might be compounded of electrons in sufficient numbers to account for their mass. For each atom nearly 2,000 electrons per unit of atomic mass would be required. The problem of atomic constitution resolved itself into one of how to maintain such systems of electrons in permanently stable régime. The early attempts had little of reality to recommend them, because by no known means could such systems of electrons be held together without assuming the existence of positive electricity in some form. But positive electricity, existing like negative electricity divorced from matter, refused to be discovered, and, in fact, still remains unknown. In Sir Joseph Thomson's model atom, the negative electrons were supposed to revolve in orbits within a uniform sphere of positive electrification of the same dimensions as the atom. It had one very great and suggestive merit, for it showed that the electrons would tend to arrange themselves in rings. If the number of the electrons were steadily increased, the newcomers would incorporate themselves into the existing outer ring until a certain number had been added, and then, if the numbers were further increased, these existing rings would become unstable, and the superfluous members would at a certain number suddenly rearrange themselves into a new permanent outer ring concentric with those previously existing.

The Periodic Law.

This simulates very well the known facts with regard to the elements as shown by the Periodic Table. Arranging the elements in increasing order of atomic mass we get the well-known periodicity of chemical properties, the tenth element resembling closely the second, the eleventh the third, and so on, hydrogen being an exceptional

THE PERIODIC TABLE

element without analogues. So that all the elements fall naturally into families, successive members in the same family being separated from one another by seven intervening elements in the early part of the table, and by seventeen in the latter part of the table. The Periodic Table is shown in Fig. 43. The elements are set down successively in order of increasing atomic weight horizontally, the vertical columns then contain families of chemically allied elements. The separate places are numbered consecutively at the top of the place. These numbers are the so-called atomic numbers. Below the name of each element is its chemical symbol and its atomic weight. The families are numbered 0, I, II, etc., and these " Group Numbers " express, with certain reservations, the usual chemical *valency* of the element —that is, the number of units of affinity with which it enters into combination with other elements. Thus, aluminium is in the IIIrd family and carbon is in the IVth. When these combine it takes four atoms of aluminium, each atom with three units of affinity, to combine with three of carbon, each with four units of affinity, the compound, aluminium carbide, being represented by Al_4C_3. After the IVth group, the elements frequently combine to form compounds with many different valencies. But here it may be stated, though the simple rule is often not followed, that the most usual valencies are either the group number or eight minus the group number. Thus, nitrogen either has five valencies or three, chlorine one or seven, and so on.

That elements possess units of combining power, or " bonds of affinity " as chemists call them, is one of the numerous facts which has been, at least partially, explained by the discovery of the electron and the fact that electricity exists in atoms no less than matter.

ELECTROLYTIC DISSOCIATION.

During the last quarter of the nineteenth century, the theory of electrolytic dissociation, put forward by

PERIODIC TABLE OF THE CHEMICAL ELEMENTS, 1920.

	Group 0	Group I	Group II	Group III	Group IV	Group V	Group VI	Group VII	Group VIII
		1 Hydrogen 1.008							
	2 Helium He 3.99	3 Lithium Li. 6.94	4 Beryllium Be. 9.1	5 Boron. B. 11.0	6 Carbon C. 12.00	7 Nitrogen N. 14.01	8 Oxygen O. 16.00	9 Fluorine F. 19.0	
	10 Neon Ne. 20.2	11 Sodium Na. 23.00	12 Magnesium Mg. 24.32	13 Aluminium Al. 27.1	14 Silicon Si. 28.3	15 Phosphorus P. 31.04	16 Sulphur S. 32.07	17 Chlorine Cl. 35.46	
A	18 Argon A. 39.88	19 Potassium K. 39.10	20 Calcium Ca. 40.07	21 Scandium Sc. 44.1	22 Titanium Ti. 48.1	23 Vanadium V. 51.0	24 Chromium Cr. 52.0	25 Manganese Mn. 54.93	26 Iron Fe. 55.84 27 Cobalt Co. 58.97 28 Nickel Ni. 58.68
B		29 Copper Cu. 63.57	30 Zinc Zn. 65.37	31 Gallium Ga. 69.9	32 Germanium Ge. 72.5	33 Arsenic As. 74.96	34 Selenium Se. 79.2	35 Bromine Br. 79.92	
A	36 Krypton Kr. 82.92	37 Rubidium Rb. 85.45	38 Strontium Sr. 87.63	39 Yttrium Yt. 89.0	40 Zirconium Zr. 90.6	41 Niobium Nb. 93.5	42 Molybdenum Mo. 96.0	43	44 Ruthenium Ru. 101.7 45 Rhodium Rh. 102.9 46 Palladium Pd. 106.7
B		47 Silver Ag. 107.88	48 Cadmium Cd. 112.40	49 Indium In. 114.8	50 Tin Sn. 119.0	51 Antimony Sb. 120.2	52 Tellurium Te. 127.5	53 Iodine I. 126.92	
A	54 Xenon Xe. 130.2	55 Caesium Cs. 132.81	56 Barium Ba. 137.37	57 Lanthanum La. 139.0	58 Cerium Ce. 140.25	59 Praseodymium Pr. 140.6	60 Neodymium Nd. 144.3	61	62 Samarium Sa. 150.4
		63 Europium Eu. 152.0	64 Gadolinium Gd. 157.3						
		69 Thulium Tm. 168.5	70 Ytterbium Yb. 172.0	71 Lutecium Lu. 174.0	72	73 Tantalum Ta. 181.5	74 Tungsten W. 184.0	75	76 Osmium Os. 190.9 77 Iridium Ir. 193.1 78 Platinum Pt. 195.2
					65 Terbium Tb. 159.2	66 Dysprosium Dy. 162.5	67 Holmium 163.5	68 Erbium Er. 167.7	
B		79 Gold Au. 197.2	80 Mercury Hg. 200.6	81 Thallium Tl. 204.0	82 Lead Pb. 207.20	83 Bismuth Bi. 208.0	84 Polonium (210)	85	
A	86 Radium Emanation (222)	87	88 Radium Ra. 226.0	89 Actinium	90 Thorium Th. 232.12	91 Uranium X₂ (Brevium)	92 Uranium U. 238.18		

Only the six spaces marked ——— are vacant places

The figures above the name of the element are the atomic numbers, and those below the atomic weights.

ELECTROLYTIC DISSOCIATION

Svante Arrhenius of Stockholm, became generally established. It asserted that compounds of the class which conduct the electric current in the state of solution, and known as electrolytes, exist in solution in a more or less completely dissociated condition, as oppositely charged positive and negative ions, the migration of which to the opposite poles constitutes the electric current.

It would be idle to pretend that complete clearness of interpretation has yet been attained, but the facts appear somewhat as follow: The elements, sodium and chlorine in Groups I and VII respectively, both act usually as elements with a single unit of valency, but they belong to, and are typical of, two distinct classes of elements. Sodium is a typical basic, metallic, or electropositive element, and chlorine is a typical acidic, non-metallic, or electro-negative element. They combine together with the utmost avidity to form common salt, NaCl. But in solution in water we are forced, by its behaviour to the electric current as an electrolyte, to recognise that the complex NaCl does not exist as such, at least for the most part. Rather, there are two new particles, " sodion " and " chlorion," which exist apart, and are called ions. The sodion—Na^+—is an atom of sodium carrying one atomic charge of positive electricity, and the chlorion—Cl^-—is an atom of chlorine with one atomic charge of negative electricity. It is as though the act of chemical combination of metallic sodium with the element chlorine was essentially the transfer of an electron, or atom of negative electricity, from the sodium atom, to the chlorine atom. The sodium readily loses a constituent negative electron to another element, such as chlorine, which will take it up. But although equal numbers of positive and negative ions may exist as separate particles when *mixed* together, neither kind can exist alone. The enormous forces of electrical repulsion between the similar charges, unneutralised by the presence of the opposite kind, effectually prevent this being even conceivable. Whether an element loses or gains one or more electrons, however, is not a self-contained property, but depends on the nature of the other element or elements in the compound formed, so that frequently elements in the later families, V, VI, and VII, which may usually tend to gain 3, 2, or 1 electrons and to act as acidic elements, may act like basic elements and lose 5, 6, or 7 electrons.

Undoubtedly, in the broadest sense, though much is not yet so clear, the chemical combining power of an element is to be explained by the inherent tendency the atom possesses either to attract from, or to yield up to, another atom, one or more electrons. The act of chemical combination, in some of the best-known and typical cases, which, in an earlier day, was depicted as due to the powerful attraction of one atom for and by another, is primarily not exerted between the two atoms, but between one of the atoms and the constituent electron or electrons of the other. Between the two *material* components of such a stable compound as sodium chloride no cohesion or attraction probably exists.

The molecule of sodium chloride, at least in the liquid state, either when fused or dissolved, consists essentially of two separate particles or ions, mixed together rather than combined, which being oppositely electrically charged, must always exist together in equal numbers in order that the whole may remain electrically neutral. But there is no definite bond of union other than this purely electrical requirement, and this refers merely to the aggregate number of each kind of particle rather than to the individuals. Apart from this limitation, the sodium and the chlorine in salt water exist separately and totally uncombined for the most part. The intensity of the electrical charge on an ion is almost inconceivably greater than any known for matter in the mass. It has been calculated that the mutual repulsion between the charges carried, for example, by the hydrogen ions, would be sufficient to burst the strongest tube that can be made, long before there was forced in as much hydrogen, in the form of ions, as would, in the ordinary state, show the hydrogen spectrum in a vacuum tube. This assumes, of course, what is really quite impossible, that such free ions could be put into a tube without being discharged by contact with the walls of the tube. The "chemical combination" of the partners in a compound completely dissociated, as sodium chloride is in liquid form, is due to a purely electrical and statistical partnership of the otherwise completely independent ions, which, in the modern view, is practically as effective in maintaining the combination as the rigid bonds linking each individual sodium atom to one chlorine atom which Dalton first pictured. This refers to the class of electrolytically dissociated substances, which comprises the acids, bases, and salts, and not to the very large class of non-electrolytes, which comprises all the organic compounds, where permanent individual unions between the atoms of the molecule undoubtedly exist.

The Outermost Region of the Atom.

Chemical changes and chemical properties, in general, deal only with the outermost region of the atomic structure, and we shall not probably do violence to the facts if, without at present attempting to review all the evidence for this conclusion, we picture it as containing a certain number of "valency" electrons. This number is the same for all the members in the same family or vertical row of the periodic table, and differs, literally, *unit by unit* in passing horizontally from one family to the next. For a certain number of electrons in the outer ring—namely, that possessed by the zero family—there is no tendency for the atom either to lose or gain electrons. The members of this family, which comprises the inert gases of the atmosphere, are totally devoid of chemical affinity. The next family, in Group I, which contains the alkali metals, has one electron more than this number, which is relatively loosely held. In all probability it moves in an orbit far external to all the rest. In the other direction, in Group VII, containing the halogen family, the number is one less than this number, and these elements readily take up an additional electron in the presence of an element of Group I which has such an electron in excess. The outer ring of electrons seems for all atoms to try and conform to a certain standard number. Atoms with less rob the ones with more, and this process probably constitutes, in the main, chemical combination. Whether the robber and the robbed entirely part company, as in the electrolytes, or remain interlocked, as in organic compounds, is a secondary consideration. We may suppose that, when the number of electrons in the outer ring exceeds a certain limit, which in the first part of the periodic table is seven, a complete new inner ring of eight electrons is formed. The chemical properties, however, depend only on the outermost ring directly, and the inner rings exert a subordinate effect. The valency of such an element and its general chemical nature resembles, therefore, the eighth preceding element. This holds in the early part of the periodic table. At the 22nd element, titanium, a new and more complicated dual periodicity commences, in which the number of elements separating the consecutive members of one family is eighteen instead of eight. A new group of three closely allied elements, the so-called VIIIth Group, now appears in the middle of the period, where previously an argon element would appear, and the next seven elements have a partial analogy to the seven preceding the VIIIth Group. The easiest way of regarding the matter is to suppose that ten metallic elements, indicated in Fig. 43 between { } are interpolated into the old short periods.

At the 57th element, lanthanum, the law suddenly and completely breaks down. A group of seventeen elements, known as the rare-earth elements, and of which two remain to be discovered, is interpolated into the series at this point. They all resemble one another and lanthanum with such extreme closeness that their separation and identification is one of the most laborious and difficult tasks that the chemist can undertake. At tantalum, the 73rd element, the series begins again almost as if it had not been interrupted, and continues normally to the end.

CHAPTER XIV

THE NUCLEAR ATOM

THE INNERMOST REGION OF THE ATOM.

Now let us see what radioactivity can tell us of the insides of these atoms, for be it remembered that though the older chemical and physical properties of matter are concerned only with the outermost shell, the seat of government which impresses upon any atom its chemical character, and which conditions that chlorine should resemble bromine and differ from potassium, is inside the atom, in a region impenetrable to the methods of investigation known at the opening of the century. From such methods we could only guess what might be inside, and the guesses never even approached the truth. But now we can send a messenger right through the unknown territory, which perchance may, on re-emergence, tell us something of more interest and value to the race than any traveller who has ever struggled back again into being from the waste places of the earth. And this messenger, whose speed must be comparable with that of light and whose mass must be comparable with that of the atom it is to invade, is the α-particle (Chapter IV.). We owe to the genius of Sir Ernest Rutherford the recognition of the importance of this new method of attacking the most fundamental of all problems, that of the ultimate structure and constitution of the atom. Together with his students, he has made a close quantitative study of the effect on the α-particle of its passage through the various atoms of matter. Though, as Bragg showed, the α-particles pass straight *through* the atoms, this is not the whole truth. Thousands of α-particles pass through thousands of atoms in their path, almost as if they were not there, suffering but slight retardation and hardly any appreciable deviation from their course at each encounter. But there occur also, and as an exception, large deflections (compare Fig. 19), and occasionally the α-particle is violently deflected through a large angle by an exceptionally close encounter, like a comet passing round the sun. It may even emerge from the side it entered. This is termed " occasional large-angle scattering " to distinguish it from the incessant very slight deviations, first in one direction then in another, according to the laws of probability, which, as a more minute examination has shown, is continually happening to the α-particle as it ploughs its way through the atoms. Inevitably this makes us view the atom itself as consisting essentially of a *very small dense nucleus* at the centre of a relatively enormous and almost empty sphere of influence containing only electrons. The α-particles, being immensely more massive than the electrons, are not seriously disturbed by the rings or shells of electrons whose revolutions determine the apparent size of the atom as fixed by the older physical methods. Against all other invaders, these swiftly revolving satellites guard the interior of the atoms as efficiently as if the atom really occupies the space to the exclusion of everything else. But such exclusive occupation of a definite volume of space by matter is an illusion. A material projectile, like the α-particle, moving at a speed the tenth of that of light, passes through all the electronic ring-systems as an errant sun might pass through the solar system. This happens many thousands of times without any serious consequences to the α-particles, or to the atomic system invaded. But an occasional α-particle finds its mark, and heads straight for the real atom—that is to say, the central nucleus in which the material as distinguished from the electrical constituents of the atom are concentrated.

THE NUCLEAR ATOM

The α-particle we know to be a helium atom of mass 4 carrying two atomic charges of positive electricity. Or, more accurately, a helium atom is an α-particle minus two electrons. In all probability the α-particle is the simple nucleus of a helium atom, the central sun, as it were, alone and unattended by any electronic satellites or planets at all. The size of this central nucleus of the atom, in relation to the apparent size of the atom, is probably of the same order of magnitude as that of the earth to the whole solar system. Rutherford, for example, from these experiments, considers that practically the whole mass of the hydrogen or helium atom is contained in a central nucleus of diameter one hundred thousand times smaller than the accepted diameter of the atom. This central nucleus carries a positive charge, to the extent of about one unit, or atomic charge, of positive electricity, for every two units of atomic mass. For each unit of positive electricity resident in the nucleus a similar unit of negative electricity, or an electron, revolves in one or other of the outer shells, so that the negative charge on the electronic systems is neutralised by the positive charge on the nucleus or material core. This model of Rutherford's differs essentially from the earlier models in that it has been based on a careful and exhaustive experimental examination of the single large-angle scattering of α-particles.

Now let us consider the exceptionally close encounters, when nucleus meets nucleus and large-angle deflection of the α-particle results. If the atom invaded by the α-particle is massive by comparison, the positively charged nucleus constituting the α-particle will be violently repelled as it impinges on the very much more intensely positively charged and much more massive nucleus of the heavy atom, and will be violently swung out of its path, much as a comet is at perihelion. It is true that the forces at work are repulsive rather than attractive, but this makes no essential difference. If the two nuclei happened to meet absolutely " head-on " the

H-PARTICLES

α-particle would be repelled the way it came almost at its original velocity.

But when α-particles traverse atoms lighter than themselves—for example, atoms of the gas hydrogen—a different state of things must obtain. Here an absolutely " head-on " collision would result in the *hydrogen* atom being repelled in the same direction as that in which the α-particle was travelling, but with a velocity far in excess of that of the original α-particle. In fact, this hydrogen atom will then behave as a new kind of radiant particle, and by virtue of its smaller mass and charge and greater velocity it should travel through the hydrogen gas far further than the original α-particles before being stopped. Marsden has shown that when the α-particles are made to pass through hydrogen and their range examined by means of a zinc sulphide screen, in addition to the scintillations given by the α-particles themselves, a few weaker scintillations, which must be due to the repelled hydrogen atoms, can be observed at distances from the source some four times greater than the α-particles themselves are able to penetrate. These new particles may be termed " H-particles " for the sake of clearness.

An Artificial Transmutation.

In 1919, by the work of Sir Ernest Rutherford, a further important step in this advance was taken, which raises the question whether a beginning has not already been made in the achievement of actual artificial transmutation to an infinitesimal extent. It has been recognised, by the late Sir William Ramsay among others, that, of all known agencies likely to be able to transmute one element into another, the α-particle, on account of its unique kinetic energy, was the most likely to prove effective. The work described shows how exceedingly difficult it is to hit the real atom exactly with the α-particle. Later results have proved that only about one out of 100,000 α-particles, in passing through one centimetre of hydrogen gas at normal temperature and pressure, produced an H-particle. Since, in this path, the number of hydrogen atoms penetrated is 10,000, in only one out of one thousand million collisions is the nucleus of the atom of hydrogen really hit. In the rare case when the α-particle actually impinges upon the nucleus, it is to be anticipated that the latter, if not an exceedingly stable system, might sometimes be broken up.

Of the common gases, hydrogen, oxygen, carbon dioxide, and nitrogen, which he exposed to the bombardment of the α-particles, Rutherford observed an anomaly in the case of nitrogen. These gases all gave the expected effects, namely, the production of "N-particles" and "O-particles"—that is to say, new rays were observed, longer in range than the α-rays, which were first thought to be atoms of these elements with a single positive charge put into violent motion by collisions of the α-particles with the nuclei of the oxygen and nitrogen atoms, always in the minute numbers to be expected from the results with hydrogen. In these cases the range of the new particle is only slightly longer than that of the α-particles themselves. But in nitrogen there were observed, in addition, particles of the long-range and other characteristics exactly similar to the H-particles produced in hydrogen gas. Only one such H-particle was observed for every twelve N-particles produced. These results strongly suggest, though they do not yet rigorously prove, that the nucleus of the nitrogen atom struck by an α-particle is occasionally shattered by the collision, and that hydrogen atoms are produced from it. It may be surmised, for example, as one possibility, that the nitrogen atom of mass 14 is converted into a carbon atom of mass 12 and two hydrogen atoms. The excessively small proportion of the nitrogen atoms penetrated by the α-particles, which are so shattered, must not be forgotten. This makes it exceedingly unlikely that such a case of artificial transmutation, if it occurs, can ever

ARTIFICIAL TRANSMUTATION

be directly confirmed by direct chemical analysis. It must also be remembered that in this case, even if it is correctly interpreted, transmutation has not been really artificially *initiated*. What has been done, at the most, is to use a naturally occurring transmutation, that can still be neither initiated artificially nor controlled, to produce a secondary transmutation. The real problem of how artificially to transmute one element into another at will remains still completely unsolved.

While this book was passing through the press, Rutherford has published further results, in which the real nature of these particles, generated by the impact of the α-rays in different gases, has been examined by the method by which the nature of the electron and the α- and β-particles has been established—that is to say, the particles were subjected to the action of electric and magnetic deviating fields, and, from the magnitude of the deflection, the mass, the charge, and the velocity were determined. This established the correctness of the earlier conclusion that the H-particles generated in hydrogen, and also in nitrogen, consisted of singly positively charged hydrogen atoms. But it was found that what have been termed " N-particles " and " O-particles " were not singly charged atoms of nitrogen and oxygen, as first surmised, but for each the same and an entirely new particle of mass 3, carrying two positive charges. On the views discussed in the next chapter they would appear to be atoms of an isotopic variety of helium, otherwise unknown.

Thus the new results confirm the conclusion that the nitrogen atom is shattered during a close nuclear collision with an α-particle, but it appears to suffer disruption in two independent ways, giving, in one way, atoms of hydrogen of mass 1, and, in the other, atoms of a new kind, of mass 3. In the case of the oxygen atom the latter particles alone appear to be produced (Sir Ernest Rutherford, Bakerian Lecture, Royal Society, June 3, 1920).

Atoms compared and contrasted with Solar Systems.

Thus, inevitably as science proceeds, the solid tangible material universe dissolves before its touch into finer and still finer particles, the unit quantities or " atoms " of positive and negative electricity. The passive attributes of matter in occupying a definite volume of space to the exclusion of other matter resolves itself into an active dynamic occupation by virtue of the sweep of the electronic satellites in their orbits round the positive central sun. But whereas, in the solar system in which we live, the central sun is both large and massive in relation to the sizes and masses of its attendant planets, in the atomic solar systems there is a curious inversion. From the facts disclosed in reference to the passage of α-particles through hydrogen, it would appear that the centres of the two colliding nuclei, the hydrogen nucleus and the helium nucleus, approach to within a distance of less than the accepted diameter of the negative electron. The central material nucleus, in which all but a negligible part of the mass of the atom is concentrated, thus appears to be at least as small as, and probably smaller than, the negative electron, the smallest particle previously known to science. Since the smaller the volume in which a given electric charge is concentrated the greater will be its mass, it may really be that the positive electron is very much more concentrated and very much more massive than the electron, and that the nucleus of the hydrogen atom, the simplest of all atoms, is in reality the missing positive electron. But this, at present, is merely a suggestion. The positive charge is the same in amount as the negative charge of the electron. For its mass to be that of the hydrogen atom, which is 1,830 times that of the electron, its radius must be 1,830 times less, or about 10^{-16} cm.

CHAPTER XV
ISOTOPES

ELEMENTS WHICH ARE CHEMICALLY IDENTICAL.

IN another totally distinct direction, radioactivity has been the means of throwing a flood of light on the nature of matter and in particular on the periodic law of the elements, which epitomises the existing chemical knowledge of matter. In the first chapter, the underlying limitations which attend all knowledge were emphasised. Such an underlying limitation is revealed by the sequence of radioactive changes. In Chapter X. (p. 154) it was shown that many of the known radioelements resemble others so completely in their chemical nature that no separation can be effected once they have been mixed, and in Chapter XII. we came upon numerous further examples of the same resemblance among the members of the thorium disintegration series. No chemist could detect by chemical analysis the separate existence of the two uraniums, uranium I and II, or of thorium and radiothorium, or mesothorium and radium, or of lead and radiolead, in a mixture containing any of these pairs. Naturally the question was asked whether any of the common elements, for which radioactive methods of analysis are not available, are, as supposed, really homogeneous elements, and whether any are mixtures of different elements, with different atomic weights, but with identical chemical properties, so merely appearing to be homogeneous to chemical analysis. Matter is, in all probability, far more complex than chemical analysis alone is able to reveal, because radioactivity has shown us the existence of elements identical in their chemical behaviour, but, nevertheless, distinct in atomic weight and in stability.

The Periodic Law and Radioactive Changes.

In 1911 the writer pointed out that the products of α-ray changes have a certain definite relationship in chemical character to their parents. The chemical properties of an α-ray product correspond with those of an element in the periodic table with group number two *less* than that of the parent. Thus, radium in Group II expels an α-particle and changes into the emanation in Group 0, ionium in Group IV changes by expulsion of an α-particle into radium in Group II, and so on. It was also noticed that the passage through the periodic table of the element undergoing change was frequently alternating, the products frequently reverting in chemical nature to that of an earlier parent. So radiothorium resembles thorium, thorium X mesothorium I, and so on. This curious atavism has now been very simply and fully explained, largely owing to the chemical investigations of Alexander Fleck in the writer's laboratory at Glasgow, who spent three years in the exhaustive study of the chemical nature of all the radioactive elements, which survive for a long enough period for their chemical nature to be determined, and many of which had previously been very imperfectly investigated from this standpoint. In consequence, the generalisation already alluded to in preceding chapters has come to light. It was seen that the expulsion of a β-particle was entirely analogous to that of the expulsion of the α-particle, but that, instead of the product possessing a chemical nature corresponding with an element in the periodic table with group number two less than the parent, it corresponded with an element of group number one greater. Hence if, in any order, one α- and two β-rays are expelled, the product is chemically of the same nature as its parent, and the curious atavism referred to above is explained. Radioactive children frequently resemble their great-grandparents with such complete fidelity that no known means of separating them by chemical analysis exists. But, of course, the two intermediate parents are readily separated. By this means all the members of the family may be recognised severally, although, but for this means, that would be still impossible.

The complete generalisation, which was put forward in 1913 independently during the same month by A. S. Russell, K. Fajans, and the writer, is illustrated by Fig. 44. The last twelve places of the periodic table, from uranium to thallium, are placed consecutively side by side, and the passage of the elements, in the uranium, thorium, and actinium series, from place to place, as the α- and β-ray changes succeed one another, is indicated by arrows. The figure is to be read at 45°, so that the lines showing the atomic weights are horizontal.

Every detail of the chemical nature of the members of the known sequences in the uranium, thorium, and actinium series, including the complicated branchings which occur towards the ends, bears out implicitly these two simple rules. Independently of their origin, atomic weights, and radioactive character—that is, of the kinds of change they are about to undergo—all the members of the three disintegration series, which, by the consistent application of these rules fall into *the same place* in the periodic table, are chemically completely identical and non-separable from one another. Hence I have termed them *isotopes* or *isotopic elements*.

THE ATOMIC NUMBER.

Confining attention to the most generally important consequences of this embracing generalisation, we may at once connect the rules with the fact that the α-particle carries a double positive atomic charge and the β-particle a single negative atomic charge. Each of the successive places in the periodic table thus corresponds

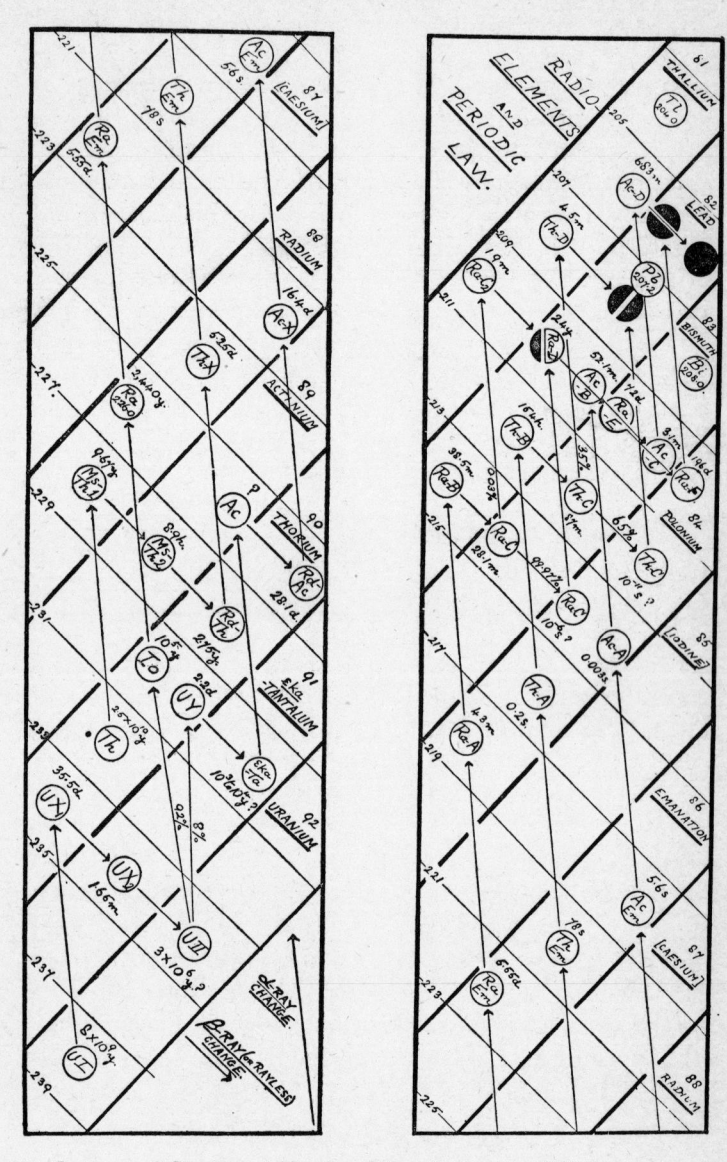

Sequence of Changes of Uranium (U) and Thorium (Th) into various Isotopes of Lead (Pb).

FIG. 44.

with unit difference of charge in the constitution of the atom. This suggestion was made tentatively by van der Broeck before it was first proved by these researches.

The discovery of the atomic nucleus by Rutherford enables us to go further. It is hardly possible to doubt that both the α- and the β-particles are expelled from the nucleus. Hence this difference of charge in the constitution of the atom in passing from one place in the periodic table to the next must be a unit difference in the net positive charge of the nucleus of the atom, and a corresponding unit difference in the number of negative electrons external to the nucleus, which compensates the positive nuclear charge and renders the whole atom neutral.

In his original theory Rutherford concluded that the magnitude of the positive charge of the nucleus was approximately one-half of the number representing the atomic weight of the elements. Now, from evidence still to be considered, it is known exactly to be equal to the number of the element in order of sequence in the periodic table, when the elements are arranged in order of atomic weight. This number is now always called " the atomic number." Usually it is rather less than one-half the atomic weight. Uranium, the last element, occupies the 92nd place in the periodic table; its atomic number is therefore 92, and its atomic weight is 238.

So far as is known the atomic number of hydrogen is one, that of helium is two, of lithium three, and so on until we arrive at uranium, ninety-two. Gold is the 79th element, mercury the 80th, thallium the 81st, lead the 82nd, and thenceforward, as shown in Figs. 43 and 44, by the numbers at the head of each place of the periodic table.

Isotopic Elements.

The generalisation proves definitely that, as regards the last twelve places in the periodic table, between uranium and thallium, the successive places correspond with unit difference of nuclear charge and unit difference in the number of external electrons as was previously assumed. But it also shows that in the ten occupied places each place accommodates on the average no less than four distinct elements. The atomic masses of the various elements occupying the same place vary in some cases by as much as eight units, and there is nothing to show that the same may not occur throughout the whole periodic table. Such groups of isotopic elements, occupying the same place, possessing the same net nuclear positive charge and the same number of electrons in their external systems, are not merely chemically identical and indistinguishable. Many of their commoner purely physical characteristics, such as spectrum and volatility, have also been found to be identical.

The existence of such isotopic elements would not have been suspected except for radioactive changes. What fixes the chemical and general material character of an element is a particular numerical charge, and this charge is not the total charge of the atom, not even the total charge of the nucleus of the atom, but is the net charge of the nucleus or the difference between the numbers of positive and negative charges which it contains. The same net charge may be, and, in the case of isotopes, is made up of different absolute numbers of positive and negative charges differing by the same amount. When an α- and two β-particles are successively expelled the net charge becomes again what it first was, and the position in the periodic table and whole chemical character also reverts to the initial state. But the atomic mass is different by four units, the mass of the α-particle expelled.

The Problem of the Ancient Alchemist.

There is one interesting point that may be referred to, which serves to show how nearly science has approached to the ancient alchemical problem of turning base metals into gold. In these spontaneous changes, if either actinium D or thorium D had elected to expel an α- instead of a β-particle, the product would have been an isotope of gold instead of lead.

Gold occupies a position in the periodic table two places removed from and before thallium, so that if thallium could be induced to part with an α-particle, the product would be an isotope of gold. If it was sufficiently stable it would be gold for all practical purposes. It is true its atomic weight and density would be somewhat greater, but otherwise it would be the same. Or, again, if bismuth could be made to expel two α-particles, or lead an α- and a β-particle, gold again would be the product. This, then, is a list of recipes for the modern alchemist, one and all indubitable, but one and all awaiting a means of accomplishment. It remains for the future to show how the nucleus of an atom can be so influenced as to be caused to eject an α- or β-particle at will. But it is a tremendous step gained to know for the first time in what transmutation really consists.

CHAPTER XVI

THE X-RAYS AND CONCLUDING EVIDENCE

The X-Ray Spectra of the Elements.

We now have to turn to yet another great advance. Beginning with the case of ordinary light, it is well known that it may be analysed into its component wave-lengths by the use of a " diffraction grating," as well as by an ordinary prism.

In the Rowland diffraction grating some large known number, usually from ten to twenty thousand lines per inch, are accurately ruled by a diamond mounted on a dividing engine, upon a plane or concave surface of glass in such a manner that all the lines are exactly parallel and all precisely equally spaced apart. The light transmitted by such a grating is split up into a large number of parallel beams which " interfere " with one another, and the result is that the direct beam is more or less extinguished, but each different wave-length of light in the beam is bent, or diffracted, from its course through a definite angle which is different for each different wave-length. So the light is resolved, or spread out, into a pure spectrum much as when it passes through a prism. Now, if the distance between the rulings—one-ten-thousandth of an inch, for example—is exactly known, the actual wave-length of each line in the spectrum may be easily and exactly calculated. A beam of X-rays, as we now definitely know, consists of a radiation of precisely the same kind as light, but of wave-length some ten thousand times shorter. Hence, to resolve it, we would require the use of a " grating " at least a thousand or ten thousand times more finely ruled than can be ruled by the most perfect dividing engine. Who could make such a grating?

But an infinitely more perfectly executed, and ten thousand times more closely packed, assemblage than the finest and most perfect Rowland grating ever made was found in 1912, by Laue, Friedrich, and Knipping, who discovered that the X-rays are regularly diffracted, like light is by the grating, when reflected from the surface of an ordinary crystal, such as rock salt, fluor spar, calcite, and the like.

In this country the discovery was eagerly taken up, and we owe to the Professors Bragg, father and son, a clear insight into the whole subject. In the crystal, as the crystallographers have, with eyes of faith, long depicted, the atoms of the substance are marshalled in a definite space-lattice of regular geometric form, so that each atom is fixed at a definite point in space at a definite distance from and in a definite angular direction to all the atoms surrounding it. The smallest number of atoms required completely to represent the pattern —so that the whole structure is made up simply by reduplicating this unit indefinitely in the three dimensions—is called the space-lattice of the crystal. Moreover, the distances between the atoms, or points, of the space-lattice is, for common crystals, just of the right order of length to resolve the X-rays in a manner precisely analogous to that in which light is resolved by the Rowland diffraction grating. If we know for any one crystal what this distance actually is, we can determine the wave-length of any X-ray from the angle at which it is reflected from the crystal.

For the ordinary heterogeneous beam of X-rays given by an ordinary X-ray tube, which corresponds to white light, the beam is resolved by the crystal into an X-ray spectrum, and the wave-length of the component radiations may be found. If we know the wave-length for any one X-ray, we can find out for any crystal, in any plane or face we choose, the precise distance apart between the atoms that make it up, and so we can construct its space-lattice.

This has given crystallographers a powerful direct method of testing the reality of the space-lattices which have been arrived at by theoretical reasoning and the power of second sight of the mathematical mind. The results already have been gratifying and remarkable. The actual spacial arrangements of the individual atoms that go to make up the crystal are now being precisely measured and explored, and, as has so frequently happened before, the patient theoretical conceptions of a generation less brilliantly equipped with experimental methods of inquiry are being triumphantly vindicated.

But it is not with this field we are now most closely concerned. It is rather with the wave-length of the X-rays, and with their period or frequency, which can be so found by this method. If we consider the unit of time, one second, in this period light or X-rays travel 3×10^{10} cms., whatever the wave-length. But in the 3×10^{10} cms. of length, or second of time, there will be about twice as many separate waves of violet light as of red light, and many thousand times more waves of any X-ray than of either. From the wave-length we can at once find the frequency or "pitch" of the radiation, or the number of vibrations per second to which it corresponds. This frequency again, in atomic solar systems, corresponds with the number of revolutions made per second by the electron in its orbit within the atom, and this depends on the diameter of its orbit. In much the same way we might speak of the frequency of a planet as the number of revolutions it makes round the sun in a century, and this depends on the distance of the planet from the sun. The rays that constitute the ordinary visible spectrum arise probably from the outermost electrons of the atom, the ones, that is, that are responsible for the chemical character and which traverse orbits of diameter of the order of 10^{-8} cm., which is the diameter of the atom, meaning by that the whole atomic system. To get waves of a thousand to ten thousand times shorter length, and frequencies a thousand to ten thousand times greater than for visible light—to get X-rays, in fact—it is clear that we have to get much nearer to the centre of the atom, into a region intermediate between that in which the ordinary phenomena of physics and chemistry originate and the innermost nucleus disclosed by radioactivity.

The γ-Rays.

By the same method of reflection from crystal surfaces some, at least, of the γ-rays have also been resolved and shown to be X-rays, but of very much shorter wavelength in general than those artificially produced. The wave-length of light is usually expressed in Ångstrom units (written Å). One Ångstrom unit is equal to 10^{-8} cm. The wave-lengths of visible light waves vary from 6,000 or 8,000 (Å) in the red to 3,500 (Å) in the violet, and to 2,000 in the extreme ultraviolet. The wave-length of the X-rays range from, perhaps, 8 Å for very soft X-rays to 0·5 Å for the most penetrating type that can be produced. But the wave-length of γ-rays is in general much less ranging from 1·2 Å to as little as 0·07. Moreover, it is believed that for the most typical very penetrating γ-rays of radium and thorium the wave-length is far too short even for the crystal to be capable of resolving them, and they may have wave-lengths 100 times shorter than the shortest yet resolved.

The existence of rays so short in wave-length and high in frequency points to a revolution of electrons in the atom in orbits of excessively minute diameter, so minute that the question arises whether the γ-rays do not really originate from electrons actually contained within the atomic nucleus. These results furnish another and independent proof that radioactive phenomena occur entirely in the atomic nucleus.

The Intermediate Region of the Atomic Structure. — The Homogeneous Characteristic X-Rays of Barkla.

A Röntgen tube gives X-rays of all wave-lengths within limits which depend on a variety of conditions, such as the nature of the metal constituting the anticathode, the degree of vacuum, and the potential difference between the electrodes. The very important discovery was made by Barkla that, when such X-rays impinge upon various metals, they will, if penetrating enough, produce new secondary homogeneous X-radiation, the properties of which are characteristic of the metal and not of the primary radiation. Ea h element, except those of less atomic weight than sodium, emits under such circumstances an X-ray of definite and characteristic spectrum, which differs from the ordinary light spectrum given by the same element in being excessively simple. Often it consists of a single strong line together with one or more weaker ones. Such characteristic X-rays belong to various series, designated the K-, L-, M-series connected in the following way: Beginning with sodium, the 11th element in the Periodic Table, the X-ray, characteristic of the element sodium, belongs to the so-called K-series, and is extremely feebly penetrating and of long wave-length, as the wave-lengths of X-rays go. Going up through the elements in increasing order of atomic weight, as far as tin, the 50th element, the K-radiation produced steadily diminishes in wave-length and increases in penetrating power, until, at tin, it is difficult artificially to generate a primary X-ray of sufficient penetrating power to excite the characteristic radiation. Hence this experimental limitation prevents this series being studied for elements of greater atomic weight.

Before this, however, beginning with the element zinc, the 30th element, in addition to the K-radiation, a new characteristic radiation of very feeble penetrating power, belonging to the so-called L-series, makes its appearance. From zinc onward this new radiation increases in penetrating power and decreases in wave-length until the last element uranium is reached. Again, at gold, the 79th element, another new series, the M-series, is first observed, very non-penetrating at first, but increasing in penetrating power to uranium.

Moseley made a systematic determination of all the wave-lengths of the principal lines of these characteristic X-rays from aluminium to silver in the K-series, and from zirconium to gold in the L-series, and discovered that they are connected together by a simple mathematical relation, involving the atomic number of the element. The square-root of the frequency (as we have seen the frequency is proportional to the reciprocal of the wave-length) is proportional to a number that increases by one in passing from any element in the periodic table to the next. In other words, the square root of the frequency is proportional to a number that increases in the same way as what we have termed the atomic number of the elements, when arranged in order according to the Periodic law.

The practical value of this discovery was great. For the first time it was possible to call the roll of the chemical elements and to determine how many there were and how many remained to be discovered. There are between hydrogen and uranium ninety-two possible elements, of which only six remain to be found—namely, the two unknown heavier analogues of the element manganese, two rare-earth elements, and the two heaviest analogues of iodine and cæsium respectively (see Fig. 43).

It is curious that the first two should still and for so long elude discovery. They would in all probability be most useful metals, allied to the noble metals in character, the first to the light platinum metals, ruthenium, rhodium, and palladium, and the second to the heavy platinum metals, osmium, iridium, and platinum.

As is well known, the Periodic Table comprises certain

exceptions. Tellurium has an atomic weight higher than iodine, though in the periodic table it precedes it, and the same is true for argon and potassium, and for cobalt and nickel. The X-ray spectra of these elements confirms the order in which they have been put by chemists in the periodic table on account of their chemical character and despite their atomic weights. This shows that it is the atomic number—*i.e.*, the net positive nuclear charge of the element, or the number of electrons external to the nucleus—which fixes the position in the periodic table, rather than, as hitherto supposed, the atomic weight. The existence of isotopic elements of identical chemical character but different atomic weight points to the same conclusion. In fact, this work on X-ray spectra dovetails perfectly into the conclusions reached, independently, in the study of radioactive change, and extends them to all the elements in the periodic table.

The Atomic Mass or Weight.

The chemical character, and even the spectrum of an element, at least to a degree of approximation attainable by common methods, depends upon the atomic shell and not upon the atomic nucleus, and the character of the shell is identical, whatever the nucleus, so long as the atomic number is the same. The atomic mass or weight, on the other hand, on the views adopted, is to all intents and purposes a property of the nucleus alone. Mass and radioactivity, the oldest and the newest properties of matter, are in this respect allied and sharply to be distinguished from all the other properties. Isotopes have in general nuclei of different mass but the same net positive charge, and therefore their outer electronic systems and all the properties which originate therein—that is to say, all properties save mass and radioactivity—are practically identical and indistinguishable.

We have seen that radioactive change afforded a very

subtle way of separately distinguishing between and of actually separating isotopes in favourable cases. In the disintegration sequence A≻B≻C≻D≻, A, B, C are *necessarily* elements completely distinct chemically and capable of easy separation by chemical analysis. But if in the three changes, one α- and two β-particles are expelled, D is *necessarily* chemically identical with A, but of atomic mass four units less.

Because of the change, D can be apprehended as an individual, and, since B and C are separable from A and in course of time turn into D, in cases when the periods are favourable, D can be separated from A. *Except for* the change, A and D would, in spite of the difference in their atomic weights, be mistaken by chemists, relying on the usual chemical and spectroscopic criteria of purity and homogeneity, for a single homogeneous element. Its atomic weight would be a mean of the atomic weights of its constituents, depending not only on the magnitude of each, but on the proportions in which they were mixed. This would apply not merely to the radio-elements but equally to all. It is therefore, perhaps, not altogether surprising that all the many efforts made to find exact numerical relations between the atomic weights of the various elements should have proved fruitless.

The Element Lead.

These ideas have been put sharply to experimental test in the case of the element lead. As the generalisation illustrated by Fig. 44 shows at once, the ultimate products of all the disintegration series in all branches, so far as they have been traced, end in the same place in the periodic table—namely, the place occupied by lead. Therefore, in spite of the differences of origin and of atomic weight, they must all be isotopes of lead, if the apparent ends of the series coincide with the actual ends and no further, as yet undetected, changes occur.

The atomic weight of ordinary lead is 207·2, whereas that of the main branch of the uranium series is 206, and that of both the branches of the thorium series is 208. The atomic weight of the end product of the actinium branch series is doubtful, but, as it is only present in small relative quantity, it may be, in the first place, neglected. Clearly, if this view is correct, the lead derived from a uranium mineral ought to have an atomic weight somewhat lower than that of ordinary lead, and the lead derived from a thorium mineral an atomic weight somewhat higher. The prediction, like so many that have been made in this subject, has been completely confirmed by experiment. Lead from carefully selected uranium minerals, not containing thorium in detectable quantity, has been found to have an atomic weight as low as 206·05. Lead from carefully selected thorium minerals containing only a small quantity of uranium has been found to have an atomic weight as high as 207·9. Chemically, they are identical and indistinguishable from common lead, which, indeed, may well be a mixture of these two isotopes in the right proportion to give an atomic weight of 207·2!

Their spectra, for all practical purposes, are identical with one another and with that of ordinary lead. But, quite recently, a minute difference of wave-length has been established in the case of one of the brightest lines, a difference that does not exceed one part in ten million or one-thousandth of the difference between the two sodium lines D_1 and D_2. It is so minute that it can only with difficulty be established by the most refined measurements. Nevertheless this difference between the spectra of isotopes is likely to prove of great importance.[1]

Agreeably, however, with what is to be expected for isotopic atoms having identical shells but nuclei of

---

[1] The ingenious suggestion has been made that it might be used to separate the isotopes of chlorine (p. 248). A beam of light filtered through chlorine will lose first the vibrations corresponding with those of the lighter isotope, since it is in predominant quantity, and may then be able to stimulate the heavier isotope only to react with hydrogen, thus effecting the separation. This is being tried at Oxford, and at the time of writing (July, 1920) the results appear most promising (T. R Merton and H. B. Hartley, *Nature*, March 25, 1920).

different mass, the densities of the different kinds of lead are different just in proportion to the differences in atomic weight. In other words, the different isotopic atoms have the same volume.

Another precisely parallel case has been established for the isotopic elements ionium and thorium. We have seen (p. 153) that, on account of its period being forty times longer than that of radium, the amount of ionium in a mineral must be something like 12·5 grams per ton of uranium, or 58 grams per gram of radium. Now all uranium minerals yet examined on a sufficiently large scale contain, probably, a larger quantity of thorium than this. It is a suggestive and unexplained point that the proportion is smallest in the secondary recent uranium minerals. In practically all the primary uranium minerals several per cent. of thorium is found. Thus, ionium can never be obtained pure free from its isotope, thorium, but from a suitable secondary uranium mineral, a preparation containing a considerable proportion of ionium, admixed only with thorium, may be separated. Such a preparation separated from 30 tons of Joachimsthal pitchblende by Auer von Welsbach, has been investigated by Hönigschmid. For pure ionium an atomic weight, 230, is to be expected, since it changes into radium with expulsion of an α-particle. The atomic weight of the ionium-thorium mixture described was found to be 231·51, whereas that of pure thorium, by the same method, was 232·12. But the spectrum of the thorium-ionium preparation was, so far as could be seen, identical with that of the pure thorium preparation, and in both no impurities whatever could be detected. The elimination of everything but ionium from the thorium by the elaborate chemical purifications adopted in the treatment of the material had been effected, but these methods are incapable of affecting, to the slightest degree, the ratio of the ionium to the thorium.

Separation of Isotopes.

It would be idle to deny that these new ideas, that different nuclei may exist in atoms which, to the chemist and spectroscopist, are indistinguishable and inseparable, cuts far more deeply into the basis of chemical theory than did the discovery of the actual disintegration of the radio-elements and of the spontaneous evolution of one element from another. It is of interest to inquire into the possibilities of separating a mixture of isotopes, or, if this is impracticable, of detecting their separate existence in a mixture without separating them. It will be obvious that any property which involves directly the atomic mass could, theoretically, if not practically, be employed for their separation and separate detection. But it is remarkable how difficult such methods are to apply to this purpose, and how few of them ever have been used as practical aids to chemical analysis. The rate of diffusion of a gas, or, less suitably, of a substance dissolved in a liquid, depends directly on the molecular weight of the substance and therefore of the weight of the separate atoms the molecules contain. Theoretically, thorium and ionium, the two uraniums or common lead itself, if it is a mixture of isotopes as is possible, ought to be capable of resolution by diffusion methods. But this has not yet been practically achieved. Other methods, such as depend upon centrifuging the mixed material, or submitting it to the process of thermal diffusion, have been proposed but not yet successfully carried out.

It would be an extraordinarily difficult and laborious piece of work, for example, to separate the constituents of the air in a pure state by diffusion, though a partial and incomplete separation by this means might easily be effected. It is not a method a chemist would employ unless he were obliged. On the other hand, though on the point there is a difference of opinion, any commonly used purely physical method other than those mentioned, such as fractional distillation, crystallisation, or adsorption, is not likely, even theoretically, to be effective in separating a mixture of isotopes. These certainly depend upon the chemical character of the element, rather than its atomic mass.

Neon and Metaneon.

Interesting, because it was discovered just at the time that the true interpretation of isotopes had been found, and also because it concerns an element very far removed from the heavy elements at the end of the periodic table undergoing radioactive change, is the case of neon and metaneon. The element neon is one of the inert gases, similar to argon, existing in the atmosphere to the extent of some twelve parts per million by volume. It is intermediate, in the zero family of elements, between helium with atomic weight 3·99 and argon with atomic weight 39·9, exactly ten times greater—both these being practically whole numbers. The atomic weight of neon is 20·2, a number differing from the nearest integer by a fifth of a unit.

As a sequel to his classical work (p. 57) in elucidating the charge and mass of the electron, which constitutes the cathode ray of the vacuum tube, Sir Joseph Thomson applied similar methods to the positively charged particles, or " positive rays " as they are called, which under certain circumstances can also be detected in the vacuum tube discharge. Here in every case so far examined the mass of the particle is never less than that of the hydrogen atom, and often it is much greater. In fact, so was developed a novel method of determining the atomic mass of elements, such as hydrogen, oxygen, nitrogen, and other gases which are present as positive ions in the vacuum tube discharge, and the molecular weight of such particles as so exist in groups of more than one atom. One of the most interesting of the numerous discoveries made was that of the gas called X_3, which has a mass three times that of the hydrogen atom, and which is, in all probability, the molecule H_3, analogous to ozone, the allotropic form of oxygen, O_3, though chemists have never yet prepared or observed the existence of such an allotrope of hydrogen.[1] But the same is true of many groups, such as CH, CH_2, CH_3, for which this new and exceedingly delicate method of gas analysis indicates at least a passing existence.

The interest of this method, depending as it does directly upon the mass of the atom or molecule, from the present point of view is that, undoubtedly, it would be capable of revealing, if they existed, in any gaseous element, the separate individual components of a mixture of isotopes of different atomic mass. It is, in fact, almost the only practical method that could do so without ambiguity. Now, in examining the positive rays produced in neon by the electric discharge, Sir Joseph Thomson and Mr. Aston found in addition to the neon atom carrying a single positive charge, Ne^+, of mass 20, a much fainter indication of another atom with a single + charge, of mass 22, which provisionally, as it could not be ascribed to a known element, they attributed to a new gas which they named metaneon.

The question at once arose whether this was a case of the isotopism with which we have become familiar in the case of lead and the radio-elements. An attempt to separate neon and metaneon from ordinary neon, by a prolonged series of fractional absorptions of the gas in cooled charcoal, effected no separation whatever. The density of the fractions separated by the process were identical and the same as before the treatment, whereas metaneon, with atomic weight 22, should have a density 10 per cent. greater than neon with atomic mass 20. But this, as we have seen, is to be expected of isotopes, for in all probability the ordinary physical properties, such as volatility, etc., are, like the chemical

[1] This differs from the new particle of mass three more recently obtained by Rutherford in the bombardment of oxygen and nitrogen atoms by α-particles, in that it carries a single instead of a double positive charge.

ISOTOPES GALORE

properties, indistinguishable. Neon remains still unresolved into its two components, though after a long series of fractional diffusion experiments some indication of a partial separation was obtained.

But the latest information confirms the existence of metaneon in the gas. Aston has developed the positive ray method of analysis considerably, so that it is capable of fixing with great precision the atomic or molecular weight of the particle causing the positive ray. His measurements showed neon to be a mixture of two gases of atomic weight 20·00 and 22·00 to within an error of one part in a thousand. So we may conclude with considerable probability that these two isotopic gases, in proportion of about 90 per cent. of the first and 10 per cent. of the second, constitute the ordinary element neon derived from the atmosphere.

The General Prevalence of Isotopism.

At the time of correcting the proofs of this book (July, 1920), this work of Aston has developed into one of the most important contributions of recent times to our knowledge of the chemical elements. The new methods, a brilliant outcome of combined mathematical and experimental ability, have proved themselves to be of extraordinary power and accuracy in the detection of isotopes and the measurement of their separate atomic weights. By altering the mode of application of the electric and magnetic deviating fields, an effect of the utmost practical service, analogous to the focussing effect of an ordinary lens on light, was secured, whereby all the particles of the same mass and charge in a narrow diverging cone of positive-rays are brought to a focus at a point, the foci for different particles lying on a straight line, in the plane of which the photograhhic plate is put. Each particle thus records its position as a spot or line on the plate, and there results an analysis of the beam into its different constituent particles, quite analogous to the resolution of light into constituent lines in a spectrum. From the position of the lines on the photographic plate, the mass of the atom producing it can be determined with an accuracy scarcely, if at all, inferior to that attained by chemical methods in the finest atomic weight determinations. But the method has the added inestimable advantage that mixtures of isotopes show their several atomic weights rather than the mean value, which is all that can be got from chemical determinations.

The results of this new method so far announced are sufficiently startling. Eighteen elements have, as yet, been examined. Of these, nine only were found to be homogeneous. The other nine consist of mixtures of from two to as many as five or more isotopes. Moreover, in every case, except hydrogen, the true atomic weight is found to be an exact integer (in terms of the atomic weight of oxygen as 16, taken as the standard of comparison) to an accuracy of one part in a thousand. For hydrogen, the atomic weight on this basis, 1·008, deduced by chemists from some of the finest atomic weight work ever performed, has been exactly confirmed. The results are collected in the table below.

"Pure" Elements.	Atomic Weight.	"Mixed" Elements.	Number of Isotopes.	Atomic Weights.
Hydrogen	1·008	Boron	Two	10·00 and 11·00
Helium	4·00	Neon	Two	20·00 and 22·00
Carbon	12·00	Silicon	Two or three	28·0, 29·0, and (?) 30·0
Nitrogen	14·00	Argon	Two	36·0 and 40·0
Oxygen	16.00	Chlorine	Two	35·0 and 37·0
Fluorine	19·00	Bromine	Two	79·0 and 81·0
Phosphorus	31·0	Krypton	Five or six	78 (?), 80, 82, 83, 84, and 86
Sulphur	32·0	Xenon	Five (?)	128, 130, 131, 133, and 135
Arsenic	75·0	Mercury	Five or more	202, 204, and three or four unresolved between 197 and 200

As shown by the intensities of the different lines, the proportion in which the isotopes are present accord well in each case with the value of the mean atomic weight as determined chemically. Thus the two isotopes of bromine are in similar proportion, but the lighter isotope of argon is barely detectable. It is thus not too much to suppose that all the atomic weights, except hydrogen, are exact integers, and that the fractional values found by chemists for some of the elements are due to their being mixtures of several isotopes.

The Problem of Transmutation.

From the picture we have formed of the general structure of the atom and the view we have of what exactly would constitute a transmutation, we may attempt, in conclusion, to consider the kind of methods by which its accomplishment might practically be attempted. It is clear that it is the nucleus of the atom that has to be changed, either by adding to or subtracting from it positive or negative charges. The subtraction or addition of electrons, so far as the outermost shell of the atom is concerned, in no sense constitutes a transmutation, but is what occurs in ordinary chemical changes. In the free state of the element the atom is electrically neutral. The number of external electrons is equal to the net positive charge of the nucleus. Subtraction of one "valency" electron or more from the outermost shell produces the positive ion, which is characteristic, not of the free element, but of it when combined with other elements to form chemical compounds. But such additions and subtractions are confined to the outermost shell. There is no exchange yet capable of being effected between the electrons in the inner completed rings and either the electrons in the outermost ring or the electrons inside the nucleus. When, however, the nucleus spontaneously ejects positive or negative charges, as it does in the α- and β-ray changes, a complete and instantaneous rearrangement of the electrons both in the completed rings and the outer shell appears to follow. In brief, to transmute an atom, the change has to be effected from within, outwards from the central nucleus. It cannot, at least as yet, be impressed upon the nucleus by any changes in the exterior electronic shell, imposed from without.

But the comparative ease with which the outer shell of the atom may be altered by chemical and also by electrical forces imposes in itself a formidable practical barrier to any more deep-seated change.

We have seen that the α-particle may be regarded as the agent most likely to break up the nucleus of an atom if it impinges upon it, and that this actually may occur in the case of the nucleus of the nitrogen atom. Is it possible artificially to generate an α-particle or one possessing a similar amount of kinetic energy?

It may be calculated that the energy of the α-particle, over the range of velocity so far studied, is such as it would acquire in passing between two points differing in electric potential by from two to four million volts. This gives a quantitative idea of the strength of the electric field likely to be required before particles analogous to the α-particle could be successfully produced.

We may be fairly certain that the only influences likely to be effective in transmuting matter will be electrical in character, and that very much higher potentials at present known or utilised in electrical engineering will have to be developed before there is much chance of success. Along this road much that is new and important will first have to be made clear. So far as it has been followed, a barrier to further progress has been reached, which may or may not prove to be fundamental. The attainment of very high potentials at present seems to be limited by the failure of the insulation. Even a practically perfect vacuum, it appears, fails to insulate, and transmits a discharge across it when the potential exceeds a certain limit.

Moseley hit upon the very ingenious idea of using the radium clock (Fig. 15, p. 59), as a method of arriving simply at otherwise unattainable potentials. If the clock there depicted is deprived of its leaves, if the insulating support of the radium can be made good enough and the vacuum sufficiently nearly perfect, there ought, theoretically, to be no limit to the extent the radium would become positively charged, and therefore to the difference of potential between it and the surrounding wall, unless, thereby, the radium products were prevented from further disintegrating and emitting their β-rays.

In practice Moseley could not, with his particular apparatus, attain a potential much above 150,000 volts. A discharge through the vacuum always occurred at this point.

The reason probably is that the loosely held "valency" electrons in the outermost shell of the atoms constituting the surfaces are dragged out of the atom by the electric field so causing the discharge. Such a change is not transmutational, but is allied to or identical with that produced by ordinary chemical agencies. It indicates that there is a definite limit to the extent to which matter can be charged, and at present this rather closes the door to further progress.

The outer regions of the atom effectively guard the inner from being attacked. If a perfect vacuum is unable to withstand the electric forces without transmitting the discharge, it may be expected that any material insulator is even less likely to do so.

Conclusion.

This must conclude the attempt to deal with the numerous and important advances made since these lectures were first given. The field of work has opened out in a number of directions previously unsuspected. The problem of transmutation and the liberation of atomic energy to carry on the labour of the world is no longer surrounded with mystery and ignorance, but is daily being reduced to a form capable of exact quantitative reasoning. It may be that it will remain for ever unsolved. But we are advancing along the only road likely to bring success at a rate which makes it probable that one day will see its achievement.

Should that day ever arrive, let no one be blind to the magnitude of the issues at stake, or suppose that such an acquisition to the physical resources of humanity can safely be entrusted to those who in the past have converted the blessings already conferred by science into a curse. As suddenly and unexpectedly as the discovery of radioactivity itself, at any moment some fortunate one among the little group of researchers engrossed in these inquiries might find the clue and follow it up. So would be diverted into the channels of human consciousness and purpose the full primary fountain of natural energy at its source, for use or misuse by men, according as to whether the long and bitter lessons of the painful past and present have even yet been really learned.

INDEX

A

α-particles, Collision of, with matter, 62-67, 223, 224
— Bombardment of gases with, 224
— Coloration of mica and gems by, 165
— Connection of, with helium, 44, 60, 93-104,
— Energy of, 61
— from radium itself, 94
— from the emanation, 79, 144
— from uranium, 149
— Individual, 42, 44-46, 61
— Limiting velocity of, 61, 66
— Mass of, 60, 98
— Number of, expelled by radium, 40, 42, 45
— passage through atoms, 220-223
— Positive charges carried by, 60, 63
— Proof of identity with helium of, 102
— Scattering of, 63, 222
— Tracks left by, 65
— Velocity of, 61, 66, 94, 161, 221, 249
α-ray product, chemical properties of, 228
α-rays, 41-67
— Absorption of, 33
— — by air, 34
— Connection between range of, and period of substance, 164
— Magnetic deflection of, 60
— Making paths of visible, 64
— Range of, 34, 45, 133, 161, 164
— — in mica, 166
— Resolution of, 41-46
Accumulation of products, 95-98, 123
Actinium, disintegration series, 186, 198-204, 207, 214, 229
— Emanation, 198, 203
— Origin of, 199, 204
— Parent of, 205

Actinium, period of life of, 198
— Production of helium from, 99, 102
— A, 198, 203
— B, C, and D, 198
— X, 198
Active deposit of actinium, 198-204
— — of thorium, 194-197
— — of radium, 137-144
— — — Residual activity from, 145
Age of the earth, 25, 75, 98, 177-183
Ages, The geological and incandescent, 179
Alchemist, The problem of the, 232
Alkaline-earth elements, 85, 105
Alternative theories of radioactive energy, 68, 89
Aluminium, 205, 213, 214
— carbide, 213
Analogies between the disintegration series, 188-191, 198
Ångstrom units, 237
Antimony, 214
Antonoff, G. N., 205
Argon, 84, 85, 97, 105, 214, 240
— atomic weight, 248
Arrhenius, Svante, 215
Arsenic, 214
— Atomic weight of, 248
Aston, F. W., 246, 247
Atom, Definition of, 105-108
— Innermost region of, 220
— Intermediate region of, 238
— Model, 212
— Nuclear, 220
— Outermost region of, 217
— Structure of, 210
Atomic disintegration, 39, 58, 67, 89, 94, 96, 98, 105, 109, 112, 155, 157, 168, 209
— — Cause of, 14
— — Multiple, 200
— mass or weight, 240, 248

INDEX

Atomic number, 231, 239, 240
— property, Radioactivity an, 12, 13, 15, 68, 74, 83, 110
— synthesis, 180, 208
Atoms, 2, 12, 40, 46, 60, 63, 66, 84, 105, 158-161
— Interpenetration of, 63
— Passage through, of α-particles, 220-223
Atoms, Solar systems compared and contrasted with, 226
Autunite, 98, 148
Average life, Determination of, 115
— — of common elements, 157
— — of emanation, 113
— — of ionium, 134
— — of radium, 117, 125, 207
— — of thorium, 207
— — of uranium, 116, 125, 207
— — Period of, 112, 207

B

β-particles, 49-59
— Charge of, 50, 51, 58
— Mass of, 57
— Tracks left by, 65
— Velocity of, 58
β-ray product, Chemical properties of, 228
β-rays, 29-66, 228, 250
— Magnetic deflection of, 48, 60
— Making paths of visible, 165
β-rays, Definition of, 139
Barium, 15, 85, 214
Barkla, C. G., 238
Becquerel, Henri, 6, 7, 128
Beryllium, 214
Bismuth, 15, 146, 148, 191, 214, 233
Boltwood, B., 125, 133
Bonds of affinity, 213
Boron, 205, 214
— Atomic weight of, 248
Bragg, Sir William, 34, 35, 45, 62, 63, 64, 220, 235
Branch Series, 201
Brevium, 150, 214
Broeck, van der, 231
Bromine, 214
— Atomic weight of, 248
Bunsen, R. W., 75

C

γ-rays, 29-32, 66, 237
— Radiograph by, 31
Cadmium, 214
Cæsium, 75, 214, 239

Calcium, 214
— absorption of gases by, 52, 101
Carbon, 106, 213, 214, 224
— Atomic weight of, 248
Carnotite, 20, 98
Cascade of changes, 74
Cathode-rays, 52-58, 210, 245
Cause of atomic disintegration, 114
Cerium, 214
Chance of disintegration, 111
Change, Law of radioactive, 112
— of radio-elements, 71, 74, 91, 92 *et seq.*
Chemical combination, Nature of, 216
— elements, bonds of affinity, 213
— — Number of, 239
— — Order of, 212
— — Table of, 214, 231, 239
Chemists and radioactivity, 109
Chlorine, 105, 213, 214, 215
— atomic weight, 248
Chlorion, 213
Chromium, 214
Cloud method of making paths of rays visible, 64
Cobalt, 214, 240
Conservation of radioactivity, 88
Constancy of radioactivity, 10, 13, 23, 24, 27, 43, 69, 70, 77, 90, 172
Control of natural energy, 5, 13, 173, 184
Copper, 214
Corpuscular theory of radiation, 38
Cosmical aspect of life, 179
— energy, 24, 120, 174, 178
Cost of scientific investigations, 19
Cranston, J. A., 204
Crookes, Sir William, 15, 42, 52, 57, 128, 165
Crookes' tubes, 52, 58, 210
Crystal, space-lattice, 235
Curie, M. and Mme., 10, 12, 13, 15, 19, 75, 83, 124, 136, 145, 198

D

"D_3" line, 97, 100, 101
Dalton, John, 106, 108, 217
Debierne, A., 99, 198, 203
Decay of radioactivity, 70, 87
Definition of the atom, 105-108
Detection of infinitesimal quantities, 17, 75, 77, 82, 85, 90, 91, 95, 109
Determination of average life, 115
Dewar, Sir James, 52
Diffraction grating, 234

INDEX

Discovery of radioactivity, 6
Discrete theory of radium rays, 40, 44
Disintegration, *see* Atomic disintegration
—, Chance of, 111
— series, Analogies between, 188-191, 198
— — of actinium, 186, 198-204
— — of thorium, 178, 186-198
— — of uranium, 121-151
Doctrine of energy, 20, 27, 37, 68, 178, 185
Dysprosium, 214

E

" E-ray," 204
Earth, Age of the, 25, 75, 177-183
— Internal heat of, 178
Earthquake routes, 180
Effects of radioactivity, 8-11, 28
Eka-tantalum or proto-actinium, 204
Electric current, Action of magnet on, 49
Electricity, Discharge of, 8, 14, 18, 34, 45, 64, 211
— Nature of, 50
Electrolytic dissociation, Theory of, 213-217
Electro-magnet, 47
Electro-magnetic inertia, 211
Electrometer, 46
Electron theory of matter, 109, 212
Electrons, 55-58, 63, 109, 210, 212, 216, 247
— period of revolution, 236
— valency, 217, 249
Electroscope, Gold-leaf, 8, 17, 42, 59, 84
Electrostatic and electromagnetic deflection methods, 55, 57, 60, 225, 245, 247
Elements, Chemical, bonds of affinity, 213
— — Number of, 239
— — Order of, 212
— — Stability of, 72, 157, 163
— — Table of, 214, 231, 239
— — Unchanging character of, 72, 73, 163, 227
— Isotopic, 229, 231
— Rare-earth, 218
— Rarity of, 155
Elixir of life, 182
Emanation of radium, 68, 77-94, 214
— α-particles from, 79, 145

Emanation of radium, Atomic weight of, 85, 103
— Average life of, 113, 116, 122
— Chemical nature of, 84, 105
— Condensation of, 80-82
— Density of, 85
— Heat generated by, 85, 86, 170
— Physiological action of, 82
— Rate of decay of, 87, 88
— Reproduction of, 88, 89, 90, 122
— Spectrum of, 85
— Volume of, 82, 119
— of actinium, 198, 203
— of thorium, 136, 190, 193-198
Emanations and radiations contrasted, 78
Emanium, 203
Energy, cosmical, Source of, 174
— Doctrine of, 20, 27, 37, 68, 178, 185
— Internal, of matter, 68, 71-73, 86, 87, 91, 96, 108, 168-176
— Measurement of, 22, 71
Energy of coal, 22, 23, 70, 120
— of radioactive substances, 3, 5, 10, 58, 62, 68, 91, 92, 172
— of radium, 22, 68, 86, 119, 171
— of uranium, 170-172
— Transformers of, 69, 90
Ephemeral transition-forms, 74, 92, 116, 121, 129, 203
Equilibrium, Radioactive, 90, 95, 117, 196
Ether, The, 37, 38, 56
Erbium, 214
Europium, 214
Evolution of elements, 134, 162, 163
— of universe, 26, 120, 175
Existence, Struggle for, 6, 184

F

Facts and theories of radioactivity, 89, 108
Fajans, K., 229
Faraday, Michael, 47, 55
Fleck, Alexander, 228
Fletcher, A. L., 166
Fluorescence, 6, 18, 31, 53, 66, 78, 79, 195
Fluorine, 214
— Atomic weight of, 248
Friedrich, M., 235

G

Gadolinium, 214
Gallium, 205, 214

INDEX

Gas, A radioactive, 77, 80, 83
Gases, bombarded by α-particles, 224
Geiger, Dr., 45
Geological bearing of radioactivity, 26, 75, 175-180
Geology, Controversy between physics and, 26
Germanium, 205, 214
Giesel, F. O., 20, 99, 203, 204
Gold, 214, 231, 233, 239
— currency, 156

H

H-particles, 223, 224, 225
Hahn, Otto, 188, 205
Halogen family, 218
Halos, Pleochroic, 165
Hartley, H. B., 242
Heat generated by radium, 18, 19, 22, 85, 119, 178
—— in the earth, 178
Heaviside, Oliver, 210
Helium, 44, 60, 84, 94-104, 209, 214
— atomic number, 231
—— weight, 245, 243
— Discovery of, 97
— Liquefaction of, 97
— Possible isotope of, 225
— Prediction concerning the origin of, 98
— Production of, by radium, 94, 99
—— by actinium, 99, 102
—— by thorium and uranium, 100
— in radioactive minerals, 96, 97
——— Volume of, 98
— Spectrum of, 99
Herschell, Sir John, 159, 162
High vacua, 50, 52
Hitchins, Miss A. F., 130, 134
Holmium, 214
Homogeneous Characteristic X-rays, 238
Hönigschmid, O., 243
Huggins, Sir William, 107
Hydrogen, 107, 214, 224, 239
— atomic number, 231
—— weight, 248

I

Incandescent age, 179
— gas-mantle, 14, 187
Increase of activity of radium with time, 16, 155
Indifference of radium to its environment, 27, 77
Indium, 214

"Induced radioactivity," 136
Inertia, 56, 211
Infinitesimal quantities, Detection of, 75, 76, 82, 85, 90, 91, 95, 109
Inglis, J. K. H., 113
Integral values of atomic weights, 243
Intermediate substances, 74, 76, 77, 131-135
Internal energy of matter, 68, 70, 71-73, 86, 87, 168
— heat of earth, 178
Interpenetration of atoms, 63
Iodine, 214, 239
Ionisation of gases, 8, 63, 64, 66
— of liquids, 215
Ionium, 133, 151, 153, 154, 164, 189, 205
— atomic weight, 243
— Average life of, 134
— Estimated period of, 134, 165
— and uranium X, Connection between, 133
Iridium, 214, 239
Iron, 106, 214
Isotopes, 133, 150, 160, 229, 231-233, 240, 248
— Separation of, 243, 248

J

Joachimsthal mine, 15, 152
Joly, John, 166, 176-178
— "Radioactivity and geology," 177

K

K-Series of X-rays, 238
Kalgurli, mines at, 132
Katrine, Loch, 125, 131
Kelvin, Lord, 20, 37, 178
Kirchoff, 75
Knipping, P., 235
Krypton, 214

L

L-Series of X-rays, 238
Lanthanum, 198, 214, 218
Laue, M., 235
Law of proportionality, 118, 123, 152
— of radioactive change, 111
Lead, 214, 231
— Atomic weight of, 241
Lead and radium, Connection between, 15, 76, 148, 241
— and thorium, Connection between, 191, 241
Life from the cosmical standpoint, 179

INDEX

Life of radio-elements, 92
— Period of average, 113
Light, Nature of, 36, 39
— Velocity of, 38, 58, 211
Limitations of knowledge, 4, 6, 66, 173, 178-180, 227
Lithium, 214
— atomic number, 231
Lutecium, 214

M

M-Series of X-rays, 238
Macdonald laboratories of M'Gill University, 89
Mackenzie, T. D., 130
Magnesium, 214
Magnetic deflection of cathode-rays, 53
Maintenance of radium, 121
— — sun's energy, 24, 120, 179
Manganese, 214, 239
Marckwald, W., 146, 147, 192
Marsden, E., 223
Mass of the electron, 55-57, 210
Matter, Electron theory of, 109
— Ultimate structure of, 209
— Unsolved problems of, 109, 206
Maxwell, J. Clerk, 158, 162, 181
McCoy, H. N., 125
Measurement of energy, 22, 71
Meitner, Miss L., 205
Mendelejeff, D., 205
Mental pictures, 109
Mercury, 85, 148, 214, 231
— atomic weight, 247
Merton, T. R., 242
Mesothorium, 187-193, 227
Metaneon, 244
— atomic weight, 248
Mica, Coloration of by α-rays, 166
Milngavie, reservoir at, 125, 131
Minerals, Helium, in radioactive 96, 97
— Lead in radioactive, 15, 148
— Quantity of radium in, 16, 75, 123, 152
— Ratio between quantities of uranium and its products in, 152
Minimum quantity of helium detectable, 101
— — radium detectable, 17, 42
Molecules, 2, 108, 158
Molybdenum, 214
Monazite sand, 186, 192
Moseley, H. G. J., 239, 249
Multiple atomic disintegration, 200

N

N-particles, 224, 225
Negative and positive electricity, 50
Neodymium, 214
Neon, 84, 214, 245
— atomic weight, 245, 248
Newton, Sir Isaac, 38
Nickel, 214, 240
Niobium, 214
Nitrogen, 213, 214, 224
— Atomic weight, 248
"Niton," 78
Nomenclature concerning atoms and molecules, 106-108
Non-separable radio-elements, 154, 187, 195, 227
Nuclear atom, 61, 210, 220

O

O-particles, 224, 225
Onnes, K., 97
Osmium, 214, 239
Ouroboros, 181
Oxygen, 106, 214, 224
— Atomic weight, 243

P

P-3 route of earthquakes, 180
Palladium, 214, 239
Parent of ionium, 133
— of radium, 122-134
Penetration test of rays, 7, 29, 30, 31, 80
Period of average life, 113
— — connection with range of α-rays, 164
— half change, 115
Periodic law, 105, 171, 205, 212, 227-229
— table of the chemical elements, 214, 228, 231, 239
Perpetual motion, 21, 24, 59
Phosphorescence, see Fluorescence
Phosphorus, 214
— Atomic weight of, 248
Photographic effects of radioactivity, 8, 14, 18, 66, 80
Physical impossibility, 25
Pitchblende, 15, 75, 127, 152, 187, 243
Planet, number of revolutions, 236
Platino-cyanides, 31, 35, 141
Platinum, 214, 239
Pleochroic halos, 165
Polonium, 16, 44, 146, 154, 199, 214

INDEX

Positive and negative electricity, 50
—— rays, 245, 246
Potassium, 105, 214, 240
Praseodymium, 214
Prediction of origin of helium, 98
Proportionality, Law of, 118, 123, 152
Proto-actinium, 205

Q

Quantity of helium detectable by spectroscope, 101
—— —— in minerals, 98
—— of radium in minerals, 16, 75, 124-127, 152

R

Radiant matter, 52, 57, 211
Radiation, Nature of, 36-39
Radiations, Complex, 28
Radioactivity, a new science, 1
—— discovery, 6, 26, 175
—— Four experimental effects of, 8
—— an unalterable atomic property, 12
Radiograph by γ-rays, 31
Radio-tellurium, 146, 148
Radio-thorium, 187-196, 227
Radium and uranium, connection between, 124-127
—— Active deposit of, 137
—— Average life of, 117, 125
—— Changes of, 136
—— Chemical nature of, 15
—— clock, 59, 249
—— Cost of, 19
—— A changing element, 73
—— emanation. *See* Emanation of Radium
—— Experiments with, 18
—— Growth of, 134
—— Maintenance of, 121-135
—— " physically impossible," 26
—— Quantity of, in pitchblende, 16
—— Radiations from, 139
—— Reproduction of, 122
—— series, 207
—— Substitute for, 154, 187, 193
—— War uses of, 19
Radium A, 89, 105, 139-144, 153
—— B, 89, 105, 139-144
—— C, 105, 139-144, 151, 164, 201
—— C', 151, 202
—— D, 153, 190
—— D, E, and F, 145-147

Radium F, Identity of, with polonium, 147
Ramsay, Sir William, 78, 82, 84, 85, 97, 99, 119, 188, 223
Ratio between uranium and its products, 152
Rayleigh, Lord, 59, 84
Rays of radioactive substances, 9, 28 *et seq.*
Recoil, Radioactive, 103, 104
Recovery of radioactivity of radium, 77, 88
Rhodium, 214, 239
Röntgen, Wilhelm K., discovery of X-rays, 6
Rowland diffraction grating, 234
Rowland, Professor, 160
Royds, T., 102
Rubidium, 214
Russell, A. S., 229
Ruthenium, 214, 239
Rutherford, Sir Ernest, 29, 30, 45, 46, 60, 78, 80, 86, 89, 98, 102, 119, 125, 136, 161, 188, 197, 220, 222, 223, 224, 225, 231

S

Samarium, 214
Scandium, 205, 214
Scattering of α-particles, 63, 222
Schuster, Arthur, 161
Selenium, 214
Self-induction, 211
Sidot's hexagonal blende, 36
Silicon, 205, 214
—— Atomic weight of, 248
Silk tassel experiment, 18, 34
Silver, 214, 239
Simplon Tunnel, Radium in rocks of, 177
Sodion, 215
Sodium, 214, 215, 238
Solar systems, compared and contrasted with atoms, 226
Spectra of isotopes, 242
Spectroscope, 75, 91, 92, 97, 99, 101, 129, 160, 163, 179, 209
Spinthariscope, 42, 44, 65
Stability of elements, 72, 157, 163
Standard, The International radium, 17
Strontium, 214
Struggle for existence, 6, 184,
Strutt, Hon. R. J. (now Lord *Rayleigh*), 59, 125, 176
Substitute for radium, 154, 187, 193
Successive changes of radio elements, 74, 77, 89, 110, 116, 129-133, 138, 145-149

INDEX

Sulphur, 214
— Atomic weight of, 248
Sun's energy, Maintenance of, 24, 120, 178-180
Synthesis of atoms, 180, 204

T

Table of atomic weights of " pure " and " mixed " elements (Aston), 248
— — disintegration series complete, 207
— — periods and quantities, uranium series, 153
— — velocities and ranges of α-rays, uranium series, 162
— Periodic, of the elements, 214
— — Chart showing sequence of α- and β-changes through, 230
Tantalum, 205, 214, 219
Tait, Professor, Recent Advances in Physical Science, 20, 25, 26
Tellurium, 214, 240
Terbium, 214
Thallium, 148, 214, 231, 233
Theories and facts of radioactivity, 89, 108
Thomson, Sir Joseph, 55, 57, 210, 212, 245, 246
Thorium, 13, 94, 97, 98, 100, 102, 133, 136, 154, 186-198, 214
— Active deposit of, 194-198
— atomic weight, 243
— halos, 166
— disintegration series, 178, 186-198, 207, 227, 229
— Production of helium from, 100
— Ultimate product of, 190, 242
Thorium A, 190, 197
— B, C, D, 164, 190, 201
— C', 201
— Emanation, 190, 193-196
— X, 190, 195
Thulium, 214
Tin, 214, 238
Titanium, 214, 218
Total energy in radium, 119
— — in uranium, 170-172
Transcendental character of radioactivity, 27, 58
Transformers of energy, 69
Transmutation, 13, 71, 72, 172, 182, 209, 223-225, 233, 248-250
Tungsten, 214

U

Ultimate product of thorium, 190, 242
— products of radium, 76, 96, 123, 147, 148, 242
Ultra-material velocities, 63, 221
Unchanging character of elements, 72, 73, 163
Unsolved problem of matter, 109, 206
Uranium, 7, 12, 97, 98, 102, 107, 116, 124, 148, 169-172, 188, 189, 194, 207, 214, 229, 239
— atomic number, 214, 231
— Average life of, 116, 125
— halos, 166
— Production of helium from, 100
— and radium, Connection between, 124-134
— I and II, 149, 165, 189, 195, 206, 227
— Y, 205
— X, 128-131, 133, 150, 188, 206, 214
— X_1 and X_2, 150
— — and ionium, Connection between, 133

V

Vacua, High, 50, 52, 249
Valency electrons, 217, 249
Value of gold, physical explanation to account for the unchanging, 156
— of radium, 19, 156
Vanadium, 214
Velocities, Ultra-material, 63
Velocity of cathode-ray particle, 58
— of light, 38, 58, 211
Visible, Making the paths of rays, 64
Volume of helium in minerals, 98
— emanation in equilibrium with radium, 82, 119

W

Wave-length of γ-rays, 237
— of X-rays, 234-238
Wave theory of light, 39
Welsbach, Auer von, 13, 243
Whytlaw-Gray, R., 85
Willemite, 35, 53, 78, 79, 81, 87

Wilson, C. T. R., 64
Writing by radium, 19

X

X-rays, 6, 30, 31, 38, 78, 210, 234
— Diffraction of, 234
— wave-length, 234-238
X_3 gas, 245
Xenon, 214
— Atomic weight of, 248

Y

Ytterbium, 214
Yttrium, 214

Z

Zero family, 217, 245
Zinc, 214, 238
— sulphide, 35, 80, 141, 196, 197, 203, 204, 223
Zirconium, 214, 239

Back End Papers.